The Wisdom Community

Edward K. Braxton

PAULIST PRESS
New York/Ramsey

Library of Congress
Catalog Card Number: 80-81053

ISBN: 0-8091-2307-X

Published by Paulist Press
Editorial Office: 1865 Broadway, New York, N.Y. 10023
Business Office: 545 Island Road, Ramsey, N.J. 07446

Printed and bound in the
United States of America

Contents

Dedicated to
Evelyn Kathryn Gardner Braxton
& Cullen Lawrence Braxton, Sr.,
selfless, loving parents,
and dear friends,
who daily teach me a wisdom
they cannot speak

Wisdom shines bright and never fades.
She is easily discerned by those who love her.
She is found by those who seek her.
She is quick to make herself known to those who desire knowledge
        of her.
Those who rise early in search of her will not go weary in the
        quest, for they will find her seated at their door.
To set all one's thoughts on her is the perfect form of prudence.
To lie awake in her cause is the short way to peace of mind.
For she herself ranges in search of those who are worthy of her.
She appears to them with kindly intent, and in all their purposes
        she meets them halfway.
The desire to learn and to understand is the true beginning of
        Wisdom.
Concern for learning and understanding means the love of Wisdom.
The love of Wisdom means the keeping of her laws.
To keep her laws is a pledge of immortality.
And immortality brings us near to God.

—from the Book of Wisdom

Preface

The Wisdom Community has emerged in my life in a gradual manner, like so many rungs of a "ladder" that has helped me to gain a better perspective on life, ministry, theology, and the Church. After sharing it privately with many others who have found it helpful, like Ludwig Wittgenstein, I have decided to offer it as a possible help to a larger public.

When I was studying philosophy in college, a Jesuit professor, David Hassel, was a significant influence in my life. He taught me to look at reality from a wide angle, to dig deep into knotty questions, to hold seemingly conflicting experiences, ideas, theories, and values in tension, and to avoid premature conclusions. In his classes, he stressed a process of personal integration and personal appropriation that went far beyond the college "paper chase" and the battle for grades. An important aspect of this synthesizing and integrating activity was open, aggressive, and consistent sharing and communication with a small group of fellow students. These gatherings were far more than "study groups." They became my first experience of a "wisdom community." I looked forward to every meeting. As they progressed, I pulled together many fragments from my earlier educational and life experiences. I also learned to articulate and come to terms with my own operative or functional beliefs and positions concerning the perennial philosophical questions and the answers of Aristotle, Aquinas, Kant, Hegel, Kierkegaard, Heidegger, Camus, Sartre, and so many others.

During my four years of theological studies, I continued to work and think in the manner of the wisdom community. As a parish priest, such a discipline was more difficult, but not impossible. I continued to pursue it, not only with priests, but also with a small number of interested parishioners who found the standard adult education program or retreat to be inadequate for them and their needs. As a doctoral student at Louvain, I attempted a more structured "program" for the wisdom community with fellow doctoral students. Between the assaults upon index cards, the search for a stray footnote, and efforts to keep the dissertation topic from growing beyond control, four of us gathered every two or three weeks for a long evening of dinner, prayer, and personal exploration of foundational questions. We were "the wisdom community."

In retrospect, I now see that a whole process, beginning even before my college experience, was laying the foundations for my subsequent thinking, teaching, lecturing, reading, writing, and counseling activities. This process contributed in a unique way to the genesis of my own developing thoughts about the possibility and need for formulating a personal synthesis, sharing the points of that synthesizing process with others, and pursuing an integral Christian humanism. More than that, these early experiences and exercises were the first sketches of "wisdom community" techniques that I later employed in educational programs. Indeed, they were the unrecognized seeds for this book. There is a very real sense in which I must express gratitude to many people whose names I never knew or no longer remember.

There are others, however, whose contribution to *The Wisdom Community* was more direct and who must be acknowledged.

The writings of Bernard Lonergan, S.J., Karl Rahner, S.J., and David Tracy have much influenced the writing of this book. Indeed, much of the dynamic of this book can be understood as an attempt to translate and apply many of the methodological insights of Lonergan and Tracy into a pastoral context. Rahner's dictum that "all theology is pastoral," as well as the content of his speculative thought, was a challenge and an assistance in bridging the worlds of "serious theology" and pastoral life.

As *The Wisdom Community* developed, it was particularly helpful for me to test my ideas with teaching colleagues. Dinner conversations and late evening walks were often the context for refining and clarifying my thoughts. In particular, Krister Stendahl, Dean of Harvard Divinity School, John Cacioppo, Professor of Psychology, University of Notre Dame, and Allan R. Laubenthal, Professor of Theology, Saint Mary Seminary, Cleveland, must be thanked for their equal readiness to listen and to speak.

I am particularly grateful to those who read the entire manuscript of *The Wisdom Community* and offered most helpful suggestions that improved the work's structure and content. They are: Daniel P. Coughlin, Director of the Center of Divine Worship, Archdiocese of Chicago; Patty Crowley, pioneering leader in many American Catholic lay movements; John S. Cummins, Bishop of Oakland, California; John J. Egan, Director of the Center for Pastoral Ministry, University of Notre Dame; Thomas J. Hickey, Director of the Cana Conference, Archdiocese of Chicago; Robert Krieg, C.S.C., Professor of Theology, University of Notre Dame; Edward J. Mahoney, Director for Clergy Education, Diocese of Burlington, Vermont; Susan Bearden McNamara, parishioner, Saints Faith, Hope and Charity Parish, Winnetka, Illinois; James Parker, Professor of Theology, Mount Angel Seminary, Portland, Oregon, and Pastor, Saint Paul's Parish, Silverton, Oregon.

As a priest of the Archdiocese of Chicago, I would not have undergone the diverse experiences that resulted in this book if John Cardinal Cody, Archbishop of Chicago, had not made it possible for me to accept invitations that took me away from Chicago. I am very grateful to him for his generosity. In inviting me to serve as "staff theologian" for the Diocese of Cleveland, Bishop James A. Hickey created a structure in which many of the ideas in *The Wisdom Community* can be tested and implemented. This new position makes it possible for the teaching and pastoral ministry of the episcopacy and the developments of contemporary theology to be in continuous and creative conversation. To Bishop Hickey, therefore, I must express singular and warm words of genuine appreciation.

Mary Margaret Bush and Susan Negolfka expertly typed the final manuscript. I am grateful for their diligence and patience.

In spite of the many outside influences, writing a book is in some ways like being a lonely islander intent on a work of concentration. Yet the islander's life is not altogether solitary. There is a small group of singular friends "in my life, for my life" who have enriched and replenished my "soul space" during the time that *The Wisdom Community* was in preparation. There is no need to name them. They know who they are: fellow priests, parishioners, and friends from the "old neighborhoods" of my life, Louvainists, caring students from Harvard, as well as the University of Notre Dame and Saint Mary's Theologate, and people whom I have met along the way. Each has made the islander's life an adventure and a song. When I think of them, my memories are happy ones, and, when I pray for them, my prayers are full of joy.

Edward K. Braxton
Palm Sunday, 1979
Abbey of Gethsemani, Trappist, Kentucky

Introduction

What is the "wisdom community"? Some recently discovered esoteric religious sect from antiquity? No, that is not it.

In its widest application, the wisdom community refers to the Christian churches. Within the limits of this book, it is a descriptive image of the Catholic Church. More specifically, the wisdom community is a metaphor for a framework and a program for renewing understanding and communication between parish priests, theologians, bishops, and the people in the pews.

The Catholic Church is a wisdom community. This is essentially an empirical statement rather than a theological one. To an empirical investigator the Church is a human institution. Doctrines, beliefs, rituals, devotional practices, intricate theoretical constructs, policies, disciplines, complex structures, and noble and ignoble deeds are all part of the Church institution and its long history. But no empirical examiner would say that that was the whole of it. Even as an empirical reality the Church is more than the sum of its parts.

The Church moves through history as the bearer of an ever developing self-understanding. Essential to this self-understanding is a posture before the world, a distillation of meaning. This interpretive scheme offers a point of view in the face of ambiguity, and suggests more than a sufficient reason for getting up each morning.

Over and above or deep within metaphysical doctrines, ceremonies, traditions, and regulations, the Church preserves and communicates a wisdom about being. This wisdom cannot be completely equated with teachings, dogmas, and intellectual theories. It is more elusive. Many people are gifted with great intelligence and learning, but wisdom eludes them. Yet, we have all met people who were profoundly wise, though their formal education was slight. I think of my aging aunt whose eyes are full of light. She listens with silent know-

1

ing to her granddaughters, who would tell her about the world, about life, and about suffering. The person whose life has led them on the path to wisdom often knows more than they can say. In many instances, they communicate and pass on their wisdom more by being than by any great pronouncement. The Church is not unlike this.

The Church as wisdom community is not the custodian of a secret knowledge or gnosticism available only to a select and elite few. The wisdom that the Church bears is available to all. This wisdom comes from the telling and retelling of the story of Jesus of Nazareth through the centuries. The empirical observer can see this in the powerful impact that the Church has had on the lives of people through the centuries. Peasants, kings, scholars, lovers, merchants, doctors, artists, cardinals, children, housewives, laborers, priests, servants, scientists, derelicts, musicians, athletes, and mystics: All of these and more have been enriched by the Church's wisdom about being. Yet, all have not "understood" the theoretical formulations of the Church's teachings. Nor have all of them "believed" all of the Church's doctrines in the same way. Still it is the Church that they would point to as the source of their liberating and integrating vision of reality, their wisdom.

This wisdom is not altogether independent of doctrines, practices, beliefs, and speculations. But it is more than that. Hence, this wisdom moves throughout the body of the Church. It is not "possessed" by the priests, or the laypeople, or the scholars, or the bishops, or the artists, in an independent or exclusive way. A ray of sunlight dancing on a piece of sculpture by an untutored craftsman may communicate more of the Church's wisdom to a faithful person than the learned sermon being delivered from the pulpit at the same time. A sister silently nursing a dying bishop may touch him with the wisdom of the Church in a way that his episcopal pronouncements never touched anyone. Though it cannot be attached to a person or office, the wisdom of the Church abides through the years.

The wisdom community is also a descriptive image for the self-conscious openness, support, and collaboration that is needed between priests, bishops, sisters, brothers, theologians, and the laity whom they serve in order to meet the present crisis. The wisdom community is a framework, a way of thinking, and ultimately a concrete activity or program that is intended to foster renewed understanding and communication between the sometimes conflicting voices within the Church. The conflict is so great in some parts of the Church that the outside observer may wonder if there is not a danger that the treasured wisdom of this community may be severely impoverished, if not lost.

What is the cause of this conflict and crisis? There are no simple answers. In part it is the confrontation with a pluralism that for many is incomprehensible or unacceptable.

II

There are many worlds. There is the world of one's concrete humanity, inner feelings, thoughts, hopes, and needs. There is the world of the local Catholic parish in which one first encountered Christianity. There is the world of the Catholic Church in ever increasing dialogue with other Christian traditions and world religions. There is the world of scholars employing the disciplines of the university to reflect critically upon the meaning of religion. There is the world of men and women of different races, ethnic groups, and different social and economic conditions suffering painful alienation with little hope that religion will be a balm for their open wounds. There is the world of ongoing socio-cultural movements that constitute the modern scene.

Many people find it difficult to live in all of these worlds. Some sever themselves prematurely from one or another. The wisdom community seeks to engage all of these worlds in an ongoing conversation so that a part will not be taken for the whole. Are worlds that are seemingly in conflict actually converging? Are battle lines being drawn too soon? Is there possibly some "higher viewpoint" from which, over time, the complementary nature of seeming contradictions may be seen? While there must be a division of labor, the wisdom community invites every member to be a part of a personal and communal integrating process according to one's own talents and circumstances.

These different worlds did not come into being all of a sudden. But many Catholics have become increasingly aware of them of late. There are many reasons for this, and certainly one of them is the ferment that led up to, and flowed from, the Second Vatican Council (1962–1965). Many bishops are startled when they hear it said that the present disquiet in the Church would not exist had there been no Council. They argue that if the decrees of the Council had been carefully studied, correctly interpreted, and responsibly implemented at all levels of the Church, then the result would have been a more orderly and less traumatic process of renewal in the Church.

But what if there had been no Council? No doubt the pre-Vatican II Church would have continued in its general style for an indefinite period of time. It would have continued to be a meaningful place for most of its members to celebrate their religious beliefs. And no doubt the Church would have continued to command respect from the larger world. Nevertheless, with the major cultural shifts going on in the larger world, the Church would have gradually become a less vital force in the lives of an ever increasing number.

With the Council, the Church entered the foray of complex cultural shifts that were altering the very foundations of Western culture. This situation, plus the inherent difficulty of large institutions in managing change on a wide scale, made it possible that what was intended as an orderly internal reform has become near revolution.

Had there been no Council, for example, there would not have occurred the widespread dis-ease that resulted from rapid liturgical changes. While the changes were generally accepted in a docile manner, their implications were far-ranging. This is true because for most people, religious meaning and value are communicated and preserved "non-linguistically" through symbols and rituals. The sudden altering of venerable foundational symbols resulted in a disorientation for many.

Had there been no Council, the response to the encyclical *Humanae Vitae* might have been different for there would have been no expectation that a "majority opinion" would have been seriously weighed. The questions of married priests and women priests would not have met with official negative responses for the present, for there would have been no environment in which they could have been asked. Furthermore, the fruitful bi-lateral, tri-lateral ecumenical deliberations between Roman Catholics and Christians of other traditions would not be awaiting implementation. The Catholic Church would never have entered into these important discussions without the Council.

The conflict between many bishops and many members of the theological community would probably not have emerged either. Prior to the Council it was more widely accepted that while theologians are important resource persons, only bishops are official teachers in the Church.

Had there been no Council, the Church would have survived and even flourished for a time and many people would have been spared confusion and pain. Many would have remained secure in a familiar and well defined framework. Numerous culturally and ethnically conditioned modes of thought, expression, and action would have continued to prevail without regard for the cultural contexts and historical circumstances in which they arose. Surely there would never have been a National Office for Black Catholics or Caucuses of Black Sisters and Clergy without the impetus of the Council. Without the Council, the shape of the Church to come might have been very similar to the Church of the past. Eventually it may have come to be regarded as a monumental cultural achievement of the past. But in the present many might have regarded it as a museum piece. Whatever one's assessment of the present dynamism in the Church, few would argue that it could qualify as a museum piece.

Broader than the question of the Church before the Council is the terrain between two distinct ways of looking at what it means to be human and what it means to be the Church. These two frameworks may be descriptively termed a "psychological" and an "ontological" view of human existence. At times they appear complementary, and at other times appear completely imcompatible.

A *psychological anthropology* tends to be concrete and existential in its emphasis, while an *ontological anthropology* tends to be abstract and essential in its emphasis. The difference between the two can best be expressed with an example. The recently promulgated revision of the sacrament of baptism as the new rites of adult Christian initiation and of infant baptism has occasioned some discussion about the differences in the two rites, and whether or not adult initiation is now to be preferred over infant baptism.

It is possible to interpret the rite of adult initiation and the renewed catechumenate as essentially, though not exclusively, working from the perspective of a psychological anthropology. This view is much influenced by the philosophical developments since Immanuel Kant's critique of earlier scholastic thought. This post-Kantian view suggests that personhood is constituted by being a conscious subject. The experienced, the known, the real, and the true are all measured by the structures of one's conscious subjectivity. For this reason the adult initiation rite stresses the conscious, aggressive, and developmental involvement of the adult Christian in stages of growth as he advances from initial interest in Christianity to being a responsible member of the Church community. The grace of baptism, therefore, requires self-involvement and personal apprehension of meaning.

The tradition favoring infant baptism is clearly working from the perspective of an ontological anthropology. Here the infant is not thought of so much as a conscious subject in the post-Kantian sense, but as a being possessing a spiritual soul. It is not the infant in his particularity as a potential existential subject that is focused upon. It is rather the infant's particularity as a unique being, loved by God and possessing a spiritual soul. This spiritual reality can, in some manner, be really and truly effected by the loving self-giving and self-manifesting of God. This presence of God's love intimate within the individual infant's soul is not experienced, known, real, or true in the sense that is essential from a psychological point of view. In the case of the infant, the sacrament symbolizes, and in some ways effects, the unmediated immediacy of God's presence as gift independent of the child's conscious status. Both frameworks provide helpful insights into what it means to be human before the mystery of God.

But the two frameworks have broader implications. The psychological anthropology tends to stress the dynamic, ongoing nature of revelation, while the ontological anthropology stresses revelation as a given and completed reality. The psychological framework takes special heed of learning as an inductive process in the concrete situation. The ontological framework gives more attention to learning as a deductive process starting with certain abstract principles of presuppositions. Again, the one calls attention to the lived experiences and needs of the individual contemporary local Church, while the other stresses important past experiences of Church tradition and the requirements of the universal Church.

These two points of view yield very different interpretations of the relationship between the mission of the Church and what must be maintained to support that mission. This in turn produces the polarization between the so-called liberal and conservative movements in the Church. Those who take a more psychological approach stress that specific structures, forms of ministry, policies, and modes of thought in the Church should be maintained only as long as they are contributing to the radical mission of the Church to preach the gospel. From this perspective it is conceivable that even long-standing traditions and teachings may give way to new developments with no essential loss to the Church's central mission. So, for example, if religious orders of teaching sisters, who have played such a crucial role in forming the American Church, were to gradually disappear, those working within the psychological framework might not be overly dismayed. It might be argued that only by such a decline will women assume a more vital presence in the Church of our day. The charism of dedicated, consecrated Christian women will not die, but it will simply resurface in a different, more vital contemporary form.

From the more ontological approach the mission of the Church is thought to be best served precisely by the maintenance of long-standing structures, practices, forms of ministry, and modes of thought.

For these are the tested and efficient ways of fulfilling the Church's timeless mission. Hence, it is better to work at strengthening the ministry of the teaching sisters and the Catholic elementary school system than to hypothesize about new forms of ministry for women.

In a pastoral context these two frameworks are painfully manifest. One priest expends his energies attempting to do all the many different things that must be done in order to maintain and strengthen the life of the parish community as it presently exists. A fellow priest regularly asks why certain things are done at all. Should the priests and the parish continue providing all services that people have come to expect over a long period of time? Are some of the many time-consuming activities of parish priests all but incompatible with their deepest discernment of their mission as priests?

The tension between these two views of mission and maintenance in the Church is part of a necessary dialectic. Two essentially positive terms, *liberal* (to free) and *conservative* (to save), are often used to describe them. Every vital community must have members with an acute sensitivity to history, tradition, and order, as well as those who are especially concerned about the present, the future, and change. This is true in the same way that every community needs its prophets, who in shrill tones and with great impatience focus the community's attention upon cutting-edge issues and problems that will not go away, as much as it needs its sages. The sage works in a quiet and disciplined way to develop solutions to urgent problems that they themselves might never have noticed had it not been for the loud complaint of the prophet. There can be no question about the constant need of the Church to be enriched by intelligent and informed liberals as well as intelligent and informed conservatives. Unfortunately, the two terms have been overlaid with pejorative connotations and caricatures that tend to make the two mutually exclusive.

According to one caricature, the "liberal" is essentially a hypocrite who is unwilling to admit that he has lost or is losing his faith. He is intellectually arrogant, irresponsible, insensitive, and destructive. He is the self-appointed underminer of authentic Catholic teaching and he is beyond argument. Orthodoxy is of no importance to him and the only real heresy is not being "relevant." He is at a loss to explain how there was an intelligentsia in the Church prior to the Enlightenment period, which he regards almost as a time of "revelation." If he would simply admit that he was a secular humanist, not a true believer, and leave the Church, then believers would be less scandalized and the mission of the Church would be advanced.

According to another caricature, the "conservative" is reactionary, brittle, defensive, threatened, nervous, and anti-intellectual. He is the self-appointed protector of the "deposit" of divine revelation and no one can dispute him on his sacred mission. Everyone who does not affirm his interpretation of orthodoxy, which is always "the mind of the Church," is suspect of heresy. He is at a loss to explain how the Holy Spirit was with Pius XII but not with John XXIII and Paul VI who triggered near radical reforms in the Church. Nor can he account for why he must be so nervously protective of divine truth. If he is correct in his loud protest that they are of God, then they will certainly survive him as well as the liberals.

These caricatures point to one of the questions that will be examined in the following pages. What are the irreducible starting points of a religious tradition? The conservative is sometimes accused of biblical, dogmatic, liturgical, or magisterial fundamentalism insofar as he equates a particular form with the reality it mediates and opposes change on principle. The liberal is ever happy to point out that what *is*, obviously is *possible*. He then proceeds to enumerate the many changes of recent decades which earlier conservatives declared could never come about in the Church.

The liberal has no difficulty pointing out the fact that just as the Church has gradually overcome biblical fundamentalism, it must now overcome a dogmatic fundamentalism that does not fully explore the historical and cultural context of magisterial statements. Yet, he may have difficulty being equally critical of the dogmatism latent in the values of contemporary culture and current theological developments. The liberal, upon reflection, must concede that he too has certain key affirmations that constitute his own irreducible starting point. The conservative, as the custodian of the rich patrimony of tradition, may feel that like Joyce's "Araby" he is compelled to bear his chalice bravely through a throng of foes.

The differences between liberal and conservative with regard to what each considers to be irreducible starting points may cause great pain and strife in the life of the Church. No intelligent and committed person easily compromises what he deems essential. In some instances, strife and conflict are apparently the only path to growth. In other instances, they result in irreparable harm.

The elusive reality of style plays a part in this conflict. The Church as a historical reality has both formed, and been formed by, diverse aspects of culture. This cultural involvement has much influenced the art, music, ritual, prayer, mysticism, and spirituality of the Church. It has also had a profound influence upon such diverse realities as the formulation of ethical value systems and the life-style of the clergy. So complex is this involvement that, paradoxically, when conservatives stand firm in defense of some rich aspect of the Church's style in order to stave off the secularizing mentality of the liberal, it may well be that what is being protected was originally adopted by the Church from an earlier secular culture. Style is a subtle reality. There is no question of the Church being without style. It would be as impossible for the Church to be without style as it would be for an individual person. For example, we sometimes hear the general descriptions "Low Church" and "High Church" with regard to liberal and conservative preferences in liturgy. It is not uncommon that Catholic people now "shop around" for a church with a liturgical celebration that they are comfortable with. One may be solemn and dramatic, while the other is informal and personal. But both are characterized by definite styles.

At first, one might think that these differences are simply matters of personal preference and different degrees of aesthetic sophistication. They are better left to the individual or local community. The problem, however, is that style is not merely the ornamentation of a common substance. In religion, style may often be a conveyer of substance.

It is possible to be enamored with style and miss the substantial reality altogether. So a conservative may favor the splendor of High Church liturgy and be moved to tears by its intimation of the awesome transcendent harmonies of the divine. A liberal may favor the unpretentiousness of Low Church liturgy and be equally moved by the gracious nearness of divine immanence. Yet both may be unwilling or even unable to love and respect the other as neighbor because of their liturgical differences!

In matters of style, the conservative is quite right in arguing that certain realities represent important cultural achievements on the part of the Church. Even if they are not absolutely essential to the heart of the Church, still they serve as an important support and enhancement of religion. Therefore, it is most imprudent to casually disregard such achievements which do not come into being overnight. The liberal is equally correct when he argues that when these important but non-essential realities are no longer enhancing and supporting the mission of the Church and perhaps even are impeding that mission, they must be altered, if not abandoned. The clash occurs, of course, when conservatives seek to attribute divine and immutable authority to style in order to protect a human achievement, and when liberals yield with reckless abandon to the maxim that whatever is changeable must be changed. Such mindless attitudes underscore the fact that it is intelligent and informed conservatives and liberals who are needed to preserve and enhance the wisdom of the Church.

III

My ministry has provided me with a number of perspectives from which to view and participate in the American Church as a wisdom community. As a parish priest in city and suburban parishes in Chicago, as a teacher in a Catholic high school, as a doctoral student at the University of Louvain, and as a campus minister at Chicago State University, I became very aware of, and very involved in, the tensions that I have been describing.

Later I served as visiting professor in Ecumenical Studies at Harvard Divinity School, as visiting professor at the University of Notre Dame, and gave retreats at a number of universities and seminaries. During that time, I addressed a large number of clergy and adults in educational programs and participated in workshops, conferences, and institutes in religious education at the regional, national, and international levels. It has also been possible for me to engage a number of bishops in frank discussion of the present state of the Church and their assessment of current theological developments. These experiences have widened the base of my experience. And with that, my sense of an unaddressed tension has increased.

In my present ministry as "staff theologian" for the Diocese of Cleveland, I work in close association with the bishop, his administrative and pastoral staff, and the seminary. I am often in different parishes in the diocese. This experience has afforded me a view of an entire diocese.

In these different contexts, I have encountered widespread bewilderment, confusion, and anxiety. In various forms and to various degrees this dis-ease seems to exist in diverse sectors of the Church community: bishops, theologians, parish priests, sisters, deacons, brothers, and seminarians, as well as the individuals and families who make up local parish congregations. The differences within and among these groups in some cases have reached open hostility and, even worse, indifference.

This growing tension does not only exist between bishops and theologians, between traditional, moderate, and progressive theologians, between younger and older generations of clergy and laity, and between bishops of one mind-set and those of another. It also exists in the heart, mind, spirit, and life-style of many individuals, whether priest, bishop, lay person, or theologian. Many individuals are not comfortable acknowledging this inner tension. But one has only to reflect on one's own life story to note the issues on which one once thought one would never change. Yet, in fact, one has changed a great deal. By a similar scrutiny one will confront the tension that sometimes exists between one's deepest inner feelings and one's public and official statements. Worse than that, one may find oneself unwilling to examine certain questions seriously. Often these questions have potentially staggering consequences with which individuals simply cannot cope.

I have written this book because a large number of people are at a loss for a sense of the whole. That is not to imply that this book gives an account of the whole or that its author is writing from some enviable universal viewpoint. *The Wisdom Community* is intended as a descriptive overview of key elements in the present ferment. Its goal is to be an aid for individuals and groups in an ongoing process of self-understanding and self-location. This can be accomplished when individuals have a structure that makes it possible for them to recognize and articulate their ever developing religious identities. A greater sense of self-location, however, is not sufficient. There is an equally honest and urgent desire on the part of many Catholic people to understand and better appreciate others no matter how much they disagree with them. Therefore, *The Wisdom Community* invites a joint effort. It is a collaborative enterprise leading to the recovery of common meaning.

The Wisdom Community is a kind of sketch book. It employs a number of descriptive models, theological sketches, thought patterns, and reference categories. Examples of these are the analysis of culture as "classical" and "modern," the analysis of human experience in patterns, the enumeration of different forms of conversion, and the methodological distinction between different modes of mediation.

They are intended as sketches, not as caricatures. Though no one of them is completely filled out or elaborated, it is hoped that their general lines are sufficiently clear that they can be recognized. They can be expanded upon by turning to appropriate works on specific topics. The book is written from a moving viewpoint that intends to help the reader in a process of bringing together central elements in the way he thinks about religion. Because of this, it is inevitable that one reader will smile knowingly to himself over a passage, while another will be indifferent to it, and yet another will feel the excitement of recognition and understanding.

The book is intended to be accessible to a diverse readership.

Hopefully, it is a book that seminarians in a theologate will find help-ful in "thinking theologically" and in becoming more enthusiastic about theology no matter how "pastoral" they envision their future ministry to be. It is also intended for priests who are seeking a frame of reference for their diverse pastoral experiences and the theological literature they read. Perhaps some religious will find in these pages some important guides for interpreting their experiences in ministry and religious life. Those charged with religious education may find this work an asset in sifting through and interpreting the ever grow-ing volume of theological literature. Bishops and theologians may find it a helpful descriptive summary of some of their common con-cerns. Christians of other traditions may find this study a useful point of entry into Catholic pluralism. For some Catholic laymen and lay-women, this work may serve as an "introduction to theology."

There are inherent problems in addressing a pluralistic reader-ship. Some of the laity, who teach every young parish priest so much of what it means to be a priest, may complain that I do not give suffi-cient examples of their experiences, anxieties, and resilience in the face of a changing Church. Have I forgotten all those conversations sitting around a kitchen table? Has my academic work dimmed my memory of the important questions and experiences that were shared there over a cup of tea? Do I not realize that so many of them have come into their own and taken hold of an adult Christian faith? Do I not understand that their time of anxiety has passed?

Some parish priests might think that I have lost touch with their world. I am rather naive if I think that the demands of pastoral minis-try will allow the leisure time needed to become involved in or start such a program as *The Wisdom Community* suggests. With the door bell and the phone never silent, and more meetings and programs than there is time for, how are priests to establish a wisdom community? This may be for those who like to speculate, but they would have pre-ferred a more immediately useful book.

Some theologians might wonder at such a book as this. Would it not be better to make a serious contribution to the field? Anyone can popularize. Is it not a disservice to give the broad outline of many dif-ficult theological issues without fully developing them? Good inten-tions are praiseworthy, but forays into "popular theology" are always dangerous. Misunderstandings and harsh judgments will come from all sides.

Some bishops might question why the book has not taken a clear-er stance in defense of Catholic teachings. What is the value of raising questions that will perplex and confound many believers? Why has the magisterium not been cited more often to answer some of the questions addressed? By setting out so many issues without giving a firm and clear answer, do we not feed the contemporary penchant for relativism?

Ultimately, it is only the concrete use of the program that will answer or validate these misgivings.

The Wisdom Community may be read in two ways. It may be read as one reads any expository work. Readers may go from page to page agreeing and disagreeing, understanding and misunderstanding, liking and disliking what they read. They may finally conclude that it was or was not "worthwhile" reading. It may be read in another way, however. It may be read as a point of departure for a genuine effort at self-understanding. In this sense, it may be read with the intention to actually form a "wisdom community." It is only by participating in a wisdom community that one can determine whether the program will work and is of value. It is hoped that many will adapt the program to their local pastoral needs and try it.

I am personally confident of the basic value and fruitfulness of the program suggested by *The Wisdom Community*. This confidence flows from my repeated use of the model as a university student, a parish priest, an adult education lecturer, a university professor, and a diocesan theological consultant. Among these successful experiments have been a group of parishioners in a suburban parish, a small band of fellow graduate students, a group of students at Harvard University, and many specially tailored workshops and retreats.

The Wisdom Community is divided into seven chapters. Chapter One, "What Happened?" provides the context by giving a descriptive analysis of some of the central factors that have so fragmented and separated the Catholic world that we may speak of the decline of common meaning. Each reader will be able to enflesh that account with the realities of his lived experience.

Chapters Two and Three, "The Turn to Interiority" (parts one and two), seek to unravel a number of the complex factors involved in a religious interpretation of reality for the contemporary person. After examining key patterns of human experience within which questions of ultimate meaning and hence the question of God are raised, I examine the crucial reality of conversion. By distinguishing religious, theistic, Christian, ecclesial, moral, and intellectual conversion, it is possible to meet in a direct way the complex horizons within which religious affirmations are made.

Chapters Four and Five, "Theology in a New Key" (parts one and two), examine the question of method in contemporary theology.

Three distinct contexts in which theological reflection takes place are outlined. *Critical mediation* is the mode of theology in the university. *Dogmatic mediation* is the mode of theology in an explicitly committed religious tradition. *Existential mediation* is the mode of theology in the socio-cultural context. These three different approaches to theology exist in a dynamic tension with one another. In the light of this tension, the questions of authority, teaching office, and certitude are raised.

Chapters Six and Seven, "The Wisdom Community" (parts one and two), provide an elaboration of the presuppositions and specific structure of the wisdom community as a program. While these chapters go into some detail, it is not the finished product that can only be determined and designed in the concrete situation by the participants themselves. It may be helpful for some to read these final chapters first.

This introduction is best concluded with an example. A family has to move. The husband is being transferred to a distant city. There is ample time to prepare for the move in an orderly fashion. All of the family's many belongings that make their home distinctly theirs are carefully packed. A new home is chosen in a neighborhood and atmosphere that is almost a duplication of their former environment. After an initial inconvenience, over time they live as if they had never lived any place else.

But now look at it this way. In the dark of night fire breaks out in their home the night before the move. There is only enough time for the family members to save themselves. From a neighbor's embrace, they watch as their home is swallowed up in flames. Yet amid their anxiety, there is quiet gratitude in their hearts that in spite of their great loss, they have saved what is most essential. They have survived as a family.

The Church at large and the American Church in particular are undeniably on the move. But one hears little consensus. Where are we moving from? Where are we moving to? How long do we have to get there? Will we know when we have arrived? The excitement surrounding three popes in as many months is not by chance. The Church is still a wisdom community. For many the present time is a "Kairos"—a fitting time or, in Newman's phrase, a "second spring." It is a time for greater self-scrutiny so as to discern rash judgments and biases, the difference between mere likes and dislikes and what is judged to be essential. It is a time to stand firm, yet remain agile and adventuresome; neither loathing the familiar nor being shocked by the novel. In short, at least for a few, it may be time for a new kind of community. Those who choose it will find it difficult. Its success is a high and distant goal. That goal, however, holds great promise. As Pope John Paul II has said, in spite of doubt, crisis, and collapse, there is a new surge of life in the Church![1]

NOTES

1. See Pope John Paul II, Encyclical Letter *Redemptor Hominis* (Vatican City: Vatican Polyglot Press, 1979), p. 15.

Chapter One
What Happened?

Introduction

Let us start with a point of agreement. Whether you are an active layperson in a parish congregation, a parish priest, a sister on a pastoral team, a university theologian, the bishop of a diocese, or an interested bystander, your own personal experiences and the experiences of your friends and colleagues convince you of the fact that "something" of major significance has "happened" to Western culture and American society in general and to the Roman Catholic Church in particular. There may be little agreement concerning precisely "what" has happened, how long it has been happening, whether or not it has ceased happening, or whether or not this "happening" ultimately augurs for good or ill for the human family and the several Christian churches. But something has definitely happened. And things are different as a result.

As for "what" has happened, many opinions are offered: the advent of secularism, a compromise approach to ecumenism, the inability to manage the momentous changes ushered in by the Second Vatican Council, a shift on the part of religion from concern about the "transcendent" and the "heavenly" to concern for the "immanent" and the "worldly," a knowledge explosion set off by biblical scholars and liberal speculative theologians, a growing lack of docility on the part of pastors to their bishops and bishops to the Vatican, a decline of vocations, and a gradual decline of docility on the part of the "people in the pews." More positively, we have seen a greater involvement of the Church at every level with the struggle for human freedom and liberation, a more collaborative relationship between bishops and theologians, attempts to concretize the Vatican Council's call for collegiality by means of the Synod of Bishops, Diocesan Pastoral Councils and team ministry, and a new fervor, confidence, and agility among many of the laity.

All of these things "happened," but I will argue that not even all of these realities together or some other unmentioned "events" constitute the full answer to the question, "What happened?" For what happened was more radical and more profound in its implications than any of these particulars. The above-mentioned developments and their counterparts in the larger society are only manifestations of a complex process of cultural and social upheaval and transformation. And it is this multifaceted process that has resulted in the "decline of common meaning."

Before examining the decline of common meaning, I believe it is necessary to give a general overview of the phenomenon of religion and to explore the relationship of religion and culture. This chapter, then, will be in five parts: (1) The Nature of Religion; (2) The Emergence of Theology; (3) The American Context; (4) The Shift from Classical to Modern Culture; and (5) The Decline of Common Meaning.

1. The Nature of Religion

It is impossible to give an adequate definition of the reality pointed to by the word "religion." There is not even a scholarly consensus concerning the etymology of the word.[1] It is better to offer elements of a description than to seek to give a definition. A first element of a description would be that religion is a response of an individual or of a people to a cluster of radical questions. Some of these questions are: What is the ultimate meaning of human existence? Do I have a personal destiny in the universe? What is the fate of the dead? What is the origin of the cosmos? Which is more lasting, chaos or order? The questions themselves may not be articulated, but a positive or religious response is manifest when a people become aware of the "sacred" dimension of reality in contrast with the "profane." This response may lead a people to populate the heavens with gods or an individual to withdraw into quiet mysticism. In either case there is at least a tacit awareness of a sacred dimension "within" or "beyond" all human experience.

The second element of a description is that this "sacred" reality is manifest by an "event" or "experience." The great religions of the world have at their foundation a celebrated real or fabled "event," series of events, or sacred persons. But *something* happens! Someone or a group sees something, hears something, dreams something, or "interprets" a series of events in a particular way. This primal "event" is seen as an "inbreak" of the sacred. This originating, engendering experience is disclosive of an unseen but abiding reality. It is, therefore, revelatory and the central persons become prophetic or paradigmatic figures. The "event" is paradoxical. Whether it is an encounter with the holy (hierophany) or a revelation of God (theophany), it remains an encounter with the "known unknown." What is revealed is revealed as mystery. The disclosure is marked by concealment. This encounter with "holy mystery" leads to the transformation of an individual or community. Among other things, it is this "event" element that distinguishes religion from philosophy. For philosophy asks some of the same foundational questions addressed by religion. But philosophy does not look to a disclosive event, "sacred history," or "sacred person" for its answer. Rather, philosophy focuses its reasoned reflections upon Aristotle's primordial "wonder" at the human condition and the universe.

A third element of a description of religion is the fact of "mediation." The inner meaning of the revelatory event that focuses one's ultimate concern is passed on or mediated through and to a community. This is of paramount importance inasmuch as it is this mediation of religious meaning that preserves and insures continuity with the originating event. This mediation of meaning is accomplished by means of signs, symbols, narratives (myths, legends, stories), traditions, factual history, rituals, cults, sacred persons, and eventually sacred texts which become the charter documents of the community, providing the community with a collective memory as well as norms for worship, belief, and order. The originating, engendering events may come to be seen as having occurred in "sacred time" and their ritual re-presentation is celebrated in "sacred space." Over time, all of the central elements of the process may become stylized and strictly regulated.

The primary concern in this process of mediation is to preserve and pass on the meaning of the engendering revelation. Therefore, the narratives that emerge may not be factual history in every detail in the strict "eyewitness" sense. So the important question may not be, "Did the encounter between Moses and the 'bush that burned but was not consumed' happen in exactly the way it is narrated in Exodus?" The question may rather be, "Does the narrative preserve and mediate the meaning of a radically disclosive, transforming, and ineffable event in Moses' life that may be termed an encounter with God?" Or more pointedly, the question may not be, "Are all the wondrous details in the infancy narratives of Matthew and Luke 'factual' in the sense that one hopes for facts in a newspaper?" But rather the question may be, "Do these narratives effectively convey the utterly unique meaning and significance that the authors ascribe to the one who was born?"[2]

When the primal meaning of a religious "event" is mediated to a people by means of narrative, ritual, and sacred texts, the several elements of "event," "meaning," and "mediation" coalesce, providing a coherent view of reality. This interpretive scheme, symbol system, or world view serves as a context within which a people draw their response to the many radical questions that spring forth from the inquiring dynamism of the human spirit. It is important to recall that for most of us these questions may rarely, if ever, be articulated in a formal or conscious manner. (See Figure 1.)

Over a period of time, the interplay of these elements constitutes the common meaning of a religious community. For the cohesiveness of a religious community, like every other community, is built upon common meaning. Common meaning exists when a people share more or less the same base of experiences, raise similar questions about those experiences, come to the same general understanding of the meaning of those experiences, make similar judgments about the truth and value of the common understanding of the shared experiences, and, finally, follow upon those judgments with common dedication and commitment to the values and truths affirmed. Such is the dynamic of love animating a family, loyalty animating a state, and faith animating a religious community.[3] (See Figure 2.)

This interlocking relationship of shared experiences, understandings, judgments, and commitments constitutes the unity of a people's religious identity. However, an important clarification must be made. The originating, engendering experience or experiences of the disclosive event is obviously not shared by all in the same manner. The direct and immediate experience of this revelatory event is reserved to the original "witnesses" who subsequently "proclaim" the experienced event and its meaning to others. This is accomplished by means of narratives, rituals, and sacred texts. These embody the common understandings and judgments about the original experiences. And, paradoxically, participation in the symbols, myths, and rituals that are mediators of the meaning of the originating experience puts a people "in touch" with the foundational event in a manner that is self-authenticating and, to a degree, "available" only to the belief community. Common commitment and ultimately common meaning result from this experience and interpersonal process.

FIGURE 1

RELIGIOUS MEANING AND THE EMERGENCE OF THEOLOGY

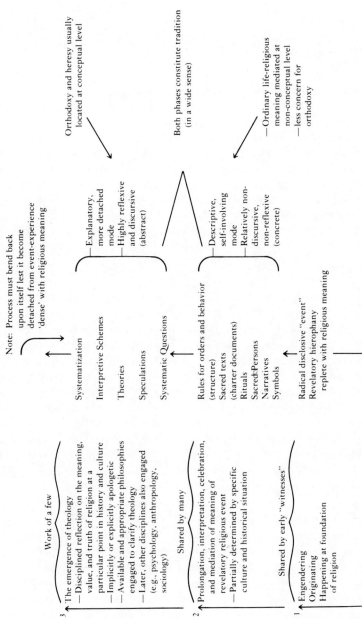

Note: Process must bend back upon itself lest it become detached from event-experience 'dense' with religious meaning

Orthodoxy and heresy usually located at conceptual level

Both phases constitute tradition (in a wide sense)

—Ordinary life-religious meaning mediated at non-conceptual level
—less concern for orthodoxy

— Explanatory, more detached mode
— Highly reflexive and discursive (abstract)

— Descriptive, self-involving mode
— Relatively non-discursive, non-reflexive (concrete)

Systematization
Interpretive Schemes
Theories
Speculations
Systematic Questions

Rules for orders and behavior (structure)
Sacred texts (charter documents)
Rituals
Sacred Persons
Narratives
Symbols

Radical disclosive "event"
Revelatory hierophany replete with religious meaning

3
Work of a few

The emergence of theology
— Disciplined reflection on the meaning, value, and truth of religion at a particular point in history and culture
— Implicitly or explicitly apologetic
— Available and appropriate philosophies engaged to clarify theology
— Later, other disciplines also engaged (e.g., psychology, anthropology, sociology)

2
Shared by many

Prolongation, interpretation, celebration, and mediation of meaning of revelatory religious event
— Partially determined by specific culture and historical situation

1
Shared by early "witnesses"

Engendering
Originating
Happening at foundation of religion

FIGURE 2

COMMON MEANING
Source and structure of community

Common meaning exists when all members of a group share all four elements

4. Commitment—Shared truths and values sustained by common symbols, by concrete deeds made manifest.

3. Judgment—Shared affirmations and negations concerning truth, value, meaning

2. Understanding—Shared desire to understand
   —Similar questions concerning truth, value, meaning

1. Experience—Shared base of common experiences

Common meaning declines when one or more of these key elements is not shared by members of a group

Note: Uniformity not required; wide range of diversity possible

e.g. —love animating diverse members of family
   —loyalty animating diverse members of state
   —faith animating diverse members of church

2. The Emergence of Theology

As a people become more sophisticated, as their culture becomes more advanced, and as they become more reflective, there emerges the possibility of theology as a reality distinct from religion. While religion is the concrete, self-involving reality by which a community relates to the "sacred," this relationship need not become self-conscious. It may remain in a concrete commonsense and descriptive form that is taken for granted. However, should some of the adherents of a religion take a self-conscious, critical, explanatory, or apologetic stance, theology (as distinct from religion) gradually emerges in the more or less systematic and philosophical reflections upon the meanings and values embodied in a religion in a particular cultural context. This development is analogous to other developments in the human community. So to the arts are added theories of aesthetics, to communities of peoples are added sociological theories, to the dynamic processes of the human mind are added the speculations of psychology and psychiatry.

Because of the gradual distinction that obtains between religion and theology, it is helpful to distinguish an *experiential dimension* of religion from the *expressive dimension*. The *experiential dimension* embraces what I have termed the originating "event" that was experienced as a revelation or disclosure of the sacred. This dimension consists of the concrete, personal, and subjective structures that shape and form religious experiences in all their variety.[4] Subjectivity and pluralism are inevitable as a result of the complexity of the human condition, the diverse contexts in which the revelatory experiences occur, and the vastness and incomprehensibility of the divine reality at the ground of the experience. The experiential dimension transforms the world view of those who have participated in the experience.

The process of prolonging, communicating, celebrating, and mediating the meaning of the transforming experience constitutes the *expressive dimension* of religion. This expressive dimension preserves and mediates the value and the reality of the experience by means of narratives, symbols, rituals. Just as the experiences of the divine are multidimensional, so also are the expressions of these experiences. The expressive dimension, therefore, may take the form of ceremonies, artifacts, oral traditions, and written texts which come to serve as charter documents that are narrative accounts of the communities' encounter with ultimate reality. Efforts to clarify the meaning of these normative texts, rituals, and experiences yield specific creedal utterances. Subsequent philosophical reflection upon the meaning and truth of these utterances produces partial or fully developed theoretical constructs and systems.[5] And this addition of technical and theoretical language constitutes the emergence of theology as we have come to know it.

This brief account of the nature of religion was deliberately generic because it makes it easier to note that, *mutatis mutandis*, all of the major religions of the East and West can be understood within this general framework. The recognition of this fact does not diminish the uniqueness of the Christian religion in any way. It does point out significant similarities between the great religions that many Catholics overlook.

Today the profound and incalculable influence of the Jewish experience and the Old Testament upon Christianity is widely recognized. The Jewish world view and the Old Testament longings, expectations, and prophecies constitute both the horizon and the context of the Christian event. Strictly speaking, the *inner* experiences of Jesus of Nazareth from his childhood through his public life (including his baptism, desert experiences, temptations, and early self-understanding) are not directly accessible to us. While many and varied opinions concerning that inner experience are put forth, they do not constitute direct knowledge. And perhaps central to that speculation are questions concerning the possibility of some utterly unique disclosive and revelatory event in Jesus' life which served as the fountain from which flowed his mediation of the meaning of who and what he was to others.

Much more can be said of friends and followers of Jesus. Their encounter with him was indeed experienced as a disclosive and revelatory event. His being was an embodiment of the sacred and his person was a theophany. His parabolic words and wondrous deeds filled out this transforming encounter. These experiences, the subsequent reflection upon them, and the integrating grasp of their inner meaning in the Pentecost "event" constituted the experiential dimension in the lives of the earliest Christian witnesses. The meaning of the Jesus "event" was preserved by his followers by recounting the story, or good news, of his transforming words and deeds (oral tradition, narratives, sacred texts) and by celebrating a sacred meal in commemoration of Jesus' final extraordinary meal with them (ceremony, ritual). Over time what emerged as a Jewish sect became a religious community unto itself with its own proper "common meaning." Hence, in Antioch the followers of Jesus are explicitly called Christians (circa 46 A.D.). They declared Jesus to be the Lord, the Christ of

God. This process constituted the beginning of what has been termed the "expressive dimension."

Over time this community of common meaning became the "ecclesia," the Church. And as it expanded and moved about, there were more and more reflections on the meanings mediated in the narratives and rites proclaiming Jesus to be the Christ of God. As this reflection took a philosophical turn, there were often bitter controversies over issues which eventually became teachings or doctrines. Eventually these doctrinal expressions took on community-wide authority as dogmas. These dogmas were further reflected upon and elaborated at particular times and in particular cultures, and the products of these reflections constituted the prevailing theology of a particular epoch. A powerful example of this is the work of Thomas Aquinas in the thirteenth century and the resultant Thomistic or scholastic philosophy and theology that held sway for centuries, even into the modern era.

The Christian religion in general and the Roman Catholic Church in particular trace their impetus to the *written* proclamation of Jesus as the Christ of God. Subsequent centuries have witnessed a great concern for adequate theoretical and technical language to express the communities' religious self-understanding. It would appear that the verbal expressions argued over and refined in the great early councils and elaborated in the highly nuanced and minutely detailed speculations of theologians were the most important of the expressive dimensions in the mediation of the meaning of the Christian event over the centuries. However, this is not exactly the case. In the world of lived religion the most important of the expressive elements were (and remain) the images, symbols, stories, and ceremonies. For these are the realities that evoke the "numinous" or mysterious reality that is at the heart of religion.

In the Eucharist and other sacraments, for example, the several elements of drama, music, spectacle, symbol, myth, narrative, sacred time, sacred place, and sacred person were brought together in a manner that deeply touched as well as formed the lives of believers, even as theoretical controversies raged. Further, the history of Western art was for many centuries dominated by Christian images. One has only to think of the following: the heroic achievement of the Gothic cathedrals with their stunning, image-filled stained glass windows and awesome spires; the inner domes of Byzantine churches aglow with their fierce images of Christ the Pantokrator; Michaelangelo's sweeping images of Genesis on the ceiling of the Sistine Chapel; countless images of the Madonna and Child, the Nativity scene, the Crucifixion, the Resurrection, and the Last Judgment; the Morality plays; the legends, devotions, and cults surrounding various religious heroes ("Saints"); the personal experiences believed to be apparitions and revelations in their own right; and the pious traditions of regional ethnic and family groups. These and many other essentially image and feeling realities constitute the "expressions" that have been most influential in communicating the common meaning of the Christian religion. It is these "concrete" mediators rather than abstract theories that for most people trigger their awareness of the gracious reality at religion's center.

In spite of the pre-eminent influence of profound feeling and emotions associated with images, it was not stained glass windows, or bas-reliefs above a cathedral entrance, or completely fictionalized artistic renderings of the Nativity that were branded heretical. The proponents of ideas and theories and the intellectual speculations that were at variance with normatively taught common theoretical meaning were branded heretics and errors. Hence, in the sixteenth century, the Council of Trent, responding to Luther and the Protestant Reformation, initiated a counter reformation by spelling out in precise detail the Catholic Church's position on certain disputed issues. And, by means of a renewed discipline, the Council tightly restructured the central elements of creed, code, and cult in the Church. And in the last century, when Pope Pius IX and the First Vatican Council, following upon the threat of the Enlightenment movement, declared the pope to be "infallible" when he teaches "ex cathedra" concerning faith and morals, the concern again was more for the discursive and verbal aspect of religious expression than for the rich symbols which provide the soil from which these verbal expressions emerge. (See Figure 1.)

3. The American Context

This background is very helpful for understanding the state of the American immigrant Church during the early and middle decades of this century. It was a minority religion, the vast majority of whose communicants were members of various ethnic groups (e.g., Irish, Polish, Italian, German) struggling to gain a foothold in the "new world."

The universal Church was organizing in a style that evoked military metaphors. The chain of command was clear from the top down: the Pope, the Vatican Curia, the local bishop, the vicar general, the monsignor who was pastor of the local parish, his curates, the sister who was principal of the school as well as superior of the convent of teaching sisters, and, finally, the laypeople in the pews. This military metaphor was carried over into titles and uniform colors for those who held certain positions of command. Life centered around the parish and often around the parish school. The parish buildings were the pride of a generous and hard-working clergy and laity alike. In most cases the pastor was the best educated and most influential member of the community.

Catholic identity and practice were fairly set. At an early age children imbibed a Catholic "self-concept" from the clear and straightforward questions and answers in *The Baltimore Catechism*. There was no question that a common meaning was mediated concerning the realities of the Trinity, the life, death, and resurrection of Jesus, the one, true Church, the need for loyalty and obedience, the sacraments, sin, grace, redemption, sexual morality, the nature and efficacy of prayer, the existence and immortality of the human soul, heaven, hell, and purgatory. There was the Catholic newspaper and the Legion of Decency to rate the moral quality of the cinema; and numerous church organizations and activities for all groups flourished. When there were pressing personal, family, or financial problems, the priest was there as a trusted and helpful guide. Many distinctively Roman Catholic postures were proudly acknowledged. Abstinence from meat on Fridays, Sunday Mass obligation, saints, special devotions, confession, large families (no artificial birth control), and pride in having a son advance to the dignity of the celibate priesthood were among them.

In the 1940's and 1950's, when many of the children and grandchildren of these loyal Catholic families became more affluent, they were educated at Catholic universities and they moved to the better neighborhoods and the tree-lined suburbs. A vigorous lay apostolate emerged in some areas, and under the leadership of forward-looking priests and laity, groups such as the Christian Family Movement, with its disarmingly powerful "See, Judge and Act" program, were developed. In small but influential pockets, groups of laity explored the challenging message of the papal social encyclicals. Others appropriated a deep and spiritual understanding of the Eucharist. The unity of the Catholic experience was especially significant when Catholics traveled abroad and found the same familiar, haunting Gregorian chant and stately liturgy.

A kind of "sacred canopy" covered the Catholic experience and galvanized the Catholic identity. Few, if any, would have called it a "Catholic ghetto" because it seemed so right. It touched people at a vital cord. It illuminated the radical questions that plagued the riddle of their existence. It gave them a zone of truth, a place to belong, a challenging vision. Tens of thousands of people benefited from this context in which to live, to grow to maturity, to choose a life-style, to respect their neighbor, perhaps to struggle heroically and silently with some grave personal or family problem, to rear their children, to rejoice at new life, to grieve in the face of mysterious, ever present death, to grow old, to hope for life eternal and to die. Perhaps the unity and effectiveness of this world view reached its pinnacle in the Marian Year of 1954.

This sketch is far from complete. It may even be something of a caricature. It is not intended to be definitive but evocative. But perhaps one or another element in the description will trigger in the reader a recollection of the mood and the style of what the American Catholic experience was for many around 1955.[6]

Two important qualities of a vital organism that were not prominent in the American scene were a sense of history and a dynamic openness to change. Because of the times, perhaps, and through no fault of their own, many laypeople, priests, theologians, sisters, and bishops were not sufficiently aware of the fact that the Church had had a long dynamic history marked by many and sometimes bold and turbulent changes. To be sure, many historical facts were known, but the implications of those facts for their own time were not always grasped. In such a stable context one was not likely to think about the fact that things had not always been the way they were and, therefore, might very well not remain the same. The fact that a particular style of Church life, or a particular understanding of Church doctrine or discipline prevailed for fifty, seventy-five, one hundred, three hundred, or five hundred years does not necessarily give it eternal significance and value, even though it may give it a certain venerable authority. A critical grasp of history reveals that the potential for sweeping change is at the very heart of the Church and its complex relationship to culture. This change may be slow and organic or sudden and discontinuous. It is primarily because these two elements of a sense of history and a dynamic openness to change were not well integrated into the conscious and existential life of the Church that most of the ministers as well as the faithful were not prepared for what happened.

4. *The Shift from Classical to Modern Culture*

During this same period when Church life, though somewhat static, was flourishing, a new dynamism was emerging in theology.

For a long time theology had settled into "schools" of thought, such as Jesuit, Dominican, Franciscan, Roman, or Louvainist. Some of these schools were not primarily occupied with new developments in theological understanding. They had devised a particular style of theology which was quite different from that of medieval openness and scientific curiosity. Narrow theological worlds, marked by a striking internal logic as well as an indifference to relevant external questions, were constructed and passed on to seminarians and future priests in a question-and-answer, or thesis, format. These texts or handbooks came to be known as the "manuals" and they took on a near absolute authority. As this was done, an ever growing number of "disputed questions" on which the schools could reach no agreement seemed to be ignored. Scripture, the writings of the Church Fathers, the decrees of Councils and Popes were used as "proof texts" which guaranteed the "truth" of a thesis without any serious consideration of the historical, social, cultural, political, or theological context and climate in which these "sources" emerged.

A small but diligent band of theologians began to take a more critical look at these sources under the impetus of renewed and serious interest in biblical, patristic, liturgical, and historical studies. These scholars were unwilling to ignore thorny "disputed questions," and their open and persistent investigation uncovered even more problematic issues. One of the central issues was a renewed appreciation of the importance of what an earlier scholar, such as John Henry Newman, was pointing to in his studies of the ongoing development of doctrine. Just how does doctrine develop and to what extent? What was the context and circumstance surrounding the composition of a controversial passage of Scripture? How can the traditional understanding of the creation narrative, which asserts that the human race came to be at one time and in one place (monogenesis), be reconciled with the scientific evidence suggesting multiple origins (polygenesis)? When Scripture scholars and theologians such as Henri de Lubac, Yves Congar, Teilhard de Chardin asked these and many other questions, they were unwelcomed since these queries seemed to challenge the very foundations of previously affirmed unchanging truths. Some looked upon these questioning scholars with suspicion. A few were even silenced. There were harsh attacks upon what theologian Garigou-LaGrange termed "la nouvelle théologie" (the new theology).

The dynamism of this new theological climate could not be stifled. These scholars, plus others such as Edward Schillebeeckx, Karl Rahner, Bernard Lonergan, John Courtney Murray, and a younger generation led by Hans Küng, continued their labors. They ushered in a new age in Catholic theology marked by a genuine grasp of historical consciousness and its myriad of implications. No longer could sources be employed uncritically for theological argumentation. Every source, whether Scripture, patristic writings, conciliar or papal decree, had to be examined critically in its own epoch, context, and horizon. Its meaning could not be automatically transposed over the centuries and into a toally different culture as if those differences were of no importance. Bishops who kept abreast of theology and were pastorally sensitive were also aware of a need for further theological development.

In retrospect, these developments seem almost providential. For when John XXIII was elected Pope in 1958, he made it clear that he would not be a "caretaker pope" by announcing his intention to summon all the bishops of the world to an Ecumenical Council. He argued that the time had come for "opening the windows" and doing some internal housecleaning so as to keep abreast with the times. In a word he called for "aggiornamento." But when the bishops sat in council, most of the pioneering theologians discussed above were also present as theological experts, or "periti," advising and assisting the bishops. As Pope John stated at the outset, Vatican II was a pastoral council, not a dogmatic one. The bold and visionary documents that were issued by the Council give clear witness that the defensive theology of the manuals would not prevail. Though all would not interpret its implications in the same manner, the bishops in principle endorsed the open, creative, positive, and dialectical methods of "la nouvelle théologie."[7] There were, of course, bishops present who were very knowledgeable about current theology and quite open. Cardinal Bea (head of the newly created Secretariat for Christian Unity) and Cardinal Meyer (Archbishop of Chicago), for example, were leaders in ecumenism and religious liberty.

The fruits of the Council are well known. Perhaps most striking to clergy, theologians, and laity alike have been the ongoing reform of the liturgy and the open and active participation in dialogue with other Christian traditions, which has as its expressed goal the reunion of the Christian family. But other things happened as well. John XXIII died between sessions of the Council and was succeeded by Paul VI, a man of a very different style and temperament. At the same time, priests and sisters began to engage in ministries not usually associated with them. Many left the active ministry. Underground movements sprang up. Church attendance declined. Confession decreased. Young people seemed disinterested in the Church even though they were educated at Catholic schools. Some priests and people balked at the liturgical changes; others thought them to be superficial and no real change at all. After a long wait, the encyclical on the regulation of human life, *Humanae Vitae*, was published. The various national conferences of bishops issued highly nuanced pastoral letters of support. Prominent theologians publicly criticized the document. Many of the laity felt vindicated by its conclusions that opposed articicical means of contraception; many others were appalled. A great deal of tension, confusion, anger, and alienation accumulated. The constant media coverage of so sensitive and crucial an issue seemed, at times, to exacerbate the problem.

Quite understandably, many people, sensing that a world that they cherished was undergoing some form of traumatic transformation, sought someone to blame. It was Pope John's fault; he never should have called the Council. Things were just fine before! It was Pope Paul's fault; he was not like Pope John and he raised false hopes by expanding his consultation and waiting so long before his birth control encyclical. It was the liberal priests' and theologians' fault for going far beyond the letter or the spirit of the Council in their pursuit for reform. It was the sisters' fault for teaching personalism to a generation of school children without teaching them Church doctrine. It was the bishops' fault for not grasping what they approved, or for turning reactionary, or for not being able to manage mammoth change. It was the conservatives' fault for docilely yielding their ancient practices and for not praying harder for the Church against the forces of evil. It was the laity's fault for not keeping up with the new theology so as to be ready to take full responsibility when they were told that, of all people, *they* were the Church. It was the fault of the media for blowing even the smallest event all out of proportion so as to give the impression that any day the Catholic Church would collapse. It was the fault of the Protestants for not constantly reminding the Catholic Church that external reform is to no avail without internal renewal.

From the vantage point of history we can see what could not be seen at the time. There is no one to blame. This in no way means that in a particular circumstance an irresponsible priest, sister, bishop, theologian, or lay person was not at fault in a specific conflict. But we can now see that the emergence of historical consciousness among theologians, the summoning of the Council, and the effort to implement its decrees within the Church all took place at a time when monumental shifts and developments were taking place in the larger culture. These sweeping transformations in secular culture were al-

ready at work prior to the period of renewal in the Church. In fact
they were in part a factor in triggering that renewal. However, during an era of unprecedented change it is not immediately obvious to
those who are living through it just how radical and irreversible it
really is. Furthermore, because the Church came into the sixties with
a somewhat insular and separatist attitude, and after a long period of
stability, it is understandable that many who were somewhat aware
that something was afoot in the larger world would have concluded
that whatever it was, it would not significantly affect the impregnable Roman Catholic Church as she attended to her somewhat overdue
internal housecleaning, or "aggiornamento."

Put more exactly, the question is not, "What happened?" but
rather, "What is happening?" in the Church as a result of what is happening in the larger culture. We can now see that multiple factors
were bringing about major changes and transformations in the general culture. Ultimately these changes are due to a gradual process of
shifting from a more classical or traditional understanding of culture
to a modern and pluralistic culture. The widespread availability of
new information and diverse experiences, due to the power of mass
media, intensified forces of change that would eventually undo or at
least reconstruct the personal, moral, social, educational, aesthetic,
political, and religious values of whole generations.

Alvin Toffler, Charles Reich, and Theodore Roszak attempted to
provide semi-popular accounts of this radical shift in works such as
Future Shock, The Greening of America, The Making of a Counter Culture,
and *Where the Wasteland Ends.* The evidence for such a transformation
may be seen and more importantly *felt* everywhere. On the surface it
was manifest in startling new styles of dress, hair, and vocabularies.
More deeply, it was manifest in the existentialist and absurdist concerns of art, literature, and films and in the new sounds in folk and
rock music. More deeply still, it was manifest in the unprecedented
social movements of the late 60's and 70's: the drug culture, the serious and not so serious turn to the religions and consciousness-raising
traditions of the East, campus unrest, a fierce and overdue revolution
on the part of oppressed black people, the anti-war movement, the
women's liberation movement, and, more recently, the previously silent voices of the homosexual and lesbian communities demanding
gay liberation. Furthermore, there were new strains on the family,
the emergence of the commune, more frequent divorce, irresolvable
conflicts between parents and adolescent or college-age children.
With the advent of refined means of contraception, technology made
it possible for the first time in the history of the race to separate sex-

uality completely from the commitments and responsibility consequent upon conception and new life.

It might be argued that all of this was an unfortunate phase in
American history. And like the nightmarish assassinations that punctuated that same era, it should be regretted and not held up as the
"new way." While this is undoubtedly true in part, a more careful
analysis suggests that these phenomena were manifestations of a
deeper and more subtle process. This process was the head-on colli-
sion of two distinct conceptions of culture.

Classical culture takes its origin in the great philosophical and artistic achievements of ancient Greece and the transformation of those
achievements by an elite segment of the peoples of Western Europe.
This classical culture was conceived as culture with a capital "C." It
was in part a matter of respected forms, good grace, style, eternal
truths, and laws that were unchanging and unchangeable. In contrast
the values, customs, mores, and styles of other peoples were thought
to be "primitive," "savage," and "barbaric." The classical view of culture focused upon the unchanging essences of things. Once this essence was grasped, the changes and developments that occurred in
concrete daily life were seen as only "accidental" and of no lasting
significance. Since it was universal, for all peoples and for all times,
classical culture was normative. Anything that was to be considered a
cultural achievement had to meet the canons of this classicist mentality. For example, Kenneth Clark in his celebrated television program,
"Civilization," and the subsequent book of the same title, considers
only the accomplishments of Western European culture as having
contributed significantly to "civilization."

Within such a prevailing culture it is not surprising that God,
humankind, the family, the Church, and the state were well defined.
Consequently biblical, philosophical, and theological categories as
well as social, political, and religious structures were quite stable.
Due to a complex history, the Catholic Church was all but inextrica-
bly wedded to classical culture. In the liturgical history of the
Church, for instance, we can find ready examples of this classical
mentality in regulations that imposed European aesthetics upon
Asian and African Christians down to the last golden tassel and rubric. In spite of the melting-pot pluralism that is thought to be char-
acteristic of America as a democracy, the American Church, like the
Church at large, has been and continues to be interconnected with elements of classical culture.

Modern culture in contrast makes no claim to be normative. The
modern mind views culture as a general notion. Its method is empiri-

cal. Therefore, it recognized culture in the customs and mores of *all* people everywhere. The modern mentality explicitly recognizes that human beings are culture-making animals and that diversity is intrinsic to this process. Modern culture is dynamic, open-ended, and on the move. It is informed, comfortable with contradictory variety, and perhaps less decisive than its classical counterpart. From the modern perspective, past cultural achievements have no absolute right to be preserved. They are rather a springboard for an unknown future. If classical culture can be characterized by an almost intrinsic intolerance for radical diversity, the hallmark of modern culture is pluralism.

Theology like any other science exists in a cultural context. When cultural foundations begin to alter their positions, there is the inevitable necessity of internal and methodological adjustments within the science. Bernard Lonergan has noted a number of important changes in the world of scientific theory, as a result of the cultural shift I have been examining. He has also noted their impact upon theology in its new context.[8] Among these are a move away from the classical concerns for absolute truth and unquestionable certitude to the modern concern for probability; a shift from concern with the changeless to an interest in development and change; a move away from a theoretical search for what is necessarily the case to a concern for an empirical search for what is, as a matter of fact, the case; a favoring of the concrete over the universal; a greater emphasis upon methodology than upon logic; a recognition that science is not a matter of permanent individual achievements, but rather an open-ended development requiring the ongoing collaboration of many.

Perhaps the most far-reaching consequence of the cultural shift in the world of science is the fact that modern science no longer considers it possible to determine the "essence" of a phenomenon. Abandoning the classical search for essences, modern science embraces pluralism and perspectivism. Pluralism accepts the fact that any reality under study may well be too rich or complex to be explained adequately by means of a single "essence." Perspectivism acknowledges that the meaning of a reality may expand or contract when examined from age to age and when viewed from diverse social, political, cultural, or psychological perspectives or horizons. Hence, in the light of Freud, Jung, Durkheim, Piaget, Kohlberg, Erikson, Skinner, and Rogers, being human can be seen as now *more*, and now *less*, than the "animal rationale" of the classical definition. In other words, the diverse data about the human condition disclosed by modern anthropology, psychology, and sociology cannot be discarded as merely "accidental." These data have gradually led to a redefinition of what it means to be human. Certainly the advent of the possibility of genetic engineering will only give impetus to the redefining process.

In this modern pluralistic context religion is examined from many points of view: the history of religion, phenomenology of religion, the psychology of religion, the sociology of religion, and the philosophy of religion. But if these disciplines remain within the boundaries set by the modern scientific method, they cannot come to any definitive conclusion about the ultimate reality with which religion purports to deal. What they can do is to describe in brilliant detail and to explain with great clarity the multiplicity and variety of the religious attitudes that humans display.

It might be thought that, since an inner renewal was at work in theology simultaneous with this radical cultural shift, theology would have remained essentially intact. But to the emergence of historical consciousness must be added the refinements of the scientific method, provocative new ways of interpreting charter documents, the collaboration of Catholic and Protestant theologians, not only with each other but also with other disciplines, and the impact of seemingly random factors that are implied by the general rubric "knowledge explosion."

Of the many reasons that might be given for why theology, and hence many theologians as well as others, underwent a radical transformation rather than minor adaptations, six are particularly significant.

The first[9] is that contemporary religious studies, faithful to the scientific method, raised serious questions about the methods, assumptions, and presuppositions of theology as it has been structured since the sixteenth century when Melchior Cano established the ten starting points from which theologians could ground their arguments. Cano's "De locis theologicis" followed classical assumptions. It viewed truth as eternal, principles as immutable, and change as accidental. But under the painstaking eye of religious studies and the historical method new and staggering questions arose. This was true because the former foundational "sources" (Scripture, patristic writings, decrees of councils and popes, and the medieval syntheses) were subjected to a scrutiny that has been more penetrating and more far-reaching than ever before.

The second reason is a consequence of the first. Namely, the Scriptures—the "sacred text" or "charter document" of the Christian religion—were submitted to the process that has come to be known as demythologizing. As far back as the second century, Scripture was

submitted to philosophical criticism when men such as Clement of
Alexandria declared that many biblical narratives must be recognized
as anthropomorphisms. For *in fact* God has no shape, does not stand,
walk, or sit, and has neither a right nor a left hand. But to this philosophical criticism have been added form criticism, redaction criticism, and the whole historical-critical method. These developments
bring forth radical questions about the composition and the historicity of the gospels, particularly about the critical infancy narratives,
miracle stories, the sayings attributed to Jesus, and the resurrection
accounts.

The third reason is the impact of modern philosophies and the
collapse of Thomism. For centuries, the ordinary conversation partner of theology had been philosophy. However, the philosophy was
of one brand, a classical philosophy derived from ancient Greek and
medieval thought. But the technical and abstract concepts of the classical Aristotelian-Thomistic framework find little resonance with the
more concrete and descriptive style of modern philosophy. On the
one hand, historicism, existentialism, process thought, phenomenology, personalism, and linguistic analysis have brought forth a brace of
new ideas, questions, methods, and techniques that have enriched the
theological enterprise with new and fertile areas of concern. On the
other hand, the very ascendance of so many acceptable philosophical
contexts has meant the eclipse of classical Thomism as the "philoso-
phia perennis." In spite of Pope Leo XIII's famous dictum "vetera no-
vis augere et perficere" in his encyclical *Aeterni Patris*, the "old"
perennial philosophy seems not to have been enriched and augmented by the new, but altogether replaced by it. The works of famous
neo-Thomistic thinkers such as Jacques Maritain and Etienne Gilson,
which would have been familiar to students of philosophy or theology in a Catholic university a few generations ago, would today go
unmentioned in many places. If mentioned, they would be criticized
for their inadequacies in meeting contemporary philosophical and
theological problems.

Even the documents of the Second Vatican Council departed
from the categories of Neo-Scholastic and Thomistic thought, favoring in their stead biblical imagery, more straightforward language,
marked more by a personalist and existentialist than a Thomistic
style. All serious theologians continue to regard Thomas Aquinas as a
pivotal figure in the history of Catholic theology. But he is not turned
to for the definitive resolution of contemporary theological debates.
What was once considered, from a classical viewpoint, to be a permanent achievement, a repository of human wisdom, a possession for all

time requiring only occasional adaptation of an accidental detail, is now regarded as, at best, one of many perspectives from which to explore the universe.

The fourth reason is rather complex. It has to do with what will later be discussed as the turn from a hard to a soft apologetics. There has been a notable de-emphasis upon the normative or dogmatic component of theology. In part this can be understood as the happy result of efforts to curb past excesses and a genuinely open attitude in ecumenical dialogue. And this is all to the good. It is now apparent that even this new attitude is marked by a dialectical tension. On the one hand, those in authority issue general directives on ecumenism, shared Eucharist, ministry, the new rites of reconciliation, or initiation in very collaborative and open tones. On the other hand, when theologians, high-level ecumenical exchanges, the local bishop, parish priest, or pastoral staff set out to implement the spirit of these guidelines in their particular situation, they are often called back by those in authority to the letter of the law.

At a deeper level the more modest approach to the dogmatic element in Catholic theology is the result of the impact of the cultural shift upon what has been termed the "expressive element or dimension" of religion when it is put into theoretical and technical language. If religious utterances are not only meaningful but also true, then in their dogmatic formulation they purport to say something about what is actually the case. Classical dogmatic theology was wedded to a philosophical framework that was thought to be able to ground critically the "truth claims" of religious discourse. Phenomenology, personalism, and existentialism do not make such claims. And indeed analytic philosophy has gone as far as to assert that religious utterances are not "true" in any traditional or verifiable sense of the term. They argue that religious utterances can be neither verified nor falsified. Such utterances may embody or be symbolic of a moral attitude or stance before the world, but they have no "cognitive" referent. They may be a privatized use of language representing a "blick" or peculiar world of religious meaning only available to the initiated. Or such language may be a paradoxical use of language so as to be "disclosive" of a depth dimension of common human experience that can only be adverted to by such "odd" discourse.[10]

The fifth reason is new and open collaboration of theology with other disciplines. If the perennial philosophy was once the privileged "handmaid" of theology, today psychology, sociology, and anthropology, to name the obvious examples, are all available as conversation partners for theology. These disciplines have diverse methods and mass complex data. Theology in the modern context seeks to be the friend of intelligence as it is represented in these other disciplines. However, the methods of these disciplines may appear reductionist as far as theology is concerned. Or the data accumulated may raise serious and not easily answered questions about former theological conclusions. Currently, this is especially true in the case of the relationship of the findings of the behavioral sciences to questions of ethics and morality.[11]

The sixth and final reason that must be noted is the complex and disputed evolution of the role of the theologian in the Church. In the modern pluralistic context, the theologian has become more and more autonomous in many cases. In the early centuries of the Church the most prolific and influential theologians were also bishops. Anselm, Ambrose, Chrysostom, and Augustine are examples. In later centuries theologians were monks who were not bishops. By the Middle Ages theologians were members of great religious communities and professors at leading Catholic universities. Such was the case with the Dominican Thomas Aquinas, at the University of Paris. The bishops continued to have the great responsibility to be the teachers of the message of Christ, but in many cases their ever growing responsibilities made them less and less able to be formally theologians.

In the modern context the theologian may labor in a Catholic university explicitly committed to the re-articulation and development of central issues in the Catholic self-understanding in some area of faith or morals. Even in that context, however, he may feel compelled by the results of his studies and personal integrity to express views that depart somewhat from the common and/or official position on the matter. The Catholic theologian may also labor at the divinity school of a secular university. In that context his more explicit commitment may be to the norms and methodologies of university disciplines. In this context his differences with official positions may be more frequent and more startling than those of his colleague in the Catholic university.[12] The divergent position expressed by contemporary theologians may be explicitly challenged or rejected by the local bishop or a body of bishops. The theologian continues to write and lecture and his views gain a hearing. Inquisitional methods of dealing with these differences are patently un-Christian. In seeking a solution, theologians can be arrogant and self-seeking and bishops can be authoritarian and defensive. However, most theologians and most bishops are not this way and regret this unfortunate stereotyping. Each is solicitous for the good of the Church. Each is further aware that the great bishop-theologians of the past were also saints!

Meanwhile parish priests, religious education coordinators, Confraternity of Christian Doctrine directors, religion teachers in Catholic elementary and secondary schools, seminary professors, and professors of theology in Catholic universities must examine a flood of new publications from popular essays to rigorously technical works. They must make practical judgments for their ministry. Inevitably some are more prudent than others with regard to the intellectual capacities and religious sensibilities of those whom they serve as well as themselves.

5. The Decline of Common Meaning

It would be incorrect to conclude that at a particular moment during, or shortly after, the Second Vatican Council the Roman Catholic Church made a corporate (i.e., laity, clergy, religious, and scholars alike) decision to disengage itself from classical culture, now recognized as obsolete, and to engage modernity, now recognized as the only viable alternative. Were that the case, the process of implementing this important consensus would be long, arduous, and traumatic because the Church has been so long enmeshed in the classical context that it is not always easy to determine whether the Church as we know it is in part the product of classical culture or whether that culture is the product of the Church.

No such corporate decision was ever made. While all *might* agree that ours is an epoch of unprecedented ferment and development, interpretations of the "meaning" of this ferment differ widely. There are those who take their stand on the cutting edge of the future, announcing their freedom in Christ Jesus, and there are those who take their stand on a past achievement of the Church, declaring that classical culture is a providential development essential for the continuation of Christianity in the West. There are those who argue that the "truths of the Church" are in essence "transcultural," and that the urgent need of the hour is not to abandon those truths for novel and transitory opinions, but to develop pluriform and contemporary modes of mediating and communicating these timeless truths. Their critics argue that when the proponents of timeless truth give examples of what they mean, they are, in fact, pointing to certain historically conditioned instances of religion's complex, ever-developing self-expression. Neither the biblical world view, nor Greek metaphysics, nor the medieval syntheses, nor the Tridentine decrees, nor contemporary theological developments escape the limitations of the context in which they were formulated. But it is countered that "within" or "behind" or "beneath" these admittedly limited articulations and expressions there rests a stream of perennial religious truth that admits of no fundamental reversal, though it may be open to a greater "development" than might have been first thought. The situation becomes worse when some "developments" are examined and they seem to be contradictory rather than complementary. H. Richard Niebuhr's study of the relationship of religion to culture provides helpful paradigms for understanding these tensions.[13]

An image may help. The Church, or better the mission or message of the Church, may be likened to an ornate jeweled cross. Over time the central pearl surrounded by rare diamonds has been overlaid with glittering semi-precious stones and even dimestore cosmetic plastic jewels that are very striking to the untrained eye. What is more, about the piece there are many small clear spheres filled with a shimmering unknown liquid. In the radiant sunlight the whole is a splendid sight. A debate arises over what is the essence of this cross. One argues that it is the simple wooden cross at the base of the artifact. But another argues that this cannot be preserved without maintaining every detail of the ornamentation. Another declares that surely the simple beauty of the pearl secured beneath the mass is the essence. Yet others protest that the ring of rare diamonds is of equal or greater import. Not a few conclude that the cosmetic bits might paradoxically be the jewel of great price. A struggle ensues with each participant convinced that he is salvaging the essence. In the midst of the conflict the glass spheres are shattered, and the elusive liquid begins to spread about, dissolve, and eat away most of the precious and common pieces. Many of the protagonists come to a halt, now convinced that it is the liquid that must be preserved. There are others who stand outside the melee confident that all the others are mistaken. They are sure that it is the radiant sunlight that is perennial and it needs no defense for it is capable of reflecting from or shining through the richest or the basest of the elements.

This image intends to describe the decline in common meaning. This decline is not the result of a smooth shift from a classical to a modern world view. It is the result of the frontal confrontation between both world views, the one declaring itself to be perennial and the other declaring itself to have eclipsed its disintegrating predecessor.

Common meaning exists when the interlocking elements of experiences, understandings, judgments, and commitments are shared in a cohesive manner by members of a group. When the cultural foundations of a society are in a period of rapid change, once stable organizations, structures, ideologies, and institutions undergo radical reorganization and re-interpretation. (See Figure 2.)

A major consequence of the decline of common meaning is an altering of the relationship of religion to the social fabric. The Judeo-Christian world view no longer provides the pervasive "sacred canopy" for society at large. It must take its place competing among many instances of meaning (i.e., scientific developments, social movements, the arts, other religions). A particular religious tradition, such as the Catholic Church, experiences a painful ambiguity within its symbols, narratives, rituals, theoretical formulations, and structures that constitute its "experiential dimension." This ambiguity then begins to undermine the "experiential dimension" that needs the "expressive element" for its existence and communication.

As a consequence of this, certain foundational realities, symbols, and concepts, such as God, Christ, Church, Protestant, redemption, priesthood, grace, sacrament, sin, soul, after-life, saint, heaven, hell, purgatory, faith, prayer, mystery, truth, orthodoxy, heresy, obedience, and authority, no longer evoke the same emotional, intellectual, spiritual, behavioral, or attitudinal responses from the pope, the curia, the various regional conferences of bishops, the various bishops within a region, the community of theologians, the people in the pews and the priests, deacons, sisters, and brothers who minister to them. So far-ranging is this pluralism that the actual formal belief of some Catholic people concerning a particular controversial doctrine may be closer to that of Christians of other traditions than it is to the "official" Catholic position. And a key reason for this is that for many, the shared base of common experiences, common understandings, common judgments, and common commitments no longer exists.

With the decline of common meaning many individual members of the Church in whatever station experience an ever growing "disease." Their personal religious self-concept is threatened by a process that seems to be flying out of control. This happens because certain "worlds" that usually exist in a mutually supportive arrangement are no longer in order. Among these are the worlds of the sacred and the profane and the worlds of common sense and of theory.

The world of the profane embraces one's ordinary experiences of everyday life. The world of the sacred embraces one's feelings, intuitions, and convictions that a transcendent, unseen power is the necessary sustainer of the profane world of everyday life. The world of common sense embraces the complex cultural achievement of a concrete historical religion with its many images, symbols, narratives, and rites which celebrate these convictions about the transcendent reality and may also be considered as occasions for genuine encounters with this fuller reality. The world of theory embraces the reflections and speculations about meaning, coherence, and truth of the three prior worlds. The world of theory by its very nature is somewhat removed and detached from the world of concrete living. During relatively stable points in history, these four "worlds" supported one another in an interlocking fashion that was all but taken for granted. Understandably, therefore, when people become aware that the shared bases of experiences, understandings, judgments, and commitments that hold these worlds together are being dislodged, they experience stress, disorientation, and dis-ease. For it was precisely this balance that made the world manageable.

An example may be helpful. A central reality in the Catholic Christian tradition is the self-identification of Jesus with bread and wine during a final meal with his followers the night before his execution. Bread and wine were basic foods in the world of ordinary life, that is, in the profane world, at the time of Jesus. In our day, while they are not seen as being quite as basic as they were in the Near East, they are certainly elements from the world of ordinary life. The person of Jesus is the supreme "disclosure event" of the sacred in the Christian tradition. So the perpetuation of the memorial meal provides a perennial encounter with the world of the sacred. This encounter and its meaning are preserved in the symbols, narratives, and rituals that compose the Eucharist. This is the world of common sense. Centuries of speculation about the meaning, truth, and method of Jesus' self-identification with bread and wine in the Eucharist have yielded two very important expressions: "real presence" and "transubstantiation." These expressions and their subsequent elaboration are in the world of technical theological language, the world of theory.

In the past fifteen years or more a number of theologians have questioned the helpfulness of the term "real presence." If Jesus is present in the assembled community of the baptized faithful, in the ministry of the priest celebrant, and in the proclamation of the gospel, are those modes of presence to be conceived somehow as "unreal" or "less real"? Furthermore, the pre-and post-Tridentine understandings of "transubstantiation" have been explored by teams of Protestant and Catholic scholars. Terms such as "transignification, transfiguration, transfinalization, or trans-symbolization" have been suggested as more helpful in conveying the meaning of Jesus' self-identification without implying an affirmation of obsolete elements of Aristotelian physics dealing with substance and accident. However, in the Encyclical Letter *Mysterium Fidei,* Pope Paul VI reaffirmed the "aptness" of the term "transubstantiation." This was all in the world of theoretical reflection upon a reality in the world of the sacred.[14]

Meanwhile a great deal happened in the world of commonsense religious practices. Prior to the reforms of the Council, the eucharistic bread was received in a very different context than it is for many today. The church space had the aura of a kingly chamber. The flicker of candlelight through red votive lamps gave the church a special aura. Sunlight danced through the multicolored stained glass windows in mystical patterns. The space was adorned with life-size images of sainted heroes of the past. The altar and tabernacle were like a throne. The ceremony was celebrated in the measured cadence of Latin. In form it was more a sacrifice than a meal. The sanctuary was remote from the people. Hushed silence was punctuated by Gregorian Chant and the sound of bells proclaiming the presence of "Christ the Son of God." The vessels were all of gold. Only the priest could touch the vessels or distribute the eucharistic breads, which in taste and substance were like no other. To receive this divine gift one knelt at the railing that separated him from the "sacred space" of the consecration. The railing was covered with a special cloth and the server carried a paten should a particle fall. And should a particle have fallen to the floor, no lay person would have dared to retrieve it. After a priest had retrieved the host, there would follow a special cleansing and purification of the area. After the reception of Eucharist one returned to one's pew in silence often to cover one's face in private prayer before this awesome mystery.

Today the space may be a multipurpose auditorium, the intimacy of one's home, or a brightly lit church marked by the bold lines and angles of contemporary architecture. The altar may not be a remote table of sacrifice but a very inviting table for a "family meal." The atmosphere is warm and friendly, maybe even conversational. An informal vernacular marks the prayers. The vessels may be ceramic, wood, or even a wicker bread basket not unlike that found in a restaurant. The bread itself in taste and appearance is more like bread. Laymen and laywomen distribute the Eucharist to the faithful, who are now standing up. The Eucharist is most likely taken in the hands and people communicate from the once forbidden cup. The approach to the altar as well as the return are marked by congregational singing. The music, now accompanied by the guitar, proclaims the goodness of "Jesus our brother." Benediction and Eucharistic processions are very simple and very rare. Eucharistic homilies speak of the gift of

Christ present as a challenge to all to help provide bread for the world.

Since religious meaning is communicated to the vast majority of people more by expressive lively symbols, images, and rituals than by technical, theoretical expressions, this example is very instructive. The highest authority in the Church favored no change in the world of theory concerning the Eucharist. But that same authority decreed a host of changes in the world of common sense. But one of the consequences of these multiple changes in the "non-essential externals" is the fact that the new expressive elements are now worlds apart from their predecessors. As a result of this Catholics of a certain type feel an acute tension at the Eucharist because the "style" (world of common sense) of the ceremony and the meaning, meaningfulness, and truth (world of theory) that they have previously appropriated are in conflict. Another type of Catholic may be more comfortable with the tension though he is vaguely aware that his "theory" about the Eucharist is being gradually reshaped by new "experience." But consider the child being prepared to receive the Eucharist for the first time. He knows nothing of the former ritual that mediated so much of the meaning of transubstantiation to his parents and grandparents. And for this reason he would have very little difficulty accepting another formulation of what he is hopefully still "experiencing" as the self-identification of Jesus with bread and wine.

When the decline of common meaning occurs in a vast meaning system such as an institutional religion, many individuals begin to lose their bearings. Trusted authorities begin to be doubted and a number of reactions set in. Authorities in this context may refer to a general symbol, such as "the Vatican," or more specifically to the bishops, the theologians, the parish priests, or the most active and articulate of the laity. Obviously these groups can be cast against each other in various arrangements and combinations. When the shared base of experiences, understandings, judgments, and commitments is intact, the meaning system and its authorities or leaders are generally highly trusted and respected. As common meaning declines, doubt may emerge as operational, ideological, ethical, intellectual, or absolute.[15]

Operational doubt may be manifest in gradual shifts in behavioral patterns. Declining presence at Sunday liturgy; lack of enthusiasm on the part of clergy and laity alike for the new Rites of Reconciliation and Initiation; no efforts to resolve differences between pastor and associate pastor or lay leaders; theologians unwelcome in certain dioceses; certain bishops ridiculed at gatherings of theologians; these are all instances of operational doubt.

Ideological doubt may be manifest when there is a growing necessity to provide a new "rationale" for continuing certain, once accepted practices. The practice could be great or small. Long tracts defending sisters in habits or priests in collars; a firm defense of a celibate male clergy, parochial schools, or the process for selecting bishops; theologians defending themselves as accountable only to their academic community; alarmist newspaper accounts of dangers or irreverence intended to terminate discussion of a thorny new theological issue; all of these can be signs of ideological doubt. It may not be that those who make the defense share in this ideological doubt. But the mode and tone of the defense bespeak an awareness that some segments are questioning with a new intensity. Hence the best available or at least the most definitive defense is put forth. If ideological doubt is deep-rooted, this action may delay but it will not forestall the crisis.

Ethical doubt may be manifest when people begin to feel in a deeply emotional way that they have been wronged or violated. "How can priests demand that I not remarry after my terrible first marriage (which I did everything I could to save), while they live comfortably and securely in the rectory experiencing none of married life's problems? Even they are free to be 'laicized' and to 'leave' the priesthood when they want to." "How can you de-emphasize devotion to Mary and suggest that some devotions are almost superstitions when my entire religious life is centered around devotions?" "How can you write a book arguing that bishops may not be literally the successors of the apostles when my whole understanding of the episcopal ministry hinges upon that succession?" "How can you demand that I no longer write or speak on this subject when I have spent endless intellectual energy substantiating my conclusions and you give me no counter evidence?" "Why are so many people allowed to stay 'in the Church' these days when they do not humbly accept all of her teachings?" Ethical doubt is very acrimonious and may lead to severe interpersonal conflicts and intense emotional reactions whether suppressed or expressed. Since it springs from deep inner emotions associated with feelings of having been wounded or betrayed, reason, argument, and evidence are not always a comfort.

Intellectual doubt is manifest when one begins to wonder about the "truth" of his religion. It may be simple or subtle. A person without a technical background in Scripture reads a *Time* magazine article that suggests that there were no Magi, wondrous star, or singing angels at Jesus' birth. He may conclude that if there were no "three kings," the whole story is probably "not true." A lay person, priest, theologian, or bishop is convinced on experiental, critical, or intuitional grounds that a high-level Church pronouncement is wrong. This anxiety festers. People then wonder if there can be error in this case, how can they be so sure that the Church is protected from error in other cases. After sympathetically and professionally examining the history of world religions, a Catholic university begins to question the seeming absolute "truth claims" of Christian doctrines. In every case, the tension is great because the persons have no theoretical, practical, or emotional context that will integrate their new insight questions and their old convictions. The matter is made worse if those around them do not understand their quandary or make light of their questions.

Absolute doubt may be manifest in apathetic disinvestment of the individual from the community. There may be no great display of emotion. There is simply a privatization process that "tunes out" those persons or structures which have been the cause of more pain and anxiety than they can handle. Absolute doubt may be marked by cynicism. A pastor retires to Florida at age sixty in good health to leave "the shambles of the Church" in the hands of the young radicals who have "destroyed the Church he served and loved."

A young suburban couple reads the *New York Times* on Sunday morning and celebrates a Bible service with their two natural children and their two adopted children of mixed parentage. They do not go to the parish church any more because they are weary of sermons condemning abortion and birth control and demanding obedience to the Church. They personally are not in favor of abortion, but they are tired of what they consider a negative Catholic over-kill. They were also very hurt when the pastor accused them of the "sin of birth control" and never said a kind word about their adoption.

A life-long Catholic quietly "drops out of the Church," declaring that he can do without the confusion and hypocrisy. Absolute doubt may be long in coming. The final act of "self-excommunication" is the summation of a gradual disengagement.

These modes of doubt are not in most cases reasoned responses to the complexities of the present Church situation. But in the face of turmoil, they are all too human and therefore understandable.

When operational, ideological, ethical, intellectual, absolute doubt are spreading through a community such as the Church, a number of responses are possible. There may be a conservative response that seeks to preserve central values even if the "system" itself will not survive. This effort, however, may bring about the response of the rehabilitator who concludes that it is only by solving the problems of the system that you will be able to preserve the values at stake. Such a response over time may set the stage for the revolutionary who concludes that the system is clearly obsolete and must be overturned for the sake of the central values. The revolutionary response is somewhat threatening and for this reason a reactionary response may set in. The reactionary concludes that the system is actually more important than the key values. Therefore, it is implicitly acceptable if you are alienated from the key values in the process of strengthening the system. At least when you finish, you will have preserved the only place where the values may be instilled anew. The presence of all of these responses simultaneously simply intensifies the disorientation of the "ordinary Catholic" trying to hold on to the basics in the face of the decline of common meaning.

To give an adequate account of "what happened?" this chapter has examined the dynamic structure of religion, the diverse modes in which religious meaning is mediated, the development of theology, the shift from classical to modern culture, the breakdown of common meaning, and the emergence of doubt. Hopefully this provides the broad framework needed for a reflective understanding of the context in which we find ourselves. The next chapters shall turn away from the external cultural situation to examine certain interior dynamics that will be helpful in a continuing process of recovery, renewal, and reconstruction.

NOTES

1. Classic introductions to the question include: Rudolf Otto, *The Idea of the Holy* (New York: Oxford University Press, 1958); Mircea Eliade, *The Sacred and the Profane: The Nature of Religion* (New York: Harper Torchbooks, 1959); Paul Tillich, "Two Types of Philosophy of Religion," in *Theory of Culture* (New York: Oxford University Press, 1959).

2. See Raymond Brown, *The Birth of the Messiah* (Garden City, N.Y.: Doubleday, 1977).

3. For a full elaboration of the function of meaning in community, see Bernard Lonergan, *Method in Theology* (New York: Herder and Herder, 1971), pp. 76–81.

4. See William James, *The Varieties of Religious Experience* (New York: Mentor Books, 1963).

5. Ewert Cousins refers to the need to recognize experiential and expres-

sive "models" in contemporary theology in his important essay: "Models and
the Future of Theology," *Continuum* 7 (1969), pp. 78–92. I am in agreement
with his key statement; "To use the concept of model in theology breaks the
illusion that we are actually encompassing the infinite within our finite
structures of language. It prevents concepts and symbols from becoming
idols and opens theology to variety and development just as the model method has done for science," (p. 82). See also Ian Ramsey, *Models and Mystery*
(London: The Oxford University Press, 1964), and Ian G. Barbour, *Myths
Models and Paradigms: A Comparative Study in Science and Religion* (New York:
Harper and Row, 1974).

6. For a provocative and unabashedly biased account of this period, see
Andrew Greeley, "Catholicism in America: 200 Years and Counting," *The
Critic*, Summer 1976, pp. 14–70.

7. The development of contemporary Catholic theology and the relationship of that theology to developments and changes in the Church's self-understanding are of crucial importance if one is to grasp the urgency of the call
for a wisdom community that will engage theologians and bishops as positive
collaborators in the ongoing life of the Church. A most helpful resource on
this topic is T. M. Schoof, *A Survey of Catholic Theology 1800-1970* (New York:
Paulist Press, 1970). This very readable volume surveys and interprets a complex process in a manner that is readily accessible to the interested reader
without a technical background in theology. It has a very helpful select and
annotated bibliography. See especially the "Foreword" by Edward Schille-
beecx as well as the following sections: "Results of a Hundred Years of Neo-
Scholasticism," "The Unchanging Truth," "The Heart of the Problem in the
'New Theology,'" and "Progress between 1950 and 1958." Significantly, all
of the authors examined in this volume are European, for these scholars were
until relatively recently the shapers of theological reflection. However, the
absence of Canadian Jesuit Bernard Lonergan from the study is unfortunate.
Even though he has not produced a vast corpus of positive theology in the
manner of Karl Rahner, his profound and original work in cognitional theory and theological method make him an equal giant on the theological scene.
While his philosophical work *Insight: A Study of Human Understanding* was
published in 1957, the full *theological* implications of that work were not apparent until *Method in Theology* appeared in 1972, two years after the Schoof
work.

8. I have been following the general outline of Lonergan's thought in the
entire discussion of the shift from classical to modern culture. See *Doctrinal
Pluralism* (Milwaukee: Marquette University Press, 1971); "The Transition
from a Classicist World-View to Historical Mindedness," "Theology in Its
New Context," "Belief: Today's Issue," and "The Absence of God in Modern
Culture," all in *A Second Collection: Papers by Bernard J. F. Lonergan, S.J.*, edited
by William Ryan and Bernard Tyrrell (London: Darton, Longman and Todd,
1974).

9. On the first four of these points I am again following Lonergan's

thought. See "The Absence of God in Modern Culture," pp. 109–111. Lonergan's own words on the present state of theology are instructive (pp. 108–109, 111):

> ... One would expect it [i.e., increasing specialization] to enable modern theology to speak of God all the more fully and effectively. However, while I hope and labor that this may be so, I have to grant that it is not yet achieved. Contemporary theology and especially contemporary Catholic theology are in a feverish ferment. A theology is being recognized as obsolete. There is a scattering of new theological fragments. But a new integration—and by this I mean, not an integration of the old type, but a new type of integration—is not yet plainly in sight. ... I should say that the contemporary task of assimilating the fruits both of religious studies and of the new philosophies, of handling the problems of demythologizing and of the possibility of objective religious statements, impose on theology the task of recasting its notion of theological method in the most thoroughgoing and profound fashion.

10. The questions raised by analytic philosophy concerning the meaningfulness and truth claims of theological discourse are many and diverse. At first glance these questions may appear remote and recondite until one is startled by the fact that the rich concept of analogy alone is not sufficient to account for the worlds that separate these two statements: (1) "My father is in the next room. He loves me very much and is very strong. If you attempt to hurt me, he will come and protect me." (2) "I believe in an all-good, all-powerful, all-knowing God who loves me as a father and will protect me from all harm." Something like Ludwig Wittgenstein's idea of "language games" seems necessary to meet the dilemma. For discussions of the problem, see John Hick, *Philosophy of Religion* (Englewood Cliffs, N.J.: Prentice-Hall, Inc., 1963), Chapters 6 and 7, "Problems of Religious Language" and "The Problem of Verification"; Frederick Ferre, *Language, Logic and God* (New York: Harper Torchbooks, 1961); *New Essays in Philosophical Theology*, edited by Antony Flew and Alasdair MacIntyre (New York: The Macmillan Co., 1964); Anders Nygren, *Meaning and Method: Prolegomena to a Scientific Philosophy of Religion and a Scientific Theology*, (Philadelphia: Fortress Press, 1971); David Tracy, *Blessed Rage for Order: The New Pluralism in Theology* (New York: The Seabury Press, 1975), Chapter 7, "The Question of God: Metaphysics Revisited."

11. This is not a new problem. Recall the tension between theology and Galileo or Darwin. While the problem is not new, its resolution is complex and seems inevitably marked by pain and excess. In the area of morality an example that is as volatile as it is complex is the relationship of the "is" of empirical data to the "ought" of moral principles with regard to sexual ethics. See Anthony Kosnik et al., *Human Sexuality: New Directions in American Catho-*

lic Thought; "Vatican Declaration on Certain Questions Concerning Sexual Ethics" (Appendix three in the Kosnik study); Philip Keane, *Sexual Morality: A Catholic Perspective* (New York: Paulist Press, 1977).

12. Avery Dulles' *The Resilient Church: The Necessity* and *Limits of Adaptation* (Garden City, N.Y.: Doubleday & Co., 1977), might be mentioned as an example of the theologian in a Church university context. Note the implicit or explicit criticisms that a number of bishops have made of his cautious suggestion that theologians have a teaching function in the Church. Note also, however, *his* reaction to the works of David Tracy and Langdon Gilkey, who write in the context of a secular university. We shall take up this question more in Chapter Four: "Theology in a New Key."

13. See *Christ and Culture* (New York: Harper Torchbooks, 1951).

14. For a full examination of the theological developments that occasioned *Mysterium Fidei* (AAS 57 [1965], pp. 753–774), see Joseph M. Powers, *Eucharistic Theology* (New York: Herder and Herder, 1967). For a contemporary theological discussion, see Tad W. Guzie, *Jesus and the Eucharist* (New York: Paulist Press, 1974).

15. I am indebted for part of this terminology to lectures by George Wilson, S.J., at the 1977 Institute for Continuing Clergy Education at the University of Notre Dame.

Chapter Two
The Turn to Interiority:
I. The Patterns of Experience

Introduction

The world of religious meaning is like a great edifice of interlocking parts. There is the foundational experiential reality which constitutes the basic encounter with the sacred. The meaning of this encounter is expressed and prolonged by symbols, rituals, narratives, and theoretical or discursive language. In the midst of a radical cultural shift, when common meaning breaks down and various forms of doubt are widespread, it is very possible for an individual or a group to focus in desperation around one or another part of the edifice as if it were the whole. One takes a stand now on this account of an ancient doctrine or on that favorite devotion as if to say that to yield here would be to concede a total collapse of meaning. And this few of us can stand.

Since inner experience is prior to, and deeper than, outer expression in religion, it is not surprising that, when the expressive dimension of religion is in flux, there is a renewed openness to self-authenticating religious experiences.

It is not by chance that recent years have seen the emergence of the pentecostal or charismatic movement, small prayer groups, the Jesus movement, the Cursillo movement, the Encounter with Christ retreats, Marriage Encounter weekends, the Search Weekend, and various sensitivity and serendipity workshops and seminars. These very diverse developments as well as many others have come about for many reasons and, in many cases, they have been signs of vitality

51

and renewal in the Church. But among other things each may be seen as elemental signs of the turn to interiority.

The turn to interiority is possible because prior to narratives, symbols, rituals, or theories there is the concrete existential subject. Every individual lives in a complex inner world. It is this inner world of dynamic interiority that is the locus of our experiences that raise questions as well as responses concerning religious meaning. With the contemporary playwright Ionesco, the turn to interiority recognizes the primacy of the question. The thematization of the proper questions is, in a sense, more important than particular responses. Since each one of us is a living document, it is not surprising that within our separate worlds of interiority the radical questions of meaning emerge at different stages of our development, with different degrees of intensity and clarity. Depending upon the adventuresomeness of our minds, the richness of our environment, and the resourcefulness of our mentors, each of us develops a greater or lesser reflective awareness of the world of interiority, a greater or lesser grasp of the questions that issue forth from this world, and a greater or lesser likelihood of recognizing appropriate answers, should they emerge.

The journey within, indicated by the turn to interiority, is a necessary and, in the main, a positive step in the process of coming to terms with how widespread is the decline of common meaning and reestablishing consensus for religious expression. The next two chapters of this book will examine the world of interiority. Each reader must use this analysis as an opportunity to explore and interpret his own interior world. Chapter Two will survey the complex patterns of human experience. Chapter Three will be a consideration of conversion as self-transcendence, as well as the relationship of generic faith to specific beliefs. This chapter will be in nine parts: (1) The "Anthropocentric Turn" and the Patterns of Human Experience; (2) The Biological Pattern; (3) The Psychological Pattern; (4) The Mystical Pattern; (5) The Social Pattern; (6) The Aesthetic Pattern; (7) The Dramatic Pattern; (8) The Intellectual Pattern; (9) Excursus: The Relationship between the Patterns.

1. The "Anthropocentric Turn" and the Patterns of Human Experience

When there is a breakdown in the world of theory which elaborates upon religious meaning, one of the most serious areas for concern is the etablishment of a meaningful context for talking of God when the theoretical arguments for the existence of such a reality are under severe scrutiny.[1] Once this happens, we are forced to confront the fact that, if there is a God at all, this being is enshrouded in radical mystery. We must concede the fact that we do not have God; God has us. Hence *all* of our language about God (including "he" language) is profoundly analogous and fearfully inadequate.

Karl Rahner has recalled Aquinas' teaching on God[2] as *incomprehensibilitas*. He stressed that this incomprehensibility stems from the very nature of the disproportion that obtains between the mystery of God and the mystery of being human.

According to Aquinas, we will know God only as incomprehensible even in direct vision of divine glory. This incomprehensibility is not a matter of a certain number of facts or pieces of information we do not yet have about God, or elements of the divine being that we unfortunately do not yet fully understand. It is, rather, God's very reality disclosed as inaccessible. This is why Paul Tillich can speak of revelation as the revelation of mystery.

While it is true that the Church has always formally acknowledged that God is mystery, this pivotal truth has not always been kept in mind. Hence, taking our lead from the profound speculations of Augustine and Aquinas, we discourse upon the inner life of the Trinity (generations, spirations, processions, etc.) as if we had first-hand knowledge or information about divine interiority, all but ignoring the fact that all such language is analogous, metaphorical, and symbolic. Furthermore, we have managed to "contain" the mystery we call God in our theories of grace and the sacraments. In this manner we have been able to clearly designate which of life's many experiences are "religious," whether or not we experience them as such, and which experiences are "merely human," no matter how disclosive of the sacred they may seem to be. Because of this we have made it more and more difficult to recognize the presence of the holy in the whirlwind or whisper of our personal life journey. In some cases, a somewhat mechanical understanding of the sacraments (*ex opere operato*) has put the worlds of the sacred and the profane in conflict rather than in dynamic tension.

When we acknowledge the near collapse of what was once a universal Catholic world view and a renewed awareness of the *mystery* of God, the turn to interiority calls for the "anthropocentric turn." The anthropocentric turn recognizes the fact that the human condition itself is laced with mystery. The human spirit is the question for which there is no apparent answer. In spite of the many technical problems that continue to be solved by the advances of science, the horizon of our questions far exceeds our answers. It is this very experience of our own incomprehensibility that provides the opening for the question of God to emerge. Hence, the "anthropocentric turn" does not begin with God as an "object" outside us to speculate about. It begins with the human condition as a locus for the impinging presence of God. The turn to interiority stresses that the recognition of this opening is not primarily the result of discursive reasoning and theoretical inquiry. It is rather a dynamic process that involves and transforms the whole person. This process of transformation will be examined in the next chapter on conversion.

The "anthropocentric turn" embraces a phenomenology of human experience in a manner that recalls Maurice Blondel's "method of immanence," in which he argued that human experience is the starting point of all understanding. For Blondel all truth leads to the enhancement of the human person. And even truth concerning the infinite or the transcendent is best encountered through reflection upon the human condition. When such reflection is pursued in a systematic way that does not abstract itself from the state of "action," that is, willing, choosing, doing, and undergoing, one comes to the question of the divine.[3]

"Human experience" is a very general term. In order to fill out that term we may speak of various patterns of human experience. Human experience may be seen in biological, psychological, mystical, social, aesthetic, dramatic, and intellectual patterns. This is not intended to be a definitive account but a helpful description. Furthermore, these distinctions are not made for their own sake. Rather, they are made to facilitate the grasp of a complex whole. When these patterns of human experience are adverted to and attended to, a range of partially formulated questions emerges. If these questions are articulated and thematized, the question of their meaning seems inevitable. Ultimately they raise the question of God.

In the stable framework of classical culture the meaning of these experiences had already been "given," so to speak, in prevailing assumptions, presuppositions, theories, social structures, value systems, beliefs, doctrines, and religious rituals. The whole was held together by common meaning. In an earlier context there occurred the problem of providing the answers to life's questions to a person long before the questions were really theirs. For example, *The Baltimore Catechism* provided a short verbal formula of faith in confessional language without due regard to the complex development of each person. As a result many people were alienated when life nudged them into asking questions of meaning in all of their existential force and they found the catechism answers to be inadequate or simplistic. Others clung to answers that sufficed when they were in third or fourth grade, fearing to allow their more mature questions to undermine their established world views and beliefs. In the present context of radical pluralism, there occurs the problem of accumulating a wide range of experiences without reflection. Due to the lack of reflection, these experiences may remain merely a random series of disconnected and radically meaningless, but occasionally "neat," happenings. The turn to interiority demands that each person get "in touch" with the inner and outer world of their many and complex experiences and inquire about their meaning.

In rendering the sequence of the pattern of human experiences as biological, psychological, mystical, social, aesthetic, dramatic, and intellectual, one does not intend a formal hierarchy.[4] Rather, the division is a logical one. The first three patterns—biological, psychological, and mystical—are accounts of the individual in his world. The next four patterns—social, aesthetic, dramatic, and intellectual—bring the individual into more or less engagement with the larger world. Furthermore, the first six patterns are more or less non-discursive, while the last—the intellectual—may be highly discursive. (See Figure 3.)

2. The Biological Pattern

The biological pattern of experience is our enfleshed condition. It is our inescapable physicalness compounded by multiple urges and instincts. Specifically it is the range of bodily processes to which we seldom advert, since they are automatic. The process by which our system fights against foreign elements and wards off disease and infection is an example. The process of digestion is another. In this pattern we can attend to the limits and the potentials of our physical form as we perfect such skills as playing the piano or skiing. The experienced skier performs a host of physical operations to perfection without adverting to them. The novice is constrained to advert to each of these operations and is convinced that they shall never be performed at all, not to mention perfected. In this same pattern we also experience an array of urges, impulses, instincts, and drives, the most complex and most pervasive of which are sexual.

Special features of our bodiliness surface when we reflect upon efforts at self-discipline and acknowledge decline. In our culture we see widespread obesity, serious problems resulting from the abuse of alcohol and drugs, as well as the continued smoking of cigarettes in spite of urgent health warnings. The development of physical depen-

FIGURE 3

THE PATTERNS OF HUMAN EXPERIENCE AND QUESTIONS OF ABSOLUTE MEANING

The question of God

Conversion

Agnosticism ← → Atheism

The Question of God

Why are all of my physical achievements marked by the undertow of decline?

Why do I personally exist in this "giftlike" human condition?

(Biological Pattern)

What is the radical source and meaning of the images and moods of my internal communication system?

(Psychological Pattern)

Who or what draws me beyond myself in ecstatic experiences?

(Mystical Pattern)

Is there a radical measure of moral goodness?

Whom may I love (and who loves me) absolutely?

(Social Pattern)

Where does the fullness of beauty abide?

(Aesthetic Pattern)

Is there an absolute "story-teller" whose "word" I may hear?

(Dramatic Pattern)

Are my life experiences, history, and the universe ultimately intelligible?

(Intellectual Pattern)

Person in concrete totality

dencies makes it very difficult for large numbers of people to discipline themselves in terms of food, drink, drugs, and smoke. Some, however, do reclaim their bodies out of respect for their health, while others may turn to fasting to show their appreciation of the plight of others or as an aid to their efforts at contemplation.

In spite of the body's power, form, grace, and stamina, it is also marked by decline. The best efforts cannot protect us from the ravage of terminal diseases and their concomitant misery and suffering. If we do not fall victim to illness, old age brings with it the weakening of our forces. Energy wanes, sight and hearing are impaired, mobility is decreased, memory fails. The upward spiral of the life adventure is confronted by the undertow of frailness, disintegration, and, eventually, death.

It is hardly possible to reflect upon the beauty, complexity, paradox, and vulnerability of our physical being without being overcome by sheer wonder and amazement. The gift dimension as well as the mystery of our existence emerges when we ponder the fact that we are not self-sustaining, self-generating, or self-actualizing. When these various responses are thematized and adverted to, the question of ultimate meaning and hence the question of God may be raised. (See Figure 3.)

3. The Psychological Pattern

The psychological pattern is our inner world. This is a world to which we often do not advert, or we consider it to be "merely subjective." It is within this inner world that flow feelings, moods, dispositions, attitudes, and affects which we may or may not be able to account for by reference to inner or outer circumstances. There may be positive feelings, such as light-heartedness, joyfulness, optimism, deep affection, and self-transcending love. Or there may be negative feelings, such as loneliness, depression, melancholy, dread, anxiety, or fear. While these moods and feelings are pre-reflexive or pre-conceptual, they do put us in touch with a deep inner reality. And in turn this complex of feelings or sentient states provides us with a way of making the larger alien world more our own.

This is especially true when these affective dispositions reach an intensity that can be termed "peak or ecstatic" experiences.[5] These experiences may be marked by feelings of dread in Kierkegaard's sense of *angst* or by the feeling of absolute dependency in Schleiermacher's usage.[6] These "ec-static" experiences may also be characterized by deep feelings that reality is worthwhile, trustworthy, gracious, and supportive. These intense inner emotions may be marked by a sense of the uncanny, an ineluctable presence, the terrifying or the "holy" in Otto's sense of *mysterium tremendum* and *mysterium facinas* (awe-inspiring and fascinating mystery).[7]

The psychological pattern of experience also embraces an inner world that is even deeper than the multiple feelings discussed so far. This is the world of images, symbols, fantasies, visions, and dreams that flood our subconscious and surface during our sleeping hours and sometimes during our waking hours in the form of startling "day-mares." Most of us tend not to take this inner world seriously and brand it as being even "more subjective" than the world of inner feelings. It is as if, when we read that certain biblical heroes came to certain religious insights or vocational decisions "in a dream," we think that this refers to peculiar "religious dreams." In spite of the pioneering achievements of Freud and Jung, many unreflective persons continue to consider the intricate and fluid images of their dreams as late-night entertainment provided by the psyche and of no "real" consequence. It is more likely, however, that they are a part of a vast network of an internal communication system working in cooperation with the feeling already mentioned for the purpose of inner harmony. Ira Progoff and his intensive journal method may assist many people to retrieve and reclaim their own valuable image world.[8] In this same pattern some individuals have striking experiences of insight, understanding, and clairvoyance.

Everyone finds himself from time to time wondering about the ever-changing world of inner feelings, affects, and compounding images and symbols. From what do they originate? Can they be accounted for in strictly bio-physical terms? Is there something I should learn from them? Are they a part of a larger whole? Can they be trusted? Is my self-consciousness marked by a kind of dialogue that suggests the presence of a possible "other"? When these various questions are adverted to and thematized, the question of ultimate meaning, and hence the question of God, may be raised. (See Figure 3.)

4. The Mystical Pattern

The mystical pattern of experience is actually the intimations of otherness alluded to in the psychic pattern when it is most intense. It is the experience of being taken from one's self. It is a paradoxical state of feeling bound in intimate communion with an incomprehensible reality that is known but unknown. An anonymous medieval mystic sought to give an account of it in *The Cloud of Unknowing.*[9] In the language of classical theology it is an all-absorbing encounter with the supernatural. In the language of secular culture it might be termed the "ultimate trip." In current theological language it is an intense experience of the human condition's openness to transcendence. In a religiously homogenous culture, appropriate symbols of these depth experiences were more readily available. Therefore, Theresa of Avila wrote of her journey into the interior Castle and a John of the Cross elaborated his ascent of Mount Carmel.[10]

In our day, language and images suggesting the nearness of the "sacred" are less common, and for this reason many people find it difficult to articulate experiences within this mystical pattern. Yet there seems to be evidence that more people than one might expect, have such experiences more than once in their lives. Nor are such experiences the esoteric preserve of an eccentric few. I think of the very normal people that I have come to know who are contemplative monks. Thomas Merton was perhaps the preeminent example. But many of his brothers at the Abbey of Gethsemani are of the same fabric and are engaged by the same "still point."

Of course, just as contemporary psychological investigation challenges most so-called para-psychic phenomena, mystical experiences are open to the questions of whether or not these experiences are explainable in terms of an individual's temperament and inner disposition. Is this encounter the result of a divine "inbreak" into a person's conscious existence, or is it a peculiar interaction of various elements in the several patterns of experience? But again, when such questions are broached seriously and their diverse elements thematized and adverted to, we face questions of ultimate meaning and hence the question of God may be raised. (See Figure 3.)

5. The Social Pattern

The social pattern of experience moves from the world of one's individuality, whether biological, intersubjective, or mystical, in order to engage others in the world of social intercourse. This world embraces one's family, associates, intimate friends, neighborhood, state, country, and, in our day, due to media and ever increasing interdependency, world.

The process of becoming ourselves, the process of individuation, requires socialization. In spite of the value of introspection, we make the greatest advances in self-understanding in the interpersonal contact with others. As we grow in maturity, we recognize that others do not exist for our "use." To a great degree, they help bring our world into being. Martin Heidegger argues that the human condition is at its root a being-with-others.

This social pattern may be examined either as a macrocosm or as a microcosm. In the macrocosm of social life we are engulfed in a fabric of ever increasing complexity. In such a fabric it is inevitable that the exercise of one person's desires and freedoms will come into conflict with those of another. When this happens, questions of social order and values emerge. How must we act in order to assure that as far as possible everyone's aims and desires will be met? Why should I be just and honest in my business dealings? Why should I be faithful to my promises? Are human decisions for good or evil measured within some larger context than the praise or scorn of others? (The complex of social, moral, and ethical experiences could be elaborated in a distinct "ethical pattern.") Ultimately the questions of societal values are a question of human meaning and the question of God may be raised.

As a microcosm the social pattern embraces the world of intimacy, our most important interpersonal relationships. While it involves us with one person rather than many, the world of intimacy is no less complex than the fabric of our larger social life. In the world of intimacy we grow to know and be known in a relationship that Martin Buber termed "I and Thou."[11] In such a relationship we do not interact with another as an "it" to be used or exploited. The other is rather the beloved, the "thou." In such a relationship we enter the world of self-disclosure and self-transcendence. Not only do we feel free to be our self in the presence of the beloved, but even more we experience ourselves as being able to be better than we were alone. This is because the intimate rapport that exists in such a relationship allows each person, by turns, to be truly responsible to the other. They are genuinely able-to-respond to each other in various and diverse moods and states. More than that, such an intimacy grants true authority. Hence, each person is capable of authoring or calling forth qualities, values, attitudes, and accomplishments which otherwise would not have been possible.[12]

Paradoxically, if one is able to develop and sustain relationships of intimacy in marriage and authentic friendships, they make one aware of a lingering existential void. To be sure, the person who deeply loves and is deeply loved, is far more enriched than the person who is estranged and alienated. Yet, an unfulfilled dimension in one's "soul-space" remains in spite of several relationships of profound affection and intimacy. Further, if one has known the wondrous joy of intimate affection that seems imperishable, one also has probably known the startling pain of the end of just such a love. With such an

experience one is again in a void. When this existential void is adverted to and brought to consciousness, we are inclined to ask: Why do
we feel this way? What is it that we long for? Who or what constitutes
our absolute fulfillment? Was Augustine right about our restless
hearts being content only in communion with absolute love? With
these questions of meaning, the question of God may be raised. (See
Figure 3.)

6. The Aesthetic Pattern

The aesthetic pattern of experience may be informal or formal.
When it is informal, it is simply participation in beauty and wonder
in its elemental sweep. It is rapture in the presence of form, color,
sound, and pattern. It is being arrested by silver green trees, silky rivers, darting stars, yellow-gold sunbursts, patterns of ice and snow
after a storm. It is sensitivity to the remarkable harmony of the human form, the prisms of light in the human eye, the cadences of another's voice, or the individuality of their gait. This informal mode of
the aesthetic pattern is capable of galvanizing the sensitive spirit so
that one can sit for hours mesmerized by the infinite variety of forms
and shades of ocean waves, the endless vistas of snow-covered mountain peaks, or the dancing rainbows of a blazing fire.

When the aesthetic pattern is formal, it is a similar experience of
captivation and participation now focused and triggered by a work of
art. It may be a Chagall canvas, an Eliot poem, a Beethoven symphony, a Bergman film, an O'Neill play, or an exceptional liturgy. The
work of art has the power to transport one to worlds that one may
never personally visit. It evokes a wide range of emotions and insights, and if it is of high quality, it has no diminishing returns in subsequent experiences.

The aesthetic pattern is not known by mere observation. Like the
world of intimacy the worlds disclosed by aesthetic experiences are
available only to the self-involving participant. Often great works of
art are cathartic. They produce a transforming encounter between
artist, work of art, and art lover. Even though art is non-discursive,
the encounter with great art may yield a sense of inner understanding. What was before only fractured and ambiguous existence, is now
participation in a hidden wholeness. Truth has been grasped, though
never discursively expressed.

In such experiences one may feel a kind of communion with the
plenitude of beauty. "Beauty is truth, truth beauty."[13] While one
need not go with Santayana in concluding that religion is but a mat-

ter of aesthetics, it can be argued that when such experiences are thematized and adverted to, one confronts questions of ultimate meaning and hence the question of God may be raised. (See Figure 3.)

7. *The Dramatic Pattern*

The dramatic pattern of experience is both individual and communal. Every person experiences it in his own concrete being-in-the-world and personal life-style. It is one's unique signature. It is manifest in one's unique physical appearance, walk, speech, style of dress, attitudes, and responses. It is what makes an individual the one and only edition of oneself. As an unrepeatable combination of all the other patterns of experience, the dramatic pattern is incarnate meaning, and it makes each of us utterly ourselves and not someone else. In a word, it is the gift of individuality.

The dramatic pattern of an individual's life is more than one's concrete uniqueness. This pattern also embraces the story or narrative by which a person integrates or interprets his life. This consists of happy memories of the past as well as hopes for the future. This embraces not only one's personal daily "story," but also the story of one's family with its myriad of customs and traditions. No matter how impoverished, deprived, or unceremonious a people may be, almost every family has stories of the "old country," "down home," or the "old neighborhood." Perhaps not as many people tell stories of their hopes and dreams of the future as do those who recount the past. Struggling young families might be a notable exception. There can be little doubt that the reason for the great impact of Alex Haley's *Roots*[14] on American consciousness is due not so much to the data he collected, as it is to the story format in which he put those data. This made the epic experience accessible to all, especially those missing a crucial link with the pre-slavery context.

The dramatic pattern of experience in its narrative and communal form is very complex. Epic stories and sagas have always been an important genre by which the human family has located itself in "history" and in relationship to the "cosmos." The narrative serves to integrate and interpret experiences that might otherwise seem discontinuous or without meaning. Such narratives may be simple or sublime and they may focus upon heroic personages[15] and cultural heroes,[16] adventure and fantasy,[17] the world views of science[18] or science-fiction.[19]

In light of the importance that the narrative form of the dramatic pattern of experience has in illuminating conversion at various stages, it is perhaps clearer why the narrative element was stressed in Chapter One as an important element in the expressive dimension of religious meaning. At the limit, human beings want to know the ultimate meaning of their personal and communal drama. In the main, they balk at Macbeth's despairing assessment that life "is a tale told by an idiot, full of sound and fury, signifying nothing."[20] The human race not only tells its "stories of the gods," but humankind also yearns to hear the story that God would tell of identity and destiny.[21] The dramatic pattern of experience, therefore, underscores our uniqueness as individuals and as a species. When the human drama is scrutinized and the perennial elements of its narrative, integrating, and contextualizing force are adverted to and thematized, one faces questions of ultimate meaning and hence the question of God may be raised. (See Figure 3.)

8. The Intellectual Pattern

The intellectual pattern is the eros of the mind to know. It is the unquenchable desire of the human mind to know everything about everything. It embraces the vast range of intelligent inquiry and understanding. Within the intellectual pattern the aggressive mind distinguishes between subject and object, between bias and evidence, between feelings and argument, between hypothesis and certitude. An inner dynamism compels the intellectual pattern to be detached, open, attentive, reasonable, and critical. The intellectual pattern nudges the reflective person from the world of common sense into the world of theory. It is at home with discursive, analytic, and theoretical modes of discourse. The intellectual pattern, therefore, must be distinguished from the first six patterns which are not dominated by this discursive and critical dynamism. The intellectual pattern recognizes that over and above the multiple meaning that may be mediated in the other patterns of human experience, there is the question of truth. What, as a matter of fact, is the case?

In its most disciplined form, the intellectual pattern becomes a series of spontaneous activities. Insights come quickly, precise formulations follow at once, significant details are noted, memory pours forth contrary instances, and imagination speedily constructs the contrary possibilities. It is this pattern of human experience that generates biology, psychology, sociology, anthropology, philosophy, theology, the sciences, and theories of aesthetics to examine, organize, interpret, and ultimately make judgments concerning the other patterns of experience.[22]

Under the sway of intellectual inquiry one examines the interlocking structure of the biological pattern, the seemingly endless
realms of the inner self disclosed by the psychological pattern, and
asks what kind of universe must there be to sustain these realities. If
these experiences are intelligible, are they part of an intelligible universe and does that universe have an intelligible ground? And this is
the question of God. Furthermore the reflective person explores the
worlds of affection, commitment, and moral responsibility encountered in the social pattern; the participation in beauty, harmony, and
illumination afforded by the aesthetic pattern; the feelings of wholeness, context, destiny, and purpose that envelops one in the dramatic
pattern; and one asks what kind of universe must there be to sustain
these realities. Is there some primary instance of moral consciousness
and beauty? Is there no radical source that grounds our hope of purpose? But this is the question of God. Finally, within the intellectual
pattern of experience we are capable of monitoring and personally
appropriating our own cognitional operations, or knowing activities.
We can clearly see that for all the knowledge that we gain by intelligent grasp and reasonable affirmation, we remain beings catapulted
into the unknown. For no matter how much we know, it is obvious
that the horizon of our questions infinitely outdistances our certain
answers. Yet our daily performances blurt out our implicit assump-
tion that the radically questionable is not without radical answer.
While we do not know everything about everything, we hold out the
hope that there is one who does. And this is the question of God. (See
Figure 3.)

The point of the preceding phenomenology of human experience
is intended to lay bare the many and diverse manners in which questions of ultimacy, meaning, and God emerge within the human person. All of the patterns are to a greater and lesser degree within the
experience of every person. But before moving from the question of
God that arises within all of the patterns of human experience to the
reality of conversion as a possible response to these questions and experiences, it is necessary to make some further comment about the in-
terrelationship between these patterns.

9. Excursus: The Relationship Between the Patterns

The first six patterns have been termed "non-discursive," while
the seventh has been termed "discursive or theoretical." Furthermore
it was suggested that it is the intellectual pattern that formally weighs
and investigates the worlds opened up by the other six. Does this

mean that the intellectual pattern is the most important of the seven, or that it is the most appropriate and valid path to truth and reality in every case? Must one be a university professor in order to master the intellectual pattern? Is there ever a time when an ordinary person with no technical training in theoretical thinking somehow "knows" more than the scholar in the library or the scientist in the lab? These are important questions and the manner in which one thinks that they are correctly answered will have direct bearing upon one's response to the suggestion that the whole Church constitutes a wisdom community.

To gain theoretical and technical expertise requires painstaking and professional discipline.

> To learn thoroughly is a vast undertaking that calls for relentless perseverance. To strike out on a new line and become more than a weekend celebrity calls for years in which one's living is more or less constantly absorbed in the effort to understand, in which one's understanding gradually works round and up a spiral of viewpoints with each complementing its predecessor and only the last embracing the whole field to be mastered.[23]

But there are many kinds of experts. The capable and dedicated wife and mother is an expert at maintaining a family. The holy person is an expert at prayer. The poor person may be expert at making much of little. The swimmer is an expert at a stroke. The true artist is expert in the use of color, phrase, and tone. But these forms of expertise are quite different from that of theoretical thinking. These experts grasp truth and apprehend the real in a manner that is quite different from the labors of the academician. While these experts have no theoretical web within which to integrate all of reality, they do have remarkable skills for meeting the specific aspects of reality with which they deal.

Theoretical language, rigorous logic, and detachment constitute one very important way of reaching reality. However, this is not the only way. It is precisely by means of a non-discursive self-involvement with intimate affection, a symphony, or a religious story that one encounters the truth of love, music, and transcendence that these encounters have the potential to disclose. The fact that one cannot be detached while actively participating within the first six patterns of experience is not an argument that these experiences are merely subjective and without truth. Involvement is more or less appropriate depending whether one is considering experiential or abstract knowledge. But *both* are forms of knowledge, and in the mature person they are complementary and not conflicting. If one concludes that the intellectual pattern is the privileged and the preferred road to the true and the real, this can lead to the rejection of more self-involving experiences.

In the area of religion this becomes especially problematic if the experiential and the expressive dimensions are completely separated. There is always the danger that symbol, narrative, and ritual are relegated to minor significance in comparison to the abstract and theoretical reflection.

The French philosopher Paul Ricoeur has stressed that narrative and symbolic are *not* merely elemental or potential meaning. They are not simply the cocoon which contains the butterfly of discursive thought. Were that the case, once the butterfly of conceptual ideas is fully developed, there would be no longer any need for the cocoon. Ricoeur argues that while it is true that symbols give rise to theoretical reflection, they do more than that. The symbol and stories with their multiple images, affects, and feelings bear the plenitude of meaning. For this reason, our thinking is ever nourished by the symbol-making power of human consciousness.[24]

It remains true, however, that the reflective activity of the intellectual pattern has a unique function. For if the other patterns are conveyers of the deepest and profoundest insights, it remains for the intellectual pattern to unravel and organize those insights in a manner that makes public discussion and examination possible. Yet the whole of the symbolic reality is always greater than any part that is submitted to intellectual analysis.

This discussion is of great importance because of a peculiar tendency one can have to equate the meaningful with the true. In the world of children we see many instances of symbols and stories that are meaningful, but, as a matter of fact, they are not true. For example, we continue to have embarrassed parents giving their children utter fictions in response to questions concerning the origin of children rather than giving them elemental accounts of the truth according to the nature of the child's question and capacity to understand. The invalid answer is "meaningful" to the child in the sense that it works. It fills an information gap. It makes sense out of a previously incoherent set of experiences. Eventually, however, the child will find that the originally meaningful answer must give way to the truth. When it does, the child's confidence in teachers and parents may be shaken.

There is a similar problem with theology. One may find that certain religious stories (narratives from the dramatic pattern of experience) render meaningful and integrate diverse experiences that one has in the psychological, social, aesthetic, and mystical patterns of experience. Within these stories things hold together in a manner that gives meaning to life. Hence the stories are fitting, congruous, and meaningful. Furthermore, these religious stories portray a world view and life-style that are considered valuable and worthwhile. They move a person and those with whom they associate toward attitudes and actions which are highly valued. When people embrace these stories as valuable and meaningful, they act in a responsible manner and collectively contribute a great deal to the enrichment of the body social.

Without adverting specifically to the intellectual pattern, one may conclude, like the child, that because the stories are clearly fitting, value-inducing, life-integrating, and meaningful, they are true and valid. But that is not necessarily the case. They may be true in the sense that they truly integrate and give meaning to my life. But the religious stories often affirm many *specific* things about life, death, and the universe. Are those affirmations correct? Can they be grounded in more than personal convictions?

If they are true, are they true literally or in some more complex fashion? Is it sufficient that they "work" even though objectively they do not conform to the way the universe actually is? Can there be diverse modes and carriers of truth? A great novel, for example, may communicate profound and lasting truths about being human even though the "plot" is not "factual."

This excursus on the complementary relationship between the intellectual pattern and the other patterns of human experience has not been intended to turn our attention from the question of ultimate meaning and hence the question of God. It serves as a necessary preparation for our discussion of conversion. For conversion involves the whole person and hence an interaction of all the patterns of experience rather than exclusively intellectual proofs.

NOTES

1. I have explored this problem more fully in my article "Knowledge of God in Bernard Lonergan and Hans Küng," *Harvard Theological Review*, vol. 70:3–4, July-October, pp. 327–341.
2. Karl Rahner, "An Investigation of the Incomprehensibility of God in

St. Thomas Aquinas," in *Theological Investigations,* Vol. XVI (New York: Seabury Press, 1979), pp. 244-59.

3. For an introduction to Blondel's thought, see Jean Lacroix, *Maurice
Blondel, An Introduction to the Man and His Philosophy* (New York, 1968). For an
account of the shift in theology from extrinsicism to the method of immanence, see Gregory Baum, *Man Becoming: God in Secular Experience* (New
York: Herder and Herder, 1970).

4. Lonergan speaks of the biological, aesthetic, intellectual, and dramatic
patterns of experience in *Insight* (cf. pp. 182–189). But there he is not exploring the world of interiority and meaning. Rather, his concern is the subjective field of common sense. John F. Haughts' *Religion and Self Acceptance*
(New York: Paulist Press, 1976) follows Lonergan also, but is closer to my
concerns when he writes of "intentional fields" as sentient, interpersonal,
narrative, aesthetic, and theoretic (cf. pp. 34–42).

5. See Abraham Maslow, *Religions, Values and Peak Experience* (New York:
Viking Press, 1970), and Peter Berger, *A Rumor of Angels* (Garden City, N.Y.:
Doubleday, 1969). David Tracy in *Blessed Rage for Order* (New York: Seabury
Press, 1975) examines the range of limit situations and limit questions in sci-
ence, morality, and everyday life in order to ground his position on the reli-
gious dimension of common human experience (cf. pp. 92–107).

6. See Søren Kierkegaard, *Fear and Trembling and the Sickness unto Death*
(Princeton, N.J.: Princeton University Press, 1968), and Friedrich Schleiermacher, *The Christian Faith,* vol. 1. (New York: Harper Torchbooks, 1963).

7. See especially Otto's treatment of the irrational and the "numinous,"
The Idea of the Holy, op. cit., passim.

8. See Ira Progoff, *The Symbolic and the Real* (New York: McGraw-Hill,
1963). Progoff's illuminating comment on the inner world of the symbolic
should be cited (pp. 99–100):

"When the symbolic dimension of existence opens itself to an individual,
his view of reality is strikingly changed. He perceives things simultaneously
on diverse levels. A new comprehension of what reality is then becomes accessible to him. It is not doctrinal, and it is not cast in terms of fixed metaphysical or religious concepts, neither ontological idealism, nor materialism,
nor any ideological dogma. It involves, rather, an open and moving relationship to principles of the cosmos, as these are reflected by an elemental symbol
in the depth of the psyche. Neutral as far as religious doctrines are concerned, and capable of moving by means of religious symbols when their
point is elemental, it establishes a personal point of contact, based not on
hearsay but on the individual's own experience. Meaning enters the existence
of modern man then by means of experiences within his psyche; for it is the
mirror in which the principles of the infinite universe are reflected for the finite person."

9. Cf. William Johnston, *The Mysticism of the Cloud of Unknowing* (New
York: Desclée, 1967).

10. For an introduction to the contemplative life by a contemporary con-

templative, see William McNamara, *The Human Adventure: Contemplation for Everyman* (Garden City, N.Y.: Image Books, 1976). See also Henri Nouwen, *With Open Hands* (Notre Dame, Ind.: Ave Maria Press, 1975); and Illtyd Trethowan, *Mysticism and Theology* (New York: Geoffrey Chapman, 1975).

11. See Martin Buber, *I and Thou* (New York: Charles Scribner's Sons, 1958); Ignace Lepp, *The Psychology of Loving* (New York: Mentor-Omega, 1963); Eric Fromm, *The Art of Loving* (New York: Harper Colophon Books, 1962).

12. For a poignant account of the struggle to balance the macrocosm with the microcosm of the social pattern, see Albert Camus, "Letter to P.B.," in *Lyrical and Critical Essays* (New York: Vintage Books, 1970), pp. 342–440.

13. From the last line of Keats' "Ode on a Grecian Urn." "Beauty is truth, truth beauty, that is all ye know on earth and all ye need to know."

14. See Alex Haley's *Roots: The Saga of an American Family* (Garden City, N.Y.: Doubleday, 1976).

15. As examples we may cite Mahatma Gandhi, John F. Kennedy, John XXIII, and Martin Luther King, Jr., as persons who are more than "remembered." Their "stories" are told over and over again, making it possible for them to loom larger than life and illuminate a world still in need of their visionary presence.

16. In America the obvious examples are the celluloid immortals of the cinema. Who would say that Clark Gable, Joan Crawford, Bing Crosby, and Elvis Presley are "dead" in American consciousness? It is their "stories" and the magic of cinema that keep them alive and provide vicarious experiences for many who were born after the physical death of the "star."

17. Note the renewed popularity of such adult fairy tales as J. R. R. Tolkien, *The Lord of the Rings* (New York: Ballantine Books, 1973), and C. S. Lewis, *The Chronicles of Narnia* (New York: Macmillan, 1977). The film *Star Wars* is of the same order.

18. See Langdon Gilkey, *Religion and the Scientific Future: Reflexions on Myth in Science and Theology* (London: SCM, 1970). For some, Darwin's evolutionary story of the origin of humankind has staggering future significance. *In Christianity and Evolution* (New York: Harcourt Brace Jovanovich, Inc., 1971) Teilhard de Chardin states: "Contrary to popular belief, it is not the scientific discovery of man's humble origins but much more the equally scientific discovery of a fantastic future awaiting man which is already disturbing men's hearts and should therefore prove the dominating concern of our modern apologists" (pp. 142–143).

19. The immense popularity of such diverse films as Stanley Kubrick's *2001: A Space Odyssey* and Steven Spielberg's *Close Encounters of a Third Kind* are a case in point. The former is a kind of visual metaphysic contemplating the question of cosmic intelligence, while the latter is a sound-and-light show celebrating friendly extraterrestrial life. *Both*, however, provide contemporary narratives of man's place and destiny in the cosmos. For a fascinating study that explores the "mythical" dimensions of such diverse contemporary

narratives and visions as the Marxist world view, comic strips, television commercials, and death of God theology, see Raphael Patai, *Myth and Modern Man* (Englewood Cliffs, N.J.: Prentice-Hall, 1972).

20. William Shakespeare, *Macbeth*, Act V, Scene V.

21. See Rainer Marie Rilke, *Stories of God* (New York: W. W. Norton and Company Inc., 1963); Tracy, *Blessed Rage for Order*. Note his provocative discussion of "supreme-fiction" in Chapter 9, "The Re-Presentative Limit-Language of Christology"; John Shea, *Stories of God* (Chicago: The Thomas More Press, 1978); William J. O'Brien, *Stories to the Dark: Explorations in Religious Imagination* (New York: Paulist Press, 1977); John S. Dunne has used the story as a voyage of understanding and discovery. This adventure requires a letting go and a "passing over" into another person's or people's experience only to return to one's own enriched and renewed. See *The City of the Gods, A Study of Myth and Morality* (London: Sheldon Press, 1975) and *A Search for God in Time and Memory* (Notre Dame, Ind.: University of Notre Dame Press, 1977).

22. For a powerful analysis of the intellectual pattern in relation to human knowing, see Lonergan, "Cognitional Structure," in *Collection: Papers by Bernard Lonergan* (New York: Herder and Herder, 1967), edited by Frederick Crowe, pp. 221–237.

23. *Insight*, p. 186.

24. This question is as complex as it is important. See Paul Ricoeur, "Creativity in Language: Word-Polysemy-Metaphor," *Philosophy Today* 17 (Spring 1973), pp. 97–111; "The Hermeneutic of Symbol and Philosophic Reflection," *International Philosophical Quarterly* 2 (May 1962), pp. 191–218; Anthony P. Cipollone, "Religious Language and Ricoeur's Theory of Metaphor," *Philosophy Today* (1977), No. 4, pp. 458–467; Ray L. Hart, *Unfinished Man and the Imagination* (New York: Herder and Herder, 1968); Louis Dupré, *The Other Dimension* (Garden City, N.Y.: Doubleday & Co., Inc., 1972); Karl Rahner, "The Theology of the Symbol" *Theological Investigations*, vol. 4 (More Recent Writings) (Baltimore: Helicon Press, 1966), pp. 221–252; Edward Braxton, "Bernard Lonergan's Hermeneutic of the Symbol," *Irish Theological Quarterly*, June 1976, pp. 186–197; Michael Polanyi, *The Tacit Dimension* (Garden City, N.Y.: Anchor Books, 1967).

Chapter Three

The Turn to Interiority:
II. Conversion—The Process
of Self-Transcendence

Introduction

The exploration of the diverse ways in which we encounter reality through the patterns of experience has hopefully served to indicate the multiple avenues in our lives where the question of ultimate meaning and thus the question of God may enter our consciousness. Each reader must explore his own interior world in order to focus upon those avenues that have been most successful for him. But no matter where one locates the question, the question cannot presuppose the response. In our day many honest and intelligent people conclude that there is no "ultimate meaning," or if there is, it cannot be known. However, Lonergan remains essentially correct when he writes:

> The question of God, then, lies within man's horizon. Man's transcendental subjectivity is mutilated or abolished, unless he is stretching forth towards the intelligible, the unconditioned, the good of value. The reach, not of his attainment, but of his intending is unrestricted. There lies within his horizon a region for the divine, a shrine for ultimate holiness. It cannot be ignored. The atheist may pronounce it empty. The agnostic may urge that he finds his investigation has been inconclusive. The contemporary humanist will refuse to allow the question to arise. But their negations

presuppose the spark in our clod, our native orientation to the divine.[1]

Our concern now is to understand better how that native "orientation" finds explicit expression in language about God, Jesus, and Church. This chapter, therefore, will move beyond the multiple experiences that raise the ultimate question to an analysis of the interior response to that question. The central reality involved here is the experience of conversion. This conversion and self-transcendence is a process of interior change and transformation that embraces the whole person. The result of this conversion process is ultimately a change in one's horizon or world view.

When one is standing by the seashore, one has a wide range of vision. Yet there are many details of seascape that are unclear, others that are not noticed, and still others that are completely out of range of the best binoculars. From a low-flying airplane, however, one can survey that same scene from a completely different perspective or viewpoint. Rocks and boulders that appeared to be the center of sight are now integrated into a vaster and more complex whole. All of this is possible because of a change in horizons or standpoint.

But what is true of our *seeing* is also true of our *knowing*. The horizon of our questions, interests, and knowledge is much influenced by the standpoint determined by the era in which we live, our social, cultural, and educational experiences, as well as the highly diverse factors of our personal development. Thus we can say that what lies within our horizon are those realities about which we have experience, interest, questions, or knowledge. Since no one has a fully universal viewpoint, other realities lie outside our horizon. But concerning them we have no experience, no interest, no questions, and hence no knowledge. Perhaps we would be interested if they were called to our attention or perhaps they are issues about which we simply do not care. Horizons may be different but complementary.

So the university theologian, the parish priest, the dedicated laywoman, and the local bishop have different horizons. But no matter how wide the range of differences may appear to be in a specific context, a measure of interdependence is recognized and the general reality of the Christian religion serves as a shared landscape. Diverse horizons may also be related in a sequence of development. So, looking at the Christian religion, we can understand that the horizons were not the same for the Jewish sect, the Church in the Greco-Roman world, the Medieval Church, the Renaissance, the Reformation, the Enlightenment, the Modern era, and the Contemporary Church. While they may be seen as parts of the development of a single whole, no two of them existed simultaneously. Finally, horizons may be in some way opposed. The scientist may know of the world of the poet but brand it meaningless. What is seen as cogent argument to one may be judged as the product of wishful thinking by another. One judges a certain course of action to be upright, another thinks it wicked. At the limit, one person is convinced that the universe is intelligible, another declares it absurd. Horizons, therefore, indicate the limits or the range of understanding we have attained, and the presence or absence of the capacity to understand even more.

Shifts in horizon may be the process of deepening, broadening, and enriching one's present horizon with new experiences and more suasive argument. But there may also occur more radical movements in which one actually changes horizons. It is a transformation that in effect rejects much of a previous stance; it signals a new beginning, full of unknown possibilities. It is not the result of cogent argument alone. Rather, it is like a wave that sweeps over the whole person. When individuals and their point of view are so transformed, the dynamic of conversion is operative in their lives.

The word "conversion," however, is somewhat problematic. Many Roman Catholics think of it as an experience available only to Christians of other traditions or those who have no religious affiliation and wish to become Catholics. While this may rightly be called conversion, conversion as it is intended here is available to, and needed by, Catholics as much as anyone else. In some Protestant communions conversion means the acceptance of Christ as one's personal savior in a highly dramatic and emotional style as with some "born again" Christians. For still others, conversion may mean a kind of gnostic election that puts one on a new spiritual plane as with some forms of Charismatic and Pentecostal experiences.

What is meant here by conversion is broader and deeper. It may or may not be a dramatic "eureka!" experience. This analysis of conversion is particularly significant for people who have been Catholics all of their lives, but have never really personally appropriated certain foundational values into their self-concept and their concrete lives. There are also those who have indiscriminately appropriated a considerable amount of "religious culture" and have equated these customs and pious traditions with a deeper interior reality. This may be a layperson, theologian, bishop, or parish priest. Such a person may be uncomfortable with the kind of personal exploration that this work is suggesting. They may feel that they do not need it. Or they may suspect it of emotionalism or a divergence from some established position. They might even be embarrassed by what they are learning about themselves as they move through the conversion process. Nevertheless, the turn to interiority requires that each one of us come to terms with the actual thinking, feeling, and believing processes that are going on within us, even if that actuality differs from what we think should be going on.

Conversion then is a process as well as an event. But the emphasis is more upon the discernment of the process than upon being startled by the event. Such a process is a change in one's world view. More than a mere development, it is a radical transformation. As a result of conversion, energies are released from all the patterns of experience and an interconnected series of changes occur in all levels of living. Dimensions or reality that previously went unnoticed take on a vivid and influential presence. Questions and issues once considered irrelevant take on high import. Others that were pressing, now sink into oblivion. When such deep changes occur in a person's understanding, knowledge, and commitments, an individual finds that not only does he change, but his relationships with others, and all of reality, also change. Conversion may take many forms. There are, for example, signs that after Vietnam, the murder of Dr. Martin Luther King, Jr., and Watergate, some Americans experienced a deep conversion in the understanding of the American experiment. Recalling the aesthetic and social patterns of experience, we can see that aesthetic conversion is the move from not noticing form, color, and tone in sculpture, painting, and music to being enraptured by them and discovering the world of art. Conversion may be interpersonal when one penetrates the value of a human being for the first time and ceases to treat others as objects. Then it is possible to encounter another not as competitor but as fellow voyager and potentially the beloved "thou" of intimate affection.

With this background it is now possible to examine specific forms of conversion pertinent to each of our interior worlds. These embrace a religious sense, a theistic affirmation, a radical response to the person of Jesus, a commitment to community, the struggle for moral responsibility as well as the liberation of intellect.[2] We will be describing conversion from the point of view of human response. To the believer, of course, this response is possible only because of divine initiatives. This chapter will be in eight parts: (1) Religious Conversion; (2) Theistic Conversion; (3) Christian Conversion; (4) Ecclesial Conversion; (5) Moral Conversion; (6) Intellectual Conversion; (7) Faith and Beliefs; (8) Conclusion.

1. Religious Conversion: The Turn to "the Holy"

Religious conversion does not mean the embracing of one of the religions. It is an attitude of wonder that may be triggered by attentiveness to any of the patterns of human experience. It may arise out of a sense of inner tranquility that cannot be explained by outer circumstances. It may arise out of a sustained sense of awe in the peak and limit experiences mentioned earlier. There may be a basic Chestertonian wonder at the fact that the universe endures. Whatever the occasion, religious conversion is more than a depth experience. It is a particular kind of *response* to such an experience that may be termed "reverence" or "awe." By means of religious conversion an individual becomes explicitly aware of the religious or sacred dimension of life that is within the horizon of common human experience. Yet this sense of abiding mystery must be adverted to and responded to if the encounter is truly to be called religious conversion. Gifted scientists as well as artists may be animated by this religious sense, but abhor traditional talk of God. Albert Einstein is an example. Robert Frost is another. Near the end of his life Frost declared: "But one thing must be said about poetry—it's the ultimate. The nearest to it is penultimate, even religion. Poetry is the thoughts of the heart."[3] The writings of Sam Keen also exemplify this dynamic response.[4] A philosophical account of this mode of conversion is found in John Dewey's discussion of the distinction between the concrete religions and a general religious sense.[5]

There is a certain amount of difficulty in speaking about religious conversion in this sense. On the one hand it may be objected that such people are simply optimists, humanists, or naturalists and there is no need to call them "religious." On the other hand it may be argued that logically there is theistic affirmation implicit in this position even if it is not thematized and articulated. However, each of us has surely known remarkable individuals who are animated by a genuine religious sense and reverent posture before the universe, but would not wish to speak of God in the usual sense. The recognition of this fact is particularly important at a crucial turning point in history such as the present. The decline of common meaning clearly indicates that available symbols, language, and arguments about God are often lacking in force and appeal for our pluriform culture. Institutional religions themselves may unwittingly distort their common affirmation of God by the exclusive use of rituals and language accessible only to a particular class or culture. This is one of the reasons why religious conversion in the broader sense discussed here tends to be more individualistic, or privatized, shying away from definitive pronouncements or technical language. There may, however, be an experiential depth to religious conversion that is quite surprising to those who think of religion only in terms of membership in one of the religions. (See Figure 4.)

2. Theistic Conversion: The Turn to God

Theistic conversion makes explicit the referent, source, or object of the feelings of awe and reverence that characterize religious conversion. When one experiences theistic conversion, one's horizon is transformed by a sense of what Paul Tillich has termed "ultimate concern." This ultimate concern is a grasp of what is truly ultimate and not simply the human exaltation of some lesser reality. Theistic conversion is a loving surrender to a loving reality that can now be explicitly named God. Theistic conversion is the affirmation of the whole person that the questions of meaning, suggested within the horizon of the various patterns of experience, have a positive, intelligible, and absolute response and ground.

This response may be deeply personal with many affinities to religious conversion. A moving example of this is found in the writings of Chiyesa, a native American of the tribe of Santee Dakota:

> In the life of the Indian there was only one inevitable duty—the duty of prayer—the daily recognition of the Unseen and Eternal. His daily devotions were more necessary to him than his daily food. He wakes at daybreak, puts on his moccasins and steps down to the water's edge. Here he throws handfuls of clear, cold water into his face, or plunges in bodily. After the bath, he stands erect before the advancing dawn, facing the sun as it dances upon the horizon, and offers his unspoken orison. His mate may precede or follow him in his devotions, but never accompanies him. Each soul must meet the morning sun, the new sweet earth and the Great Silence alone!
>
> Whenever in the course of a daily hunt the red hunter comes upon a scene that is strikingly beautiful or sublime—a black thunder cloud with the rainbow's glowing arch above the mountain, a white waterfall in the heart of a green gorge; a vast prairie tinged

FIGURE 4

CONVERSION AS SELF-TRANSCENDENCE

Transformation of Horizon

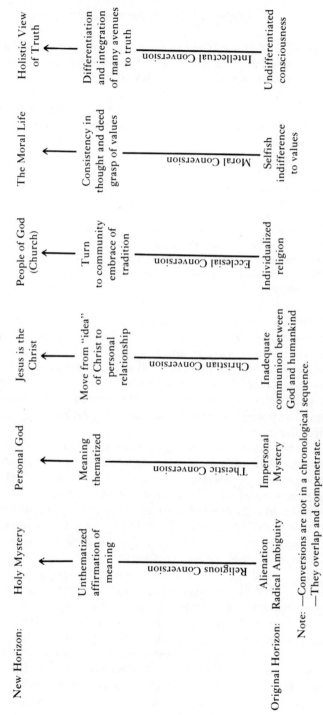

New Horizon:

| Holy Mystery | Personal God | Jesus is the Christ | People of God (Church) | The Moral Life | Holistic View of Truth |

Original Horizon:

Note: —Conversions are not in a chronological sequence.
—They overlap and compenetrate.
—One or another may be absent.
—They all interact in a mature Christian identity.

with the blood red of sunset—he pauses for an instant for the attitude of worship. He sees no need for setting one day in seven as a holy day, since to him all days are God's.[6]

Within the Catholic tradition Jesuit poet Gerard Manley Hopkins gives expression to a similar experience in "The Wreck of the Deutschland":

> I kiss my hand
> To the stars, lovely-asunder
> Starlight, wafting him out of it; and
> Glow, glory in thunder;
> Kiss my hand to the dappled-with-damson west:
> Since, tho' he is under the world's splendour and wonder,
> His mystery must be instressed, stressed:
> For I greet him the days I meet him, and bless when I
>   understand.[7]

Theistic conversion tends away from the open-endedness of religious conversion. The reality of God is specified by a barrage of analogous expressions. God is affirmed as person, pure spirit, absolute being, all-knowing, all-powerful, all-good, and eternal. The unconditional acceptance of the reality of God calls forth responses that are akin to falling in love. It is not simply the result of a rational thinking process. But while it clearly is not fully rational, it need not be termed "irrational."

A better term might be "trans-rational." It is an obvious but significant fact that only those who already believe in God expend their intellectual energy attempting to demonstrate rationally that there is an objective referent to that term. And only those who consider themselves atheists expend their energies attempting to demonstrate that there is no such referent. In either case the affirmation or the negation by the total person precedes the theoretical apologia. Proofs of God's existence are the work of believers who wish to indicate on publicly arguable grounds that the faith which they possess is not unreasonable. But the genesis of that faith was not reason alone.

Returning to the analogy of human affection, one is not required to ground critically the conditions of the possibility for loving a particular person before one embarks on the adventure of love. Yet when one experiences genuine love, there is a certain sense in which the experience is self-validating and self-authenticating for the person involved. Still, after the fact, one can make critical observations to show the "reasonableness" of one's experiences. So, too, in theistic conversion one does not first prove the reality of God beyond doubt as a detached philosopher and then commit oneself to this proven reality.[8]

Religious and theistic conversion taken together provide a broad horizon of experiences and insights that make us much more aware than we tend to be of a crucial fact: The God of Jesus is the same God of the great world religions. Following Friedrich Heiler, Bernard Lonergan summarizes areas common to such world religions as Christianity, Judaism, Islam, Zoroastrian Mazdaism, Hinduism, Buddhism, and Taoism. Each of these traditions affirms the following in their diverse ways (see Figure 4):

> There is a transcendent reality ... immanent in human hearts: ... he is supreme beauty, truth, righteousness, goodness ... love, mercy, compassion ... the way to him is repentance, self-denial, prayer; that the way is love of one's neighbor, even of one's enemies; that the way is love of God, so that bliss is conceived as knowledge of God, union with him, or dissolution into him.[9]

3. Christian Conversion: The Turn to Jesus as the Christ

As we have seen, a theistic conversion acknowledges the universal orientation of the human spirit toward mystery and the fact that the reality intended by the word "God" is the ground of that mystery. But the human response to the mystery of God is possible only because of God's universal openness to the human condition. Christian conversion is the specification of that orientation of humankind and that outreach of God by means of the focal reality of Jesus exalted as the Christ. Theistic conversion is specified as Christian conversion when the "event" of God's self-disclosure is recognized supremely in Jesus. In Old Testament language it is the replacement of the heart of stone with the heart of flesh and the heart of flesh becoming effective in good works through human freedom that results in one's total transformation. In the idiom of the Apostle Paul, Christian conversion is experienced as God's love flooding one's heart through the Holy Spirit received as gift. In the expressions of Augustine, Christian conversion may be termed "operative and cooperative grace." In explicitly Christological, creedal, and liturgical language, Christian conversion is the affirmation that Jesus is the Christ of God. It is a vital participation in his birth, life, ministry, teachings, execution, and transcendence of death. It is moving from the state in which one does not experience the disclosure of the Holy One in the Paschal Mystery to the state of appropriating that experience. It is this past, present, and cosmic event precisely recognized as "event" in one's personal existence that constitutes Christian conversion.

Christian conversion, therefore, is not only a transformation of horizon that allows one to affirm that life has ultimate meaning. It is also an encounter with Jesus that renders his very person as the central symbol announcing that, rumor to the contrary notwithstanding, the story of the human race is going to turn out all right. In a word, it is the affirmation that Jesus as the Christ of God is the good news.

Christian conversion is an intensely personal reality. No one can experience Christian conversion for any one of us. Neither parent, nor priest, nor friend, nor teacher, nor bishop can replace the individual in this experience. It can be accomplished only by the individual opening himself up to the reality of Jesus. Christian conversion in this sense is not accomplished by means of infant baptism. It is the result of a mature, conscious involvement with the person of Jesus as required by the bold new rite of adult initiation. When this happens, Jesus becomes not a name, not a holy card picture, not a stained glass window image, not a set of rules, but a person who makes the love and justice of God tangible and with whom one has a true and personal relationship. Through Christian conversion one puts on Christ. (See Figure 4.)

4. Ecclesial Conversion: The Turn to Community

Just as the reflection on the patterns of experience advanced from the individual to the communal, in the same manner the discussion of conversion now advances from the individual to the communal experience. Religious, theistic, and Christian conversions are by nature existential and intensely personal experiences of transformation. Ecclesial conversion, however, is the turn to others. With ecclesial conversion the transformation process is celebrated and supported in community. Ecclesial conversion is the recognition of the value of history, tradition, order, and the need for a division of labor. It is a sense of peoplehood. Ecclesial conversion is not content with a "Jesus and me" attitude, no matter how genuine. Ecclesial conversion is a dynamic that binds one to others who share the experience of the Jesus event, and who wish to celebrate and perpetuate that experience in word, sign, sacrament, and deed. It is joining company with the pilgrim people of God, gathered in the Spirit and seeking to be the contemporary embodiment of Christ.

Ecclesial conversion partakes of common meaning. Therefore, if the analysis in the first chapter is correct, it is to be expected that in an epoch of unprecedented disputes over common meaning, ecclesial conversion becomes for some problematic, for others impossible, and for still others, irrelevant.[10] Two simple examples illustrate my point. At the moment when it has become customary to exchange the greeting of peace in the Sunday liturgy, one still notices individuals with no intention of greeting anyone. They may even protest that, "It's optional!" Many such people would never miss a Sunday liturgy, yet the nature of their ecclesial identity is such that this gesture seems inappropriate and out of place. They have a highly individualized sense of what it means to be a *member* of a Church community.

As a second example, consider the university student who has been reading about the joint theological statements coming from official Roman Catholic dialogue with Anglican, Lutheran, and other Christian traditions. More importantly, the student has experienced the genuine faith and devotion of Christians of other traditions. Such a person may begin to wonder about talk of the "one true Church" and question why should one be a member of a specific tradition when all traditions have their noble elements as well as their documentable great faults.[11] It is in a sense easier to embrace or to reject an absolute. For this reason it is not difficult to understand the anxiety of an Archbishop Lefebvre and his vocal or silent sympathizers who feel betrayed by a Church that is disengaging a static style and returning to the dynamic and organic style of earlier centuries. In the contemporary ecumenical context ecclesial conversion is not enriched by a nervous defensiveness. It must be marked by a genuine regard for other Christian churches as well as other religions. This more open attitude need not lead to indifference. It is not a non-reflective attitude of: "Let a thousand flowers bloom!" Ecclesial conversion is the embrace of one's vital tradition as the witness of truth, while recognizing the historical limitations of that tradition. Mature ecclesial conversion is capable of deep and positive commitment without defining other Christian traditions in negative terms. Such a Christian is comfortable with the genuine value found in other traditions. This is a highly nuanced posture that is perhaps not easily achieved without a measure of intellectual conversion which is yet to be discussed.

Because the Church is a multidimensional reality with a long and complex history, and because every human spirit is marked by a particular temperament, needs, and dispositions, an individual's ecclesial conversion may favor one or another dimension of the Church. This may even lead some to overlooking, rejecting, or even denying aspects of the Church's self-understanding that are of lasting import. Others will defend obsolete cultural practices as the heart of the Church.

It should not be surprising that some think of the Church primarily as a juridical institution with beliefs to be affirmed and rules to be obeyed in order to merit a spiritual reward. Others think of the Church as a community of the faithful (*Koinonia*) bound together in genuine interpersonal relationships under the power of the Spirit. Still others think of the Church as the most apt sign or sacrament of the loving favor of God among his people with whom he has a covenant. From another perspective the Church may be viewed more fittingly as a scout going before the larger world seeking out where the Lord may be found, or a herald proclaiming the good news that is found in the word and person of Jesus Christ. Yet another possibility is that the Church should not be turned in upon itself and alienated from the world. It should be an open, servant community. As a catalyst for change and development the Church must be on the cutting edge of those movements that seek to bring about freedom, justice, equality, love, and peace in the concrete social order.[12]

It is easy to say that the Church is a mystery and hence is all of these and more. Such seemingly inclusive attitudes may overlook the point that in fact an individual or group embodies an operative ecclesiology that actually supports one aspect and opposes another. Nor does it face the dilemma of what does one do when one aspect seems to be in conflict with another. Is there some implicit hierarchy? And if there is, how is that hierarchy determined?

Because of the many changes that have resulted from the Second Vatican Council, more and more people experience ecclesial conversion as conversion to a community on the move. *Ecclesia semper reformanda.* For this reason ecclesial conversion may be seen not so much as faith in the Church, as it is responding to the call of the Spirit to assemble as the Church and proclaim, celebrate, and incarnate one's faith in the mystery of God disclosed in Jesus, the Christ.

Hence Karl Rahner, reflecting on the present ferment in the Church, can anticipate that the shape of the Church to come will be marked by greater openness, practical ecumenism, more democratic styles of government, and strong socio-political involvement in activities that will confront the fierce consequences of what is sometimes termed "social sin" in the local neighborhood, the ghetto, or the Third World.[13] (See Figure 4.)

5. Moral Conversion: The Turn to Values

Moral conversion is the move from words and ideas to actions and deeds. These actions and deeds, however, do not flow from the need to satisfy one's own desires but from values that have been grasped and interiorized. Moral conversion is the struggle to attain self-consistency between the values one affirms and the deeds one incarnates. It is the never-ending quest for authenticity in one's public as well as private worlds. The person whose horizon is transformed by moral self-transcendence struggles with Saint Paul, knowing that that which he should do he does not do; and that which he should not do he does. Morally converted persons know that by actions and deeds they are creating the one and only rendering of themselves in the dramatic pattern of experience and they want that to be their best self. Moral conversion is the journey toward an integral and mature self-identity. This is possible because of the dynamic nature of our inner freedom as well as our ability to apprehend value.

Moral conversion is realized when we choose the truly good over the apparently good. Under its sway we even stand firm on values when values are in conflict with personal convenience, satisfaction, or gratification. It is speaking the truth when dishonesty would spare us blame and embarrassment. Moral conversion is not a respecter of person or office. A priest may recognize it in a teenager. A housewife may witness it to a bishop.

Moral conversion is difficult. To be fully open to it we must each be continually aware of developments in our complex human condition. We must be vigilant so as to recognize patterns of progress and decline. We must ever scrutinize our personal responses to values and honestly recognize the implicit scale of preference that we unwittingly assign to them. Aristotle was correct in observing that genuine moral knowledge is the proper possession only of the morally good person. Until we are such persons, we must each keep advancing, changing, learning, and yielding to the self-correcting process of this radical conversion.

Robert Bolt provides a heroic image of moral conversion in his interpretation of Thomas More. When he is asked to swear to the Act of Succession against his conscience, More counters:

> When a man takes an Oath ... he's holding his own self in his hands. Like Water. And if he opens his fingers *then*—he needn't hope to find himself again.... If we lived in a State where virtue

was profitable, common sense would make us good, and greed would make us saintly. And we'd live like animals or angels in the happy land that *needs* no heroes. But since in fact we see that avarice, anger, envy, pride, sloth, lust and stupidity commonly profit far beyond humility, chastity, fortitude, justice and thought, and have to *choose, to be human at all* . . . Why then perhaps we *must* stand fast a little—even at the risk of being heroes.[14] [Emphasis added.]

Moral conversion may be generic and then it inquires about appropriate general over-arching values that guide one's life. It may be specific and then it inquires about the appropriate, specific values that are at stake in specific situations. Finally, it may be existential, and then it inquires about what values are to be, as a matter of fact, embodied or rejected when acting in a concrete existential situation.

The morally converted subject may affirm values to be absolutely absolute, absolute, relatively absolute, relative, or absolutely relative. If a value is absolutely absolute, it is seen as binding all persons, at all times and in all circumstances. It admits of no exceptions. If a value is absolute, it is seen as practically binding all persons, at all times and in all circumstances. But at least hypothetically it admits of possible exceptions. If a value is relatively absolute, it is seen to bind most people at most times and in most circumstances, but exceptions are real and accepted. If a value is relative, it is seen as binding only certain persons at certain times and in certain specific circumstances. Finally, if a value is affirmed as absolutely relative, individuals in their particular time and circumstance must determine the presence or absence of binding force.

Moral conversion and the appropriation of values obviously embrace an immense range of issues and situations. There is one's personal life, family life, and larger social life. There is the complex world of business and finances on the local, national, international, and multinational scales. There is the world of nations in relation to their citizens and citizens in relation to their nation, and nations in relation to each other. There are the special problems of the interdependencies and responsibilities of the First, Second, and Third Worlds.

The specific issues are literally too numerous to even name. Some can be indicated by the following questions. What is my responsibility to care for my health? When may I discontinue efforts to sustain the life of the terminally ill? What is my responsibility to overcome racist and sexist attitudes within myself and the larger society? Is it ever permitted for me to take what is not my own? Does society have the authority to execute those who commit monstrous crimes? As an employer, is it ever just for me to pay my employees less than a living wage? What is the value of my word? Am I ready for the responsibility and commitments of marriage? What do I do in the face of a marriage that has become destructive of all involved? Am I free to enter a second marriage? When, with whom, how, and in what circumstances may I express my sexuality? Are pre-marital sex, adultery, and masturbation always wrong? What is the appropriate response to a homosexual or lesbian orientation? What methods are fitting ways to realize the goal of responsible parenthood? Should I invest money in companies that perpetuate various social injustices? Do I have any responsibility for correcting environmental abuses? May a nation contemplate nuclear war? Ought science to pursue all of the possibilities of genetic engineering? Under what circumstances may fetal life be terminated?[15]

In seeking to answer these and many other questions, a person may be informed or uninformed. One may be open to the truth whatever it may be or one may be selfishly predisposed. In the face of the more difficult questions, one may be diligent or superficial. One may be inclined to *autonomous* ethical decision making in which one feels that one must decide for oneself without being overly influenced by the opinions of others. One may be *heteronomous* in one's approach, seeking only to obey some external authority to whom one has abdicated moral decision making as well as moral responsibility. Or one may take a *theonomous* approach in which one seeks to augment one's personal discernment of appropriate decisions by means of the wisdom of the larger community as well as a prayerful openness to the promptings of the divine presence.

If the other modes of conversion are at play in the consciousness of a person seeking to live out the freedom as well as the responsibility of moral conversion, one's attitude will more likely be theonomous than autonomous or heteronomous. Taking the conversions in a reverse order, intellectual conversion (which is yet to be discussed) will prompt an individual to become well informed on the whole range of questions and information that may be relevant to the issue that is being decided. Ecclesial conversion will prompt inquiry into the wisdom of the tradition of one's community to see if there have been long-standing positions taken by those in positions of responsibility. These will be prayerfully and seriously examined and never casually discarded. Furthermore, ecclesial conversion will automatically prompt an openness to the example, inspiration, and wisdom of one's fellow church members whose lives may be of high virtue. If

Christian conversion is truly operative, then one's personal relationship with Christ will compel a prayerful openness to the movements of Christ's Spirit, perhaps especially in reading the Scripture. Religious and theistic conversion will mean a deep longing to live authentically before the mystery of God with a patient and tranquil confidence during periods of discernment, as well as trust in God's favor if one *truly* acts with a pure heart.

Clearly, moral conversion is not a once-and-for-all accomplishment but a life process. A number of psychologists have examined the process of moral development. Lawrence Kohlberg, expanding upon the pioneering research of Jean Piaget, has identified six stages of moral development. These six stages may be described in a summary way as: (1) the obedience to avoid punishment stage; (2) the "you scratch my back and I'll scratch yours" personal needs stage; (3) the "be good in order to win approval" stage; (4) the law and order stage; (5) the legal or social contract stage; (6) the universal ethical principle stage. Kohlberg's findings suggest that moral values are grasped over time and in rather distinct stages. He suggests a hierarchy that moves from an elemental "avoid pain, seek pleasure" stage to the level of mature and personal commitment to universal moral values.[16]

Without canonizing or absolutizing Kohlberg's stage theory, one can recognize the fact that Catholics, like anyone else, may be at very different stages in the process of moral development. They, too, experience a certain amount of disequilibrium as their "life-world" demands that they enter a new stage. Which stage is appropriate for a mature Catholic? No doubt there would be some dispute as to whether stage six should be considered the appropriate stage for the mature Catholic in the area of moral conversion. Is it too autonomous? Others might argue that the sixth stage or perhaps even a seventh stage of "theocentric" ("Christocentric"? or "ecclesiocentric"?) self-transcendence is certainly the ideal for every adult Christian. Still others would complain that sometimes the style, if not the content, of Catholic moral pronouncements does not take into account any developmental model and as a result retards individuals at the law and order stage (4) or even the reward and punishment stage (1).

When we take a developmental approach to the process of moral conversion and the personal appropriation of values, we become more aware of the question of "subjectivity" and "objectivity" in moral decision making. Is the prayerful, informed following of one's conscience that differs with official teaching concerning a difficult question being "merely subjective," while the prayerful and informed following of an official teaching that is actually at variance with one's conscience being "more objective"? This is not a false or simple question. Let us take a recurrent example from the sacrament of reconciliation concerning divorce and remarriage. A validly married Catholic obtains a divorce after exhausting every means of salvaging an utterly unlivable marriage. (Anyone who has been involved in marriage counseling as a parish priest or who has struggled through a divorce knows that such situations are all too real.) Subsequent to the divorce the party enters a second marriage and wishes to remain an active member of the Church. The "pastoral reasoning" in response to this kind of situation may be the following. In contracting the second marriage the person has violated the "objective" moral order. However, due to the pressures of their particular circumstances and perhaps their invincibly erroneous conscience, they do not personally ("subjectively") suffer any culpability or guilt.

The problem with this posture is twofold. First of all, a mature Christian who is seeking to live an authentic life will not be content to think that what he has done is objectively wrong (he has violated an absolute absolute) but subjectively, he is excused (making the value in effect an absolute or a relative absolute). If the value at stake is "objectively speaking" an absolute absolute, he will want to struggle to bring his subjective situation into conformity with it.

The second part of the problem is the dichotomous use of language where objective denotes good and subjective denotes bad. Such language obscures a simple fact. Every human being is a subject. Everything we experience, understand, affirm, or deny we do as subjects. Our dynamic orientation is toward authentic and mature lives as subjects. Literally speaking, therefore, no one lives in the objective moral order. Even if it is argued that right reason and revelation (in a strictly propositional sense) mediate the objective nature of the human condition (e.g., through Scripture, natural law theory, and tradition), it would still be mediated by subjects to subjects. The impression is sometimes had that a select group of people are capable of freeing themselves of every aspect of *their* subjectivity so as to obtain information about the objective moral order and then report it back to others who otherwise would be confined to the world of their subjectivity. But this is obviously not the case. All of us are subjects. But that is not to imply, therefore, that our moral decisions are "merely subjective" in the sense of whim and caprice. Fidelity to our native orientation toward authenticity, our reflective capacities, and the deepest insights of a profound religious tradition all make possible the apprehension of true values as well as specific imperatives.

Even if one concedes that some moral values are not absolute absolutes but rather normative ideals (hence absolute or relatively absolute), the subjective-objective problem may persist. Take the still emotion-laden and complex question of the methods employed by a couple to ensure responsible parenthood by limiting the size of their family. One couple may concede that the teaching of *Humanae Vitae* is a normative ideal that, at present, due to their own weaknesses and limitations, they are not able to live up to. To the degree that this departure from the normative ideal is sinful, they seek forgiveness and they strive to better approximate what they hold to be a true value.

Another couple may have three children of their own and three that are adopted. They do not consider their use of contraceptives to be a regrettable departure from a normative ideal, but a positive factor in their effort to live up to the ideal of responsible parenthood. They are distressed when they are told that they should work to overcome their invincibly erroneous conscience which is causing them to offend the objective moral order. After a long and difficult period of discernment they are convinced that fidelity to the generic value of fully responsible parenthood demands that they not heed a specific, even authoritative, exhortation against contraception.

These examples make it clear how profoundly difficult the subjective-objective question really is. Facile solutions of either a traditional or a progressive kind will not really meet the urgent pastoral need of the couples involved. At a Continuing Education program these questions were raised with a group of priests who had had many years of experience. A majority of them confided that they feel uncomfortable on the one hand defending certain moral values as "objective absolute absolutes," and on the other hand acknowledging the "objective" authenticity of people's concrete decisions. Some thought that as difficult as some particular cases may be, it would be chaotic to blur the line between subjective and objective. "Any lawyer will tell you that hard cases make bad laws." Others declared that honesty required that they simply admit that in the concrete order authentic subjectivity is the only objectivity that is meaningful or attainable.

No serious and pastorally sensitive priest, theologian, bishop, or layperson would argue for a simplistic resolution to this very real dilemma. Perhaps the decline of common meaning is more evident on questions of morality than in any other area of the life of the Church. The dialogue envisioned by "the Wisdom Community" seeks to bring people to an honest and trusting sharing of their differences in the hope of gradually regaining areas of common meaning. (See Figure 4.)

6. Intellectual Conversion: The Turn to a Wholistic View of Knowing

In discussing the intellectual pattern of experience, we have already adverted to the human capacity to penetrate, distinguish, analyze, differentiate, and integrate under the impetus of the unrelenting desire to understand. Intellectual conversion is the process of reflecting upon these activities and penetrating the knowing process in a way that further expands our horizons. This process gives us the capacity to move comfortably in and out of diverse worlds that at first blush seem diametrically opposed. Intellectual conversion is the liberation of intellect and the unification of mind. Recognizing the complexity of human understanding, intellectual conversion refuses to submit to a sacrifice of intellect. For truth is one.

Therefore, if conflicts obtain between the worlds of science, aesthetics, psychology, sociology, philosophy, theology, and historical theory, it is due to insufficient understanding about the different ways in which language may be employed, or there is unstated bias or confusion about diverse areas of competence. It may also be due to the fact that issues are insufficiently mature or there is just plain error. Intellectual conversion acknowledges the self-correcting process of learning, and foresees that over time, seemingly contradictory positions may well be shown to be complementary from a higher viewpoint. Of necessity, intellectual conversion recognizes the collaborative nature of all efforts at human understanding.

To begin with, intellectual conversion distinguishes between the readily available everyday world of immediacy and the more remote world reached indirectly. A child living in the world of immediacy may think that knowing is something very much like taking a good look, and objectivity is seeing what is out there and not seeing what is not out there. This immediate world is what we encounter with our senses of seeing, tasting, touching, and smelling. But as every adult knows, there is a much larger world than the crib or the playground. This larger world is not entered through personal sense experiences alone. Sophisticated cultures have a vast complex of achievements that all play a part in our encounter with the larger world. Those achievements are constantly advancing or declining, and individuals as well as whole reflective communities examine past and present achievements to assess their validity. Hence knowing is not merely taking a good look. It is a complex and recurring activity. It is confronting the world as a whole, raising questions, formulating hypotheses, weighing evidence, making judgments, believing the judgments of others, and making commitments to act on these judgments.

It is obvious enough that in practical affairs most people are nudged rather spontaneously into intellectual conversion. We realize that appearances are not everything. What we see may not be what we get. To be certain, we look for sufficient evidence and sufficient reason. But this spontaneous conversion may not hold when one turns from the practical affairs of daily life to the subtle questions of philosophy and theology.

If the process of intellectual conversion is thoroughgoing, one not only asks the question: What am I doing when I am knowing? One also asks: Why is doing that knowing? And what do I know when I am knowing? In order to answer these questions one is constrained to monitor not only all the patterns of human experience but also the whole world that is implied by the word "interiority." The answer requires the full grasp and appropriation of one's subjectivity and the structure, norms, and potentials of one's conscious activities. This is accomplished by heightening one's awareness of the dynamic processes of human consciousness. While this is not easy, it is not as difficult to perform as it is to give a verbal account of the performance. The result of this attending to oneself attending, is the awareness that experience, understanding, judgment, and commitment are the recurrent elemental structures of human knowing.

Intellectual conversion facilitates a new and deep awareness of the fact that there are many patterns of human experience. Hence human consciousness flows in many and diverse modes. It is polymorphic. When the polymorphic, or multidimensional, nature of human consciousness is adverted to, it becomes possible to distinguish, untangle, or differentiate these complementary modes.

Intellectual conversion distinguishes different realms or worlds of meaning. It recognizes the world of common sense and practical daily life. This world does not define or elaborate universal principles. It is a storehouse of practical wisdom that is apt for particular situations. But there is also the world of theoretical or scientific meaning. In this world, rigorous logic and articulated methods govern the activity of defining and establishing systematic relationships.

Since all of the patterns of experience potentially bring a person to the question of God, there is also the world of religiously differentiated consciousness. In this world, already examined as religious and theistic conversion, one lives in deep awareness of the divine. And this awareness prompted by asceticism may advance and culminate in the recollected silence of mysticism.

Intellectual conversion allows for the multiple differentiation of conscience. It recognizes that within the different realms or worlds different procedures and attitudes will be more or less operative. As a result of intellectual conversion one is free to move comfortably from the world of common sense to the world of theory without experiencing any great incongruity. However, a person living mainly in the world of undifferentiated consciousness may be baffled by the plurality. Such a person prefers a homogeneous world. To accommodate these desires we are ever tempted to reductionism.

So if the procedures of common sense which aptly meet the questions of ordinary life are correct, then the formidable methodologies of theoretical investigation must be intellectual arrogance or error. Or if theory is to be accepted, then common sense must be overcome as a hangover from the primitive and pre-scientific early days of the race. If the serenity of religious contemplation is of value, then perhaps the labors of the scholar are in vain or a threat.

Undifferentiated consciousness is at a loss as to how the worlds of common sense, science, scholarship, and religion can be integrated. In the present ferment the ability to allow issues to mature with a sufficient accumulation of evidence and to respect the collaboration of diverse specializations is of singular import if we are to penetrate the potentially complementary nature of diverse world views. Hence a person who cannot make certain critical differentiations accomplished by intellectual conversion is apt to feel a great deal of tension that may be resolved by oversimplification of the issues. Note, however, that intellectual conversion cannot impose a false harmony. At the limit, what is so is so, and what is not is not.

The dynamism of intellectual conversion may have a purifying as well as an integrating effect. It purifies by its power to recognize in religion the tendency to embellish mystery with magic and to taint symbol with superstition. Through the analysis of culture and ethnicity, intellectual conversion comprehends why a type of religious devotions that flourish in France, Spain, or Mexico, for example, would not originate in Germany, Switzerland, or the Netherlands. It is integrating insofar as, over time, intellectual conversion prompts one to recognize that the Christ of the Catholic Church and the Christ of other Christian traditions is one Christ. Strictly speaking, there can be no Anglican, Lutheran, or Roman Catholic Christ even though there may be crucial diversity in the symbols and theories that mediate the one Christ. Furthermore, intellectual conversion acknowledges that the God of Jesus is not only the God of Moses but also the God of Mohammed, the Buddha, the philosopher, and the scientist. For while the paths to God may be many, God is one.

By means of its purifying and integrating power, intellectual conversion initiates a process of reflective criticism that overcomes the negative undertow of biblical, liturgical, doctrinal, or juridical fundamentalism. While affirming God as the reality toward which authentic religious symbols, rituals, narratives, and theories point, intellectual conversion concedes that if God is God, all such pointers are historically and culturally conditioned. No human formulation can be absolutely true with exactly the same meaning for all peoples, at all times, and in all places. For as circumstances and cultures change, humankind's self-perception changes and religious utterances undergo a transformation of meaning. This, of course, is not a particularly radical concession; it is simply the consequence of taking seriously the limits of language, the historicity of the human race, and the permanence of mystery.

Biblical fundamentalism takes its stand on the literal truth of a Scripture passage. There is no differentiation made between the biblical stories (which may not be literal historical facts in every case) and the abiding religious truth these narratives convey. Liturgical fundamentalism reduces ritual to rubricism. There is no differentiation between the culturally conditioned signs, ceremonies, and symbols of the liturgy and the timeless reality in which one is invited to participate. Doctrinal fundamentalism equates the full reality of the Christian mysteries with innately limited verbal expressions of the *Magisterium* or the speculations of theologians. Juridical fundamentalism takes its stand on particular laws, rules, practices, and customs as the necessary way of preserving the identity and values of the Church community. There is no differentiation that recognizes that practices which were apt at one juncture in history may not be apt in the present context. Indeed the unyielding maintenance of such practices may contribute to the undoing of cherished values.

Each of these forms of fundamentalism results from a desire for certitude that would lift Scriptural texts, liturgical rites, and doctrinal pronouncements out of the historical and cultural contexts in which they were developed. Proponents of such fundamentalism in its extreme form are startled when even the Church itself acknowledges the need for the most contemporary Scripture scholarship, the adaptation of the liturgy to diverse cultures, and the nuanced understanding of the development of doctrine.

Intellectual conversion reaches a special depth when it recognizes that in spite of wide-ranging power it still has native limitations. And while the labors of the intellectual life in its most disciplined and technical form are the vocation of a few, the love of God is offered to all. (See Figure 4.)

Within the world of interiority we have enumerated the reality of conversion in several modes that we have termed "religious, theistic, Christian, ecclesial, moral, and intellectual." It is important to note that while the sequence has an inner logic, it is not intended as chronological or hierarchical. When the various conversions are operative within an individual or a group, they are related in a compenetrating, overlapping, and sometimes dialectical manner. Therefore, like the patterns of experience, conversion has been unravelled in this manner in order to facilitate understanding. Concretely, various combinations of these modes of conversion are ongoing simultaneously in any one or group of us according to our personal history, context, and horizon.

It would be foolish to imagine a neat sequence from religious to intellectual conversion or the same constellation of conversions in every individual. This is why it is possible to encounter the brilliant scholar who relegates all religion to superstition, the saintly church woman who knows nothing of the labyrinths of speculative theology, the priest who enters the ministry under the sway of ethnic and cultural values but with no deep personal sense of Christ, the bishop who is dedicated to the Church as he understands it but sees no need to keep abreast of theology, the admitted atheist advancing sublime and heroic moral values in a manner that puts religionists to shame, the artist who experiences mystical union with God but brands institutional religion pharisaical. The multiple forms of conversion are not respecters of person or office. None of them is present "automatically." Hence we may be surprised by the narrow-mindedness of a scholar and the intellectual curiosity and discipline of a laborer.

If all six forms are operative in an individual, there remains the key question of how that particular individual integrates them. Which conversions are given the privileged position? In making a moral decision, for example, a person may uncover insights that seem at variance with the Church's reflections on the issue. But these reflections are highly prized due to ecclesial conversion. If the tension cannot be resolved, one may eventually give precedence to the Church's self-understanding, while another may favor the fruits of intellectual investigation. Or a strongly felt Christian conversion may put a person at variance with the dictates of both ecclesial and intellectual conversion. If such tensions are persistent and concern issues and values of great import, it is possible that, over time, one will feel

compelled to leave behind a previously embraced horizon. For besides conversions there are breakdowns.[17]

7. Faith and Beliefs

When we reflect upon conversion as a cluster of compenetrating
and ongoing activities of self-transcendence, we are necessarily within the world of interiority. And the world of interiority is the world
of subjects. There can be no such thing as conversion in general. The
several modes of conversion occur in actual living persons in history
or they simply do not exist. And this living response to the call to self-
transcendence or conversion is often described by the general term
"faith." Wilfred Cantwell Smith is underscoring a fact that is as obvious as it is overlooked when he states:

> The study of a religion is the study of persons. . . . Faith is a quality
> of men's lives. 'All religions are new religions, every morning. For
> religions do not exist in the sky somewhere, elaborated, finished,
> and static; they exist in men's hearts.'[18]

Because the highly personal nature of faith as the response to the
impulse of conversion is easily overlooked, one often finds that one or
another element or dimension of religion's self-expression (symbol,
ritual, narrative, theory, practice, laws) is spoken of as if it were inter-
changeable with faith. So when someone does not enter into the accepted meaning of a particular ritual, or disputes the common interpretation of a particular narrative, or questions the present value
of a venerable theological pronouncement or violates the common
law of the Church, it may be observed that such a person has little or
no faith. This, of course, is not necessarily the case.

All acts of religious expression are attempts to objectify an interi-
or reality. This interior transformation is, in turn, prompted by the
gift of God. Therefore, "expressions" of faith have a normative function. They strive to keep the individual and the community in communion with the transforming power at the heart of conversion.
However, they cannot be equated with faith, which is the personal
transformation due to conversion. Smith calls these indispensable expressions "cumulative tradition," and by that he means:

> the entire mass of overt objective data that constitute the historical
> deposit, as it were, of the past religious life of the community in
> question: temples, scriptures, theological systems, dance patterns,

legal and other social institutions, conventions, moral codes, myths, and so on; anything that can be and is transmitted from one person, one generation, to another, and that the historian can observe.[19]

Generic faith as the transformation of horizon due to the real and operative presence of conversion can be distinguished from specific beliefs in a way that may be very helpful for the kind of sharing and communication that a wisdom community is intended to foster.

The new horizon that results from conversion gives one what we may term a "personal experiential base." And this self-validating experience is the generic and faithful response to mystery, God, Jesus, community, moral value, and intellectual discipline. So the reverent awe and trust of religious conversion are more generic than the specific affirmation of God. But the affirmation of God is more generic than specific affirmations or beliefs about how God is God. And the affirmation of Jesus as the Christ is more generic than specific affirmations or beliefs about how Jesus can be the Messiah.

The affirmation of communion with the followers of Jesus is more generic than specific affirmations and beliefs about which community of Jesus' followers is the "one true Church." The affirmation of value over satisfaction is more generic than the specific affirmation or belief that this or that value is absolutely absolute or absolutely relative. Finally, the affirmation of the freedom of intelligence and the unity of truth are more generic than the specific affirmations or beliefs that certain judgments are in fact true.

When we see faith as generic and belief as specific, we establish ample flexibility for discussing the diversity of world religions and the diversity within specific religious traditions. This is true because it emphasizes the broad base of what is held in common by the generic faith response without denying what may be hotly disputed concerning specific beliefs. This differentiation allows that while the response to Jesus may be one of genuine conversion marked by living faith, one might not affirm or find equally compelling various specific philosophical and theological speculations that have taken on a normative character in the tradition.[20]

This distinction does not intend to imply that faith in this generic sense is all that matters and that specific beliefs are merely accidental. For the converted horizon of faith is the very viewpoint within which specific beliefs are adverted to, understood, affirmed, or denied. But this is not always the case. Many people embrace a host of beliefs of quite varying importance without ever distinguishing them from the broad foundational faith. The distinction does, however, in-

tend to stress the fact that while the faith response of one who is under the impetus of conversion is likely to be in part occasioned by
some element of "cumulative tradition" or "expressive dimension,"
the faith transformation cannot be equated with specific affirmation
or denials of specifics. For prior to linguistic discourse there is a radical "inner word" that cannot, in every case, be measured by the outer
word or expression. Hence the radical referent of conversion is the
experienced reality within the individual that puts them "in touch"
with the mystery of God, the person of Jesus, the call to community,
the thirst for the truly good, and the self-correcting dynamism of intelligence.[21]

An important clarification is in order here. To stress that multiple belief systems may in fact be outgrowths of radically compatible
conversion experiences is not to say that individual Roman Catholic,
Anglican, or Lutheran Church communities have not the right to invite their members to assent to the "outer word" by which the particular community is commonly recognized. Furthermore, such affirmations are clearly intended as articulations and affirmations of faith.
However, a careful perusal of history reveals the fact that the Catholic Church's own understanding of the meaning of its normative language as well as its selection of issues about which normative
assertions and assents must be made and called for, have differed
much from context to context and from age to age. Any sensitive parish priest knows that within his congregation he will find a range of
specific beliefs that is about as wide as the range of separated Christian churches. This is inevitable due to the unique spiritual journey
of every person. Hence the judgment that one is or is not a fully orthodox member of a particular tradition is not necessarily to affirm or
deny that one is within the ambit of faith and conversion. For the ultimate absolute point of reference is not the verbal expression but the
individual's response to the inviting presence of the mystery of God.

8. Conclusion

This third chapter has been an exploration of the world of interiority. By reflecting upon the questions of meaning raised within the
many patterns of human experience, we have identified the self-transcending response to these questions as a basic change of horizon or
conversion. This yielding to the call to conversion has been named
"faith," while specific formulations or understandings of the process
have been termed "beliefs."

One important consequence of the turn to interiority that in turn results from the radical cultural shifts discussed in the first chapter is the tendency towards a "soft apologetic" in favor of an earlier "hard apologetic."

A *hard apologetic* appeals more to argument and obedience, while a soft apologetic appeals more to experience and authenticity. A hard apologetic takes its stand on rational arguments for the existence of God, "historical" evidence to show that the New Testament authors were trustworthy eyewitnesses, scriptural arguments (from miracles and testimonies) that Jesus is the Son of God, scriptural and historical arguments to show that the Catholic Church is indeed the community established by Jesus to witness to his ministry. And within this community, the Spirit has providentially provided that those who are the official teachers (bishops) are gifted with the charisms needed to authentically proclaim and interpret the Gospel message. An appreciative and obedient hearing of this teaching is expected on the part of those members of the Church who may have many other gifts but are not the official teachers.

The *soft apologetic* does not deny argument and obedience any more than the hard apologetic denies experience and authenticity. But the point of emphasis is different. The foundational personal experiences of religious, Christian, ecclesial, moral, and intellectual conversion are essential. Argument and obedience are necessary, but they are subsequent and subordinate. While office must be respected, real authority is not automatic or *ex officio*. Spiritual and intellectual authenticity is looked for in the bishop, priest, or theologian to give credibility to their teaching. The sweep of intellectual conversion challenges the unquestioned authority of arguments and texts employed by hard apologetics. Where there may have appeared to be only one theology, many theologies clearly emerge. We will explore the impact of the turn to interiority upon theology and its relationship to the Church in the next two chapters, "Theology in a New Key."

NOTES

1. Lonergan, *Method*, p. 105.
2. For the *generic* account of conversion I am follow Lonergan. See *Method*, pp. 235–44. Note, however, that while he speaks only of religious, moral, and intellectual conversion, I distinguish religious conversion from theistic conversion, specify Christian conversion to provide the necessary focal symbol, and add ecclesial conversion to include the important communal

dimension of conversion. See Charles Curran, "Christian Conversion in the Writings of Bernard Lonergan," *Foundations of Theology: Papers from the International Lonergan Congress 1970*, edited by Philip McShane (Dublin: Gill and Macmillan, 1971); Donal Dorr, "Conversion," *Looking at Lonergan's Method*, edited by Patrick Corcoran (Dublin: The Tabbot Press, 1975), pp. 175–86; Hans Küng, "The Other Dimension," *On Being a Christian* (Garden City, N.Y.: Doubleday and Co., Inc., 1976), pp. 57–88; finally, for a helpful account of the process of conversion or transformation illustrated by ordinary life examples, see Rosemary Haughton, *The Transformation of Man: A Study of Conversion and Community* (Springfield, Ill: Templegate, 1967).

3. See Lawrence Thompson and R. H. Wimmick, *Robert Frost: The Later Years, 1938–1963*, p. 238; see also Loren Eiseley, *The Unexpected Universe* (New York: Harvest Book, 1969).

4. See Sam Keen, *Apology for Wonder* (New York: Harper & Row, 1969).

5. See John Dewey, *A Common Faith* (New Haven, Conn.: Yale University Press, 1934).

6. T. C. McLuhan, *Touch the Earth: A Self Portrait of Indian Existence* (New York: Outerbridge and Dienstfrey, 1971), p. 36.

7. Gerard Manley Hopkins, "The Wreck of the Deutschland," *The Poems of Gerard Manley Hopkins*, edited by W. H. Gardner and N. H. MacKenzie (London: Oxford University Press 1970), p. 51.

8. See Küng, *On Being a Christian*, pp. 73 ff.; also see John Dunne, *The Reasons of the Heart* (New York: Macmillan, 1978).

9. Lonergan, *Method*, p. 109. See also Friedrich Heiler, "The History of Religions as a Preparation for the Cooperation of Religions," *The History of Religions*, edited by Mircea Eliade and Joseph Kitagawa (Chicago: University of Chicago Press, 1959), pp. 142–53; Wilfred Cantwell Smith, *The Meaning and End of Religion* (New York: Mentor Books, 1964); John Hick, *God and the Universe of Faiths* (New York: Macmillan Press, 1973).

10. A central part of the problem is the fact that, due to the decline of common meaning, the once admired Church now seems in disarray. In more tranquil days one could see in the Church a haven of stability and certitude. For it was, "a uniquely continuous and consistent history, the blend of venerable age and vigorous youth, a powerful organization, sprung from humble roots, spread throughout the world, with hundreds of millions of adherents and a strictly ordered hierarchy, a cult of rich tradition and noble in its solemnity, a profound system of doctrine theology [Sic], the comprehensive cultural achievement, in the secular sphere, of building up and molding the history of Christian Europe, modern social teaching." Hans Küng, *The Church*, translated by Ray and Rosaleen Ochenden (New York: Sheed & Ward, 1967), p. 25. This challenging and somewhat controversial work explores at great length many of the questions that would fill out this sketch of ecclesial conversion.

11. I have explored the peculiar problems of the university student in relation to ecclesial conversion in my essay "A Catholic at Harvard," *National Catholic Reporter*, September 30, 1977, pp. 7,9 ff.

12. Avery Dulles elaborates on these descriptions by examining the Church under different "models": institution, mystical communion, sacrament, herald, and servant. See *Models of the Church* (Garden City, N.Y.: Doubleday & Co., Inc., 1974). See also Dulles' previously mentioned *The Resilient Church*; E. Schillebeeckx, *Christ the Sacrament of the Encounter with God* (New York: Sheed & Ward, 1963); Richard P. McBrien, *Do We Need the Church?* (New York: Harper & Row, 1969); idem, *Church: The Continuing Quest* (New York: Newman, 1970).

13. Karl Rahner, *The Shape of the Church to Come*, translated by Edward Quinn (New York: Seabury Press, 1974), Part Three, "How Can a Church of the Future Be Conceived?" This remarkable book is deceptive in its brevity and its simplicity. It would serve as an excellent piece of common reading to initiate the dialectic of a wisdom community. Note the similarity between Rahner and Dulles on the future Church. *Models of the Church*, pp. 188–92; see also Lonergan, "The Church and the Churches," *Method in Theology*, pp. 367–68.

14. Robert Bolt, *A Man for All Seasons* (New York: Vintage Books, 1960), p. 81. For a biblical example, see the story of Eleazer, who chose death over violating his conscience and scandalizing youth (2 Maccabees 6: 18–30).

15. There is a great body of literature to address these questions. Some key sources are: Daniel Callahan, *Abortion: Law, Choice & Morality* (New York: The Macmillan Co. 1972); Charles E. Curran, *Christian Morality Today, The Renewal of Moral Theology* (Notre Dame, Ind.: Fides, 1966); idem, *Catholic Moral Theology in Dialogue* (Notre Dame, Ind.: Fides, 1972); idem, *New Perspectives in Moral Theology* (Notre Dame, Ind.: Fides, 1974); Joseph Gremillion, *The Gospel of Peace and Justice: Catholic Social Teaching since Pope John* (Maryknoll, N.Y.: Orbis Books, 1975); James M. Gustafson, *Christ and the Moral Life* (New York: Harper & Row, 1968); "Genetic Science and Man," *Theological Studies*, 33 (entire issue); Stephen J. Kelleher, *Divorce and Remarriage for Catholics?* (Garden City, N.Y.: Doubleday & Co., 1973); Paul L. Lehmann, *Ethics in a Christian Context* (New York: Harper & Row, 1963); Richard McCormick, *Ambiguity in Moral Choice: The 1973 Pere Marquette Theology Lecture* (Milwaukee: Marquette University Press, 1973); John J. McNeill, *The Church and the Homosexual* (Kansas City: Sheed, Andrews and McMeel, Inc., 1976); Reinhold Niebuhr, *Moral Man and Immoral Society* (New York: Charles Scribner's Sons, 1960); Timothy E. O'Connell, *Principles for a Catholic Morality* (New York: The Seabury Press, 1978); Karl Rahner, "On the Question of a Formal Existential Ethics," *Theological Investigations*, Vol. 2, "Man in the Church" (Baltimore: Helicon Press, 1966); John Rawls, *A Theory of Justice* (Oxford: Oxford Paperbacks, 1971); John H. Yoder, *The Politics of Jesus* (Grand Rapids, Mich.: William B. Eerdmans Publishing Co., 1972).

16. For an introduction to Kohlberg, see Ronald Duska and Mariellen Whelan, *Moral Development: A Guide to Piaget and Kohlberg* (New York: Paulist Press, 1975).

17. Horizons that were once seen as an upward spiral may come to be rejected as a mere rut. What one experiences as a conversion may be observed

by another to be a decline. For an elaboration of "breakdowns," see Lonergan, *Method*, pp. 243–44.

18. Wilfred Cantwell Smith, "Comparative Religion: Whither and Why?" *The History of Religions*, op. cit., p. 34; in *The Meaning and End of Religion*, op. cit., p. 71, Smith elaborates on this statement:

> My faith is different from my brother's. This is a fact. The faith of one of my neighbors (or readers) is different from that of another. This is an inference, but can hardly be gainsaid by anyone who takes evidence seriously. From data such as these the historian must start looking further afield and more widely in time; if one may infer anything at all in these matters one can hardly but recognize (and the more sensitive one is, the more surely one recognizes) that Tertullian's faith was different from Abelard's, Constantine's different from Zwingli's, St. Teresa's different from John Knox's, Harnark's different from William Jennings Bryan's. At a less elite level, the faith of a Roman proletarian catacombist or martyr was different from that of a hanger-on of the Crusades, and both of these from the faith of a modern Bible-belt farmer.

19. Smith, ibid., p. 141.; see also W. C. Smith, "Faith as a Universal Human Quality," Bea Lecture, Woodstock College, March 18, 1971 (unpublished manuscript); Walter E. Conn, " 'Faith' and 'Cumulative Tradition' in Functional Specialization: A Study of the Methodologies of Wilfred Cantwell Smith and Bernard Lonergan," *Sciences Religieuses/Studies in Religion*, Winter 1975, pp. 221–46.

20. James Fowler correctly observes that religious pluralism is not simply the obvious differences between the great world religions (horizontal pluralism). It is also the differences that obtain within specific religious traditions (vertical pluralism) due to differing stages of faith development. See James W. Fowler, "Faith Development Theory and the Aims of Religious Socialization" (unpublished manuscript), October 1975.

21. See E. A. Burtt's discussion of Christianity and Existentialism in *In Search of Philosophic Understanding* (New York: Mentor Book, 1965), pp. 77–112.

Chapter Four
Theology in a New Key:
I. The Question of Mediation

Introduction

Chapter One began by inviting diverse readers to a consensus. No matter what one's background or perspective may be, all would admit that something has happened to the Catholic Church in the last decade and a half. There followed an overview of the decline of common meaning. This fourth chapter begins with equal confidence that each reader will also affirm that as a result of the decline of common meaning and the turn to interiority "something" has also happened to theology. Again there may be as many different opinions and evaluations of what happened to theology as there are of what happened to religion. But in any case, things are not the same.

Throughout this work, it has been stressed that religion and theology, while interrelated in a complex fashion, are not the same. By means of the expressive dimensions or components of symbol, narrative, ritual, and community norms, religion proclaims and celebrates the originating revelatory and experiential encounter with the holy mystery of God. Much of religion as it is lived by individuals is a pre-conceptual or at least non-conceptual reality. Various individuals or groups, of course, may have a greater or lesser interest in certain theoretical questions. And this interest and subsequent understanding may help them better synthesize the diverse elements of the religious world view by means of which they render life experiences meaningful.

Theology, however, is the self-consciously discursive and concep-

tual activity of reflecting upon the meanings, values, attitudes, and interpretations of reality that are mediated by religion to individuals
and to a whole culture. This reflection may defend, interpret, challenge, clarify, or apply to concrete situations the meaning and truth
that religion proclaims. It should be obvious that religions issue forth
theologies, but theologies do not produce religions. Many individuals
can live out their religious lives completely oblivious of, and indifferent to, the stormy battles of theology. And while theology may appear to be able to exist without religion, it actually feeds upon it.[1] For
without religion, the symbols, rituals, values, beliefs, and texts upon
which theology reflects would not exist in a vital way. In the Roman
Catholic tradition theology has long played a supportive and apologetic role in favor of religion. In the present ferment, however, that
does not always seem to be the case and hence particular difficulties
arise. This chapter will explore the new pluralism in contemporary
theology. This chapter will be in six parts: (1) The Question of Method; (2) The Question of Mediation; (3) Critical Mediation; (4) Dogmatic Mediation; (5) Existential Mediation; and (6) Conclusion.

1. The Question of Method

Like any other discipline, theology is pursued by means of implicit or explicit methodology or methodologies. Among other things,
method offers an organizational framework. Such a framework is ex-
tremely important if one is to interpret and integrate the results of
the factors we have been discussing. Chief among them are: the shift
from classical to modern culture; the role of conversion; the distinctions between faith and beliefs, religion and theology, and a hard and
a soft apologetic. In this context, it is not surprising that there should
be an intensification of interest in questions of theological method.

Theological method recognizes diverse areas of competence, the
division of labor, and the necessity of collaboration. Bernard Lonergan has met this organizational issue by suggesting that there are
eight distinct but functionally related specialities in theology.[2]

Methodology consists of distinct but interrelated activities, collaborating in appropriate patterns that are reduplicable and that lead
to real advances rather than a rut or even decline. As Lonergan puts
it, "A method is a normative pattern of recurrent and related operations yielding cumulative and progressive results."[3] In the modern
context, the method that Lonergan proposes for theology is necessarily empirical. For this reason the privileged documents of Scripture
and tradition may not be viewed as trans-cultural premises from

which certain deductions may automatically be made. Rather they are seen as data that must be examined in their historical context and analyzed according to contemporary procedures and techniques.

There are eight specialized activities in Lonergan's method. Four look to the past tradition: (1) Research, (2) Interpretation, (3) History, and (4) Dialectic; and four look to the present situation: (5) Foundations, (6) Doctrines, (7) Systematics, and (8) Communications. (See Figure 5.)

(1) Research. The Christian experience has been mediated to us by means of symbols, rituals, narratives, beliefs, doctrines, speculations, and heroic deeds which have been recorded in documents and diverse artifacts. Therefore, there is a need to accumulate these documents by the best scientific means available. This will mean assembling the critical editions of all relevant texts and artifacts so as to determine as accurately as possible the exact content or significance of these works. This entire and ongoing process is the first speciality, Research.

(2) Interpretation. Since these documents and artifacts preserve religious meaning, it is important to know as clearly as possible what the authors or artists meant when they wrote or created in their particular historical contexts. It is equally important to know what similar or different meanings these works may have called forth in subsequent historical periods and new circumstances. By means of all the available methods of literary and cultural analysis, effort must be made to understand what meaning was intended and what new meanings have emerged. This painstaking hermeneutical (or interpretation) process comprises the second specialty, Interpretation.

(3) History. The third speciality is history. Here one seeks to examine the fate of various interpretations, meanings, and events as they moved through the centuries of history. Which one advanced and which one declined and why? What provoked past differences that produced not only different theologies but eventually different Christian churches? History seeks to uncover the relationship between authors, ideas, and documents. How do key individuals, events, circumstances, documents, and ideas relate to those that went before, followed, or were present at the same time? The specialist as historian is engaged in a long and critical process that seeks not only to interrelate diverse interpretations and complex events but also to uncover

FIGURE 5

CONVERSION AND THEOLOGICAL ACTIVITY

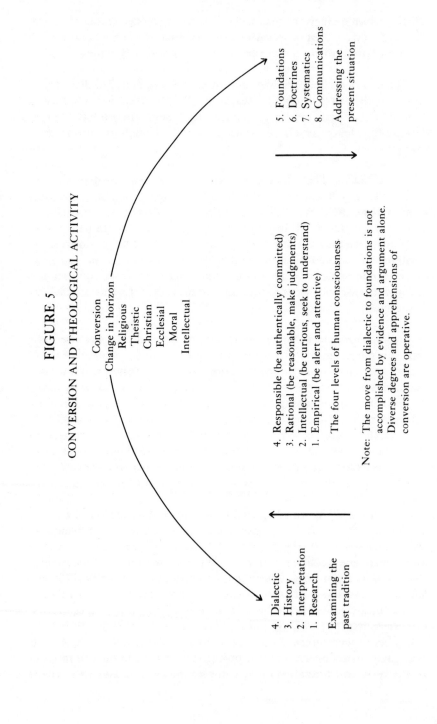

Conversion
Change in horizon
    Religious
    Theistic
    Christian
    Ecclesial
    Moral
    Intellectual

5. Foundations
6. Doctrines
7. Systematics
8. Communications

Addressing the
present situation

4. Responsible (be authentically committed)
3. Rational (be reasonable, make judgments)
2. Intellectual (be curious, seek to understand)
1. Empirical (be alert and attentive)

The four levels of human consciousness

Note: The move from dialectic to foundations is not
accomplished by evidence and argument alone.
Diverse degrees and apprehensions of
conversion are operative.

4. Dialectic
3. History
2. Interpretation
1. Research

Examining the
past tradition

what *in fact* was ongoing in history that sparked the multiple, even contradictory, interpretations.

(4) Dialectic. The past, like the present, is marked by differences and conflict. Eventually the question of who is correct or incorrect arises as well as the related question of the grounds for affirming a correct position and rejecting as incorrect a counter-position. Here is needed the crucial fourth functional speciality, Dialectic. Dialectic has a high and distant goal. It is not content with narrow horizons. Hence it strives for a comprehensive viewpoint, a framework or set of frameworks that make it possible to coordinate and integrate the numerous viewpoints that are manifest at a given moment of religious history or in a whole movement of history. This way it is possible to determine whether differences are absolutely irreducible, whether they are actually the multiple factors of a larger complex whole, or whether time will reveal them to be interlocking stages by which a single development is unravelling. In this manner, dialectic is able to recognize variously differentiated human consciousness as well as completely undifferentiated consciousness. It notes, for example, those who can and cannot distinguish the various kinds of truth found in science, philosophy, common sense, religion, theology, and the like.

Dialectic is more than comparison. It is also criticism. By means of criticism dialectic seeks to uncover viewpoints that are not coherent and arguments that are not sound. Dialectic, then, is an open, honest, and challenging interchange which can welcome participants with genuine differences. Over time, the interchange will determine whether these differences are real or apparent. Minor differences can be put aside so that the real issues can be engaged and hopefully resolved.

The resolution of difference recognized by dialectic will not be accomplished by investigation and argument alone. This is why it is within dialectic that Lonergan locates the process of conversion, which has been elaborated in the previous chapter. The reason for this is the important realization that the resolution of real conflicts is not self-contained within research, interpretation, and history alone. Evidence and argument must be carefully weighed, but they cannot give the whole account of how the questions, broached in dialectics, are ultimately resolved.

Is the religious interpretation of reality meaningful and true? Is the theistic interpretation of the religious sense meaningful and true? Is the Christian interpretation of theism meaningful and true? Is the ecclesial interpretation of the Christian reality meaningful and true? If the ecclesial interpretation of the Christian reality is meaningful and true, is the Roman Catholic interpretation of "Church" meaningful and true? If the Roman Catholic interpretation of "Church" is meaningful and true, is it the only interpretation that is meaningful and true? If other interpretations are possibly meaningful and true, then how are they to be determined and recognized?

Is this particular theoretical account of the Church's self-understanding merely adequate for the present context, the best possible for the present context, superior and normative for the foreseeable future, or absolute, definitive, and irreformable? When questions such as these are finally answered with confidence and conviction, it is not by means of diligent intelligence alone. The various degrees and forms of conversion are at play as the tension is resolved.

(5) Foundations. Conversion, then, makes possible the transition from the dialectic of the past to the foundations of the present. It is important to recognize that one does not move to the fifth speciality, Foundations, by evidence, tradition, and argument alone. In an older "hard" apologetic, it might have been argued by Catholics that the application of the first four specializations to Scripture and early Church history would clearly and objectively show that Peter enjoyed a primacy among the Apostles. Further, the Bishops of Rome succeed to that divinely established primacy. However, Orthodox, Anglican, Lutheran, or Baptist scholars could examine the exact same evidence and not come to the same conclusion. The reason for this may be that the evidence is ambiguous or that, if it is clear, the prior convictions of the investigators have influenced the accumulation, selection, and interpretations of the same data. In other words, conversion is present. One already has a firmly held position and the theological activity aims at providing an apologetic for the existing conviction.

We have already seen that religious, theistic, Christian, ecclesial, moral, and intellectual conversions constitute the basis for the interior world of the mature Christian. It is the objectification or articulation of these conversions into basic horizons that establishes one's foundations. When authentic conversion is thematized, one has the necessary foundations for moving on to doctrines, systematics, and communications. Foundations are one's point of departure on the question of God, Jesus, Church, the moral and intellectual life. Foundations, however, do not consist primarily of proving a premise, such as the inerrancy of Scripture and/or of the Church, from which multiple conclusions can then be logically drawn by theologians. It is rather the result of a radical change in the theologian allowing one to move from the *indirect* discourse of recounting the diverse convictions of others in the past to the *direct* discourse that declares what one believes to be the case in the present.

(6) Doctrines. The horizon or view of reality embraced by foundations makes it possible to apprehend or formulate doctrines. As the sixth speciality, Doctrines articulate particular judgments of fact and value. These affirmations and negations embrace moral, ascetical, mystical, pastoral, as well as dogmatic, theology. Doctrines seek to expose as clearly as possible the commitments made by converted subjects in a particular tradition and at a particular time. By making more specific the features of the horizon entered by means of foundations, doctrinal judgments seek to affirm (incompletely but still truly) salient features of the religious, theistic, Christian, ecclesial, moral, and intellectual interpretation of reality. In the language of the previous chapter, it may be said that, while foundations constitute the horizon of generic faith, doctrine constitutes the horizon of specific beliefs.

(7) Systematics. Left alone, religious doctrines may appear strange or problematic because of the peculiarities of language, the era in which they were formulated, or the diverse differentiations of consciousness that may or may not distinguish the literal from the symbolic mode of speech. To meet this problem there is a seventh speciality, Systematics. The systematic theologian is concerned with understanding the doctrines that have been affirmed, ordering them in a coherent way and highlighting the not always obvious ways in which they may relate and hold together. In its refined form systematics works out a technical and philosophical language as well as a highly speculative mind-set so as to deal with seeming inconsistencies and errors. Ever seeking an overall whole, systematics draws insights from many technical fields as well as everyday life so as to meet the demand of intellectual conversion for coherence and to make more luminous the Christian mysteries. Systematics is concerned not only with the internal coherence of doctrines. It also seeks to integrate religious convictions with whatever is known in other areas of human life.

(8) Communications. The end result envisioned by theological method is not a set of coherent speculations but the transformation of

people in their concrete and perhaps unsophisticated life situation. Hence the eighth and final speciality is Communications. Here the highly technical activities of the previous specialities must engage a vast array of interdisciplinary collaborations and diverse cultural, ethnic, social, political, educational, and intellectual conditions that typify the human family from age to age and from place to place. In this way communications is at the service of religion. It is the "pastoral art." It seeks to develop appropriate rituals, symbols, ceremonies, and practices to celebrate and intensify the world view made possible by conversion.

This calls forth the important skills of pastoral theologians, religious educators, catechists, liturgists, preachers, musicians, poets, artists, and media experts. This will require the use of genuine and indigenous religious art, rather than mass-produced "plastic crucifixes" that "communicate" institutional affiliation but no religious meaning or value. A great sensitivity to the positive values and the potentially religious significance of realities that are cherished by people of different classes, cultures, races, and regions is needed if this speciality is not to become negative indoctrination that imposes a foreign culture and cast of mind on a people in the name of a universal religion.

In local communities, Catholic university presidents, principals of Catholic secondary schools, and directors of Catholic elementary school systems have great responsibilities. Laypeople, brothers, sisters, permanent deacons, parish priests, and bishops must strive to keep abreast of the most important results of the theological process so as not to be overwhelmed when a gradually developing issue bursts forth in the popular media. Theologians who engage in continuing education programs have a special responsibility to remain in contact with the life experience of so-called ordinary parish life so as to temper and adapt their observations to real pastoral needs in a way that enhances the growth of the local church more than it spreads confusion and ill will.

Communications may be the crucial functional speciality at this juncture. One of the reasons for this is that while what is communicated is in a written form, it is often not read or only partially read. So when the Vatican issues a carefully worded document, or a theologian publishes a highly nuanced book, many people (especially the laity) never see the text itself. Instead, the most provocative ideas in these works are taken out of context and proclaimed on television news or the newspaper under such headings as: "Pope deplores...";
"Theologian denounces..."; "Scholars question..."; "Church for-

bids. . . ." As a result, many people are entangled in a maze of misinformation and confusion from which they cannot easily escape. Since the Church is competing with the powerful impact of the terse and instant images of modern media, neither the pulpit nor the adult education class is adequate to meet this problem.

Communications must not be seen in a paternalistic sense as the techniques, programs, and efforts on the part of the Church (meaning priests, theologians, brothers, sisters, and bishops) to "reach" the people (meaning the laity). Communication must be an upward and downward spiral. Since all of the diverse people make up one Church, it is as important that there be structures by which priests in parish ministry communicate with university theologians, and leaders of parish communities communicate with bishops and other leaders. Indifference to or misuse of communication on the pastoral level can render all of the activity of the seven other specializations a mere exercise.

2. The Question of Mediation

This brief overview of the eight interconnected areas of theological specialization makes it obvious that it is no longer possible for any one person to be expert in all disciplines and competencies that move one from initial inquiry (research) to end result (communication). Now more than ever there is a conscious and explicit acknowledgment that the theology of the future will be the result of a division of labor and ongoing collaboration between specialists. What this overview does not provide is an explicit account of precisely how one moves from dialectic (the past tradition) to foundations (the present situation).

Conversion is obviously the catalyst. But it has already been noted that an individual may rank the values of one conversion over another. The horizon of one theologian may be dominated by ecclesial conversion, another by intellectual conversion, and yet another by moral conversion. In each case the other conversions may be present but to a subordinate degree. This is especially true when one wants to ascertain on what authority one's foundations can be termed more or less probable or even certain. How is one to know that one's starting points are in fact irreducible? What should those starting points be? The recurrent affirmations of the religious tradition? The recurrent patterns and operations of one's scientific method? The urgency of the concrete situation and the authenticity of one's discernment?

To answer these questions we must recognize the *de facto* situation that contemporary theology exists in at least three distinct contexts or communities. Thus there are three distinct modes of mediation operative in the move from dialectic to foundations. These modes of mediation may be termed the "Critical" mode, the "Dogmatic" mode and the "Existential" mode. Each one corresponds roughly to a distinct zone of discourse or conversation partners of theology. These are the university world or the academy, a specific ecclesial or Church tradition, and the specific socio-cultural matrix that a theologian may be addressing or from which he may be speaking.[4]

The first (Critical) takes its stand on the authority and truth-finding power of its methodology. The second (Dogmatic) takes its stand on the authority and truth of a privileged tradition. The third (Existential) takes its stand on the authority and truth that is manifest when central beliefs or themes of the Christian tradition authentically engage the urgent social, cultural, or political issues of the day or the personal life world of the individual Christian.

3. Critical Mediation: Theology in the University Context

Theology in conversation with the academy is dominated by intellectual conversion and its mode of mediation is essentially, though not exclusively, critical. Theology in the university context attempts to provide a refined and sophisticated account of the meaning of the Christian tradition in such a way that reasonable people employing the rigorous methods of the academy will be able to comprehend theology, whether or not they are explicitly religious, because of the internal coherence of evidence and arguments and because of sympathetic vibration with their own human experience. Theology in this mode is especially concerned to maintain honest, open, critical, and collaborative inquiry in the manner proper to an authentic climate of unbiased learning and study.

Because of this, theology in a university is particularly concerned to show that religious truth claims can be vindicated or rejected when measured by commonly accepted methods of academic inquiry. This process is carried on by employing the special resources of philosophy, sociology, psychology, anthropology, and other university disciplines. Philosophy, however, remains the most important partner of university theology, especially when it is seeking to give a clear account of the truth claims that religion proposes as answers to life's fundamental question. Depending upon the philosophical framework, truth may be defined as that which is internally coherent, that which is verified, that which is adequate to common human experience and language, or that which is disclosive of depth dimensions of reality. In this manner a theologian may explain what he means by "true," make explicit his truth claims, and defend them on grounds that are available for objective evaluation by all reasonable and intelligent people.

Theology in the university setting, therefore, argues that religion addresses fundamental human questions and claims to provide answers for these questions. It should be expected that intelligent and fair-minded people will give these claims a public hearing. Therefore, even if a theologian is as a matter of fact an explicit believer in a certain tradition (ecclesial conversion), he will make his argument on strictly scholarly and publicly available grounds. Convictions, personal faith, and beliefs, no matter how sincerely held, cannot serve as public grounds for defending his religious truth claims. The highest authority rests in the publicly available tools and methods of intelligent and disciplined inquiry. However, it should be noted that commitment to various schools of thought and intellectual bias may still diminish the scholar's success at attaining a detached and objective viewpoint.

Much influenced by the Enlightenment, critical mediation does not hide from evidence of modern physical and life sciences that, for example, make it impossible to continue to affirm a literal interpretation of the biblical story of creation. Nor can it blindly defend a literal understanding of biblical inspiration in the light of modern historical studies of the composition of Scripture. A significant presupposition of critical mediation is that there is no area of religious faith, belief, or practice that is sacrosanct or untouchable. The irreducible starting points are not particular beliefs but rather the scholarly requirements of critical methodology.[5] If fidelity to this methodology calls cherished traditional beliefs into question or even concludes them to be "erroneous," the method is not abandoned in favor of the "beliefs."

The critical mode of mediation, therefore, embraces the "faith of secularity" in the ultimate value and worth of the human condition, and it suggests that the same critical reflection and unyielding discipline that characterize analysis in other areas can be employed to argue cogently that the key Christian symbols are the fitting fulfillment of the hopes of this secular faith. Because of this critical posture, theology in the academy is slow to proclaim that contradictions, inconsistencies, and conflicting evidence can be covered over by the statement, "Well, it's a mystery." While ultimately, mystery may have to be acknowledged, mystification, bias, or bad scholarship must

be abhorred. Critical mediation may well concede that there are other, seemingly self-authenticating ways of coming to religious convictions besides critical investigations. But these are not admissible in a
public discussion.

One might be tempted to call this approach a reworking of what
was once called "natural theology" or "philosophy of religion" and
not theology at all. Natural theology goes as far as it can in answering
ultimate questions with "unaided reason." Philosophy of religion is a
detached analysis of the philosophical presuppositions of religion.
But it is argued that, because of the explicit commitment to reflect seriously upon the truth claims and cognitive content of the Christian
tradition, critical mediation is a kind of fundamental theology. One of
its goals is to demonstrate the legitimacy of religious discourse, and
this legitimacy can be grounded by accepted university disciplines
without recourse to creeds or beliefs. This critical mode of theology
intends to treat only foundations (the issues of generic faith). It does
not embrace doctrines and systematics (specific beliefs). Because of its
"suspension of belief," some church leaders, church scholars, parishioners, and secular observers may confront this critical style of theology with the charge of false pretenses. Generic optimism about life's
meaning cannot be equated with the horizon of Christian faith. For
this reason the university theologian of this sort for some becomes a
scandal, a kind of "unbelieving theologian." His critics claim that he
is engaged in "understanding seeking faith" when the church community knows full well that all authentic theology must start with
"faith seeking understanding."[6]

The theologian writing in the critical mode faces a dilemma. On
the one hand, in spite of all his efforts to establish the value and validity of core Christian symbols on public grounds, many of his colleagues in the secular university may find his enterprise to be suspect
because his very undertaking implies more than mere interest. Some
form of prior commitment to the symbols under investigation seems
implied. On the other hand, there may be conflict with the church
tradition from which he probably came. This tension takes two
forms. First of all, the generic faith horizon that he is able to ground
critically seems somewhat impoverished, governed by intellectual
and perhaps implicit religious conversion.[7] His colleagues from the
church tradition may applaud these "foundations" as a significant advance for the general dialogue between religion and secularity, but
they are convinced that they will never serve as foundations for a fundamental theology of the Christian faith unless that faith is explicitly
thematized, affirmed, and addressed.[8] The second and more serious

tension results from the confrontation between what the critical theologian considers to be the positive findings of his discipline and the specific affirmations of the church tradition.[9]

Let us consider an example. The Christian tradition has long proclaimed a hope in life beyond the grave. The liturgy proclaims that, "Life is not ended but merely changed." This hope has been traditionally expressed by reference to the biblical image "the resurrection of the body" or the more Greek philosophical speculations concerning the native "immortality of the human soul." The theologian in the academy may conclude that he can affirm neither the resurrection as the literal resuscitation of dead bodies nor the metaphysical truth of Aristotelian-Thomistic hylomorphism. He may be uncomfortable with talk of "after life" and the "souls of the faithful departed," if such expressions are accepted as literal or ordinary language when he considers them to be symbolic ways of pointing to an abiding hope and an impenetrable mystery. If he chooses to use such language, therefore, his interpretation and understanding of it may be radically different from that of many members of the Church community. Or he may privately believe with the Church, but feel that no public case can be made for this belief. Still his labors might be very helpful in demonstrating to fellow scholars the validity of the question of human survival as well as the value of examining the Christian symbols that seek to respond to that question. More and more Catholic scholars study and teach theology in secular universities where this critical mode of theology is operative. Some of those teaching and studying in Catholic universities and seminaries are much influenced by the writings and conclusions of this "scientific" model of theology. Other Catholic scholars reject the radical implications of the critical mode or sharply distinguish between genuine Catholic theology and philosophy of religion. There is, therefore, a built-in tension between critical and dogmatic mediation. (See Figure 6.)

4. Dogmatic Mediation: Theology in the Church Context

Theology in conversation with an ecclesial tradition is dominated by ecclesial conversion and its mode of mediation is essentially, though not exclusively, dogmatic. The theologian in the Church context reflects upon the key elements of the world view of a specific ecclesial tradition to which he is explicitly committed. Therefore, as a Lutheran, Anglican, or Roman Catholic, such a theologian seeks to re-articulate the deepest insights of that tradition's self-understanding

FIGURE 6

THE THREE CONTEXTS OF THEOLOGY

	The World of the Church	The World of the University	The World of the Socio-Cultural Situation
1) Primary Conversation Partner			
2) Dominant Mode of Conversion	Ecclesial	Intellectual	Moral
3) Irreducible starting points	Privileged tradition: —Scripture —normative judgments of legitimate authority	Methodology, skills, and techniques of scholarly community	Relating central themes of religion to concrete social, cultural, political, and emotional situations of a people or an individual
4) Mode of Mediation	Dogmatic: —explicit religious commitment presupposed —deepen understanding of and explain doctrine and its development —radical reinterpretation or rejection may be penalized by Church	Critical: —explicit religious commitment not required or decisive (may be present) —possible to reject or radically re-interpret specific beliefs and docrines without penalty from academy	Existential: —explicit religious commitment, present doctrines, and scholarly findings employed as needed for the religious interpretation and transformation of situation —selectivity may be questioned or penalized by Church or academy
5) Prevailing Understanding of Truth	Fidelity to authentic tradition and teaching	—Internal coherence —Disclosive power —Weight of evidence	—must be transformative of concrete situation —relevant to individual
6) Tension	Faith seeking understanding?	Understanding seeking faith?	Value of faith and understanding measured by particular situation only?

7) Who?	—Those with teaching authority (Bishops) —Church theologians	—Some Church theologians —Philosophers of religion —University theologians	—people in general —University theologians —Bishops —Church theologians
8) Goal	Faithful and relevant re-articulation of authentic Church teaching for present moment in the Church	Examine and show grounds for relevance and validity of questions addressed by religion	Provide a theology for existential life world, e.g., liberation, feminist, black theologies —Facilitate personal synthesis and religious integrity for individual
9) Principal Specialties	Doctrines and Systematics	Dialectic and Foundations	Dialectic, foundations, doctrines, and communication

Note: These three contexts are interrelated.
Lines separating them are not absolute:
—Each benefits from and challenges the other.
—Scholars, those in pastoral ministry, as well as the laity, are more or less in a particular context according to circumstances and explicit reflection.

and witness concerning God, Jesus, Church, the moral life, etc., in the manner that best communicates with the contemporary world. In some cases this may be an unbending repetition of past doctrines, but it is more likely to be an informed effort to communicate the genius of a living tradition. Such a theologian's goal, therefore, is not only the continuity and renewal of one's specific tradition but also the development of sensitivities and techniques appropriate to the long-term goals of an ecumenical and pluralistic age.

Dogmatic mediation may be less concerned with the public modes of argument and definitions of truth that characterize critical mediation. This need not be due to a lack of intellectual sophistication so much as to the different presuppositions of a distinct context. In this context, tradition is recognized as the bearer of truth in such a way that the theologian may assume or take for granted the essential truth claims of earlier apologetics. The classic utterances of the tradition for which the theologian seeks to provide a contemporary interpretation or reinterpretation have a privileged position. Theology in the ecclesial context is no less concerned with truth than is theology in the academy. It is precisely because of its concern for truth that it places the final authority and criteria for truth not so much upon rigorous methodologies or public modes of argumentation as upon the central outer words or expressive dimensions of the tradition which are affirmed as being disclosed, revealed, and guaranteed by a Divine Spirit abiding in the Church. Paramount among these would be the sacred narratives that constituted the community's charter documents (Scripture). In the Catholic context, the patristic writings, the decrees of councils and Popes constitute a living interpretative tradition that complement the Scriptures. In a less technical, but no less real, manner, the rituals and symbols of liturgy are authoritative mediators of religious truth as well.

Depending on the degree of differentiation involved, dogmatic mediation may argue that its irreducible starting points are generic biblical proclamations such as "Jesus is Lord." Or it may seek to be more precise by affirming the decrees of the Council of Nicea to be the normative linguistic expression of that biblical witness. It may be more specific still in selecting the detailed elaboration of that normative statement by a specific theological school to be the most fitting, or even the only acceptable, rendering of the inner meaning of the creedal statement. Therefore, in the language of the previous chapter, dogmatic mediation embraces faith in general as well as beliefs in particular.[10] And these may or may not distinguish the specific horizons of theistic, Christian, ecclesical, moral, and intellectual conversion.

Because it is explicitly "faith seeking understanding" and not "understanding seeking faith," dogmatic mediation is not dismayed by the fact that its irreducible starting points are not critically grounded by the standards of university scholarship.

When dogmatic mediation moves from dialectic to the present situation, foundations, doctrines, and systematics may not be clearly and formally distinguished in every case. Consequently even within the context of dogmatic mediation there is a wide spectrum of positions. One theologian, church leader, or lay person may consider the Scripture, with its very diverse forms of expression, to be the one absolutely irreducible starting point. Others may hold that the spirit-guided interpretation of the Scriptures in the early Councils must be *equally* embraced as an irreducible starting point if confusion and ambiguity are not to become widespread. But among those who affirm the councils, some will argue that their decrees are the absolute and irreformable formulations of generic faith as well as specific beliefs. They are the "deposit" of faith. To others, however, these irreducible starting points must not be seen as transcultural, a-historical "deposits" of absolute truth. They must be examined and interpreted in the light of their contexts. In this way it becomes apparent that a doctrine moves through history as implicit, explicit, denied, defended, defined, ignored, retrieved, and clarified. Because of these internal differences, views on the nature, development, and reformability of foundations, doctrines, and systematics cover a startlingly wide spectrum within the present-day Catholic tradition.[11]

The relationship between dogmatic mediation to critical mediation is a complex one. The range of that relationship extends all the way from a completely undifferentiated mind set that secures the truth of its absolute religious convictions by asserting in a blatantly anti-intellectual manner, "Thank God, I don't have to be an intellectual to be saved!" to the sophisticated and highly nuanced scholarship of theologians in Church-affiliated universities, who employ many, if not all, of the critical methods of their counterparts in a secular university.

Hence dogmatic mediation collaborating with critical mediation in a Church university has no difficulty acknowledging the fact that the Genesis account of creation does not provide accurate cosmology, science, or geography. Because of the presence of the differentiation of consciousness made possible by an operative intellectual conversion, dogmatic mediation can easily embrace the findings of critical investigations concerning the age and early formation of the material universe as well as the long and gradual evolution of the human species. For this is not at variance with the radical "religious" meaning of the creation narratives which affirms that neither the universe nor the human race is a random happening or intrinsically evil. They come forth blessed by the eternal creative power of God. Should critical mediation assert that there is no sense in which "creation" may be applied to the universe or that it is a misleading "metaphor," some proponents of dogmatic mediation might well disagree. In their view critical mediation would then be overstepping its boundaries and attempting to answer an essentially religious question with a scientific answer.

The account of sin in the Adamic narrative is another important example. Because contemporary biblical scholarship accepts many of the methods and findings of critical mediation, many theologians, Church leaders, and laity may well allow that the story of Adam and Eve is not a literal, historical event. There never was a "preternatural state" in which men lived without labor and women gave birth without pain. Nor is God a wrathful Shylock who foreordains that the guilt of "original sin" be passed on to every generation in a biological fashion and who will only be placated by the blood of his divine Son.

However, the story is no mere fable. As a mediator of religious meaning via narrative, it is a universal parable replete with religious timeless truth that cannot be mediated in any other manner. For this reason dogmatic mediation would balk if critical mediation suggested that *since* the "Adamic Myth" is not literally true, the categories of "sin" and "redemption" lose their validity and meaning. In fact the concession that the Adamic narrative may not be a point-by-point account of a historical event may well make *more* apparent its transhistorical and timeless religious meaning.[12]

The interplay between critical and dogmatic mediation results in an important dialectic. The secular university theologian may wonder why the Church university theologian feels he must hold on to certain core affirmations as if protecting "something" from the bright lights of critical investigation. So his "conservative tendencies" are noted. But a bishop, from the viewpoint of his special pastoral and teaching ministry, may find the Church theologian distressingly liberal, particularly when he applies critical methodology to the New Testament. The bishop may well applaud and encourage scholarship while cautioning that there should be no departure from "sound Catholic teaching." However, a particular segment of the clergy and laity who are not technical theologians might wonder at the bishop's leniency for allowing the theologian to "tamper with the truths of faith."[13]

Each moment in this dialectic is indicative of an instinctive awareness of the Church community that its living tradition is the bearer of interpretations of reality whose truth value does not hinge essentially upon the results of critical investigation no matter how sound and accepted this methodology may be. The internal tension within the tradition is caused by a lack of consensus. Is the irreducible starting point on the question of sin and redemption, for example, the literal account of "the fall" in Genesis? Or is it rather a universal meaning "behind" or "within" that account and open to various interpretations? Is it a particular philosophical or theological interpretation of that core meaning as, for example, refined by Augustine's thought on original sin? Is it a normative linguistic creedal formula determined by a Church council at a particular point in history? Obviously there is more or less room for exploration, development, and even correction depending on where one draws the line. But *whatever* position one takes, you are faced with the question of tradition.

All acts of human understanding are influenced to some degree by tradition, point of view, and a certain predisposition or prejudice. Since critical mediation is much indebted to the Enlightenment, it shares in the Enlightenment's program to overcome the prejudgments and commitments of a religious tradition insofar as such predispositions confine the sweep of rational inquiry. But paradoxically the Enlightenment spirit itself suffers from a kind of narrow-mindedness or prejudice. As the German philosopher Hans-Georg Gadamer expresses it, "The fundamental prejudice of the Enlightenment is the prejudice against prejudice itself, which deprives tradition of its power."[14]

Unfortunately in English the word "prejudice" has come to have only the negative connotation of an unfounded judgment as in the case of ethnic, racial, or religious prejudice. But in the light of the finite and historical mode of human existence, we are forced to recognize the presence of positive as well as negative prejudices in our lives. Negative prejudice may result from rushing to premature conclusions with insufficient evidence. This may be due to a predisposition to accept whatever is novel. Negative prejudice may also be due to an unreflective acceptance of long-standing tradition and the views of those in authority. This reflects a predisposition to accept what is old or established.

The Enlightenment was certainly correct in drawing the distinction between conclusions reached by the force of one's own reason and conclusions accepted because of faith in the authority of others.

When the weight of the authority of a document (Scripture) or a ministry (Bishop) sways our judgments, clearly a kind of predisposition or prejudice is functioning. However, besides negative prejudice, there is positive or legitimate prejudice. Legitimate prejudice can be the source of truth and freedom rather than error or constraint.

The essence of authority is not the demand for blind obedience in opposition to freedom, autonomy, and reason. True authority does not demand abdication of one's reason but the use of it in the recognition that another's knowledge, insight, information, range of understanding, or charisms are superior to, or at least different from, one's own. For these reasons we give another's judgment precedence over ours. This is why if authority is to be effectively exercised, the superior qualities of knowledge, understanding, and holiness must be genuinely acquired. If one who wields authority is in fact incompetent, he will eventually lose force over the minds and hearts of the governed because he cannot lead or inspire.

But what is true of an individual may be even more true of a tradition that is both ancient and vital. In reaction to the Enlightenment, the Romantic movement defended tradition against an exclusively negative interpretation of authority. Tradition and custom have a real authority over our attitudes and our behavior even though the truth of what tradition transmits to us cannot be grounded by reason alone. Structures of education, social order, family life, and religion depend upon this for their continuity. Such a recognition of tradition need not lead to "traditionalism," which absolutizes tradition in all its detail, as a historically given reality in an antithetical relationship with reason, freedom, and autonomy. A living tradition and the investigative techniques of the Enlightenment need not be opposing prejudices. They are rather complementary. Their reciprocal relationship can advance the coherent perception of reality at a given moment of history.

Gadamer turns to the concept of "classic" as it is used in aesthetics to exemplify his positive interpretation of the significance of tradition. As we saw in Chapter One, an earlier notion of classic which canonized the techniques and achievement of a particular period as normative is no longer universally recognized. However, there is still a sense in which the term "classic" can be attributed to certain creations of the human spirit. These are works that are such timeless penetrations of the particular in a certain context that they have the power to illuminate the universal in a manner that is transformative of those who encounter the work with an attentive spirit. A novel, a painting, or a musical composition attains classic power not because its creator followed the conventions of a particular era, to convey the concerns, affirmations, and values of that era, but because the creator was inspired to use creative genius in a manner that produces a work that transcends the limitation of a particular age and addressed any person of any age in the depths of their being.

> "The Classical is what resists historical criticism because its histori-cal dominion, the binding power of its validity that is preserved and handed down, precedes all historical reflection and continues through it."[15]
>
> "(The Classic) speaks in such a way that it is not a statement about what is past, a mere testimony to something that still needs to be in-terpreted, but (it) says something to the present as if it were said specially to it."[16]

The Enlightenment prejudice makes it impossible to experience fully "aesthetic conversion" and encounter the truth-disclosing pow-er of the art work. The Enlightenment attitude assumes the art work to be an object to be studied by what it wrongly believes to be exhaus-tive objective criteria. To really encounter and be moved by the clas-sic work of art one must bring an attentive spirit that is willing to embrace the "particular" on its own terms.

The most indifferent or critical observer of Christianity would acknowledge that the Christian tradition proclaims a vision of reality that has classic power to illuminate and transform. And this "classic" vision has considerably influenced the lives of individuals, whole peo-ples, and cultures. This has been accomplished by the personal appro-priation of that particular tradition in such a way that its truth-bearing and transformation power are manifest. We have only to think of Francis of Assisi, Joan of Arc, Thomas More, Julian of Nor-wich, John XXIII, Martin Luther King, Jr., or Dorothy Day.[17] These, many others, and the less celebrated persons that touch our individ-ual lives give ample evidence that the "prejudice" of dogmatic media-tion via tradition may be a prejudice in favor of the authority of truth, liberation, and sanctity.

Dogmatic mediation, therefore, moves from dialectic to founda-tions trusting in the "reflective tradition" of ecclesial conversion real-izing, as Michael Polanyi observes, that it knows more than it can tell.[18] And of course, to those within the dogmatic tradition that tacit knowledge is anchored in more than the very real transformative power that comes from participation in a vital and classic tradition. Their ultimate trust is that the Holy Spirit, who elected them to be hearers and proclaimers of the word, guides this privileged tradition by means of the common faith of all as well as the teaching charism of the bishops. (See Figure 6.)

5. Existential Mediation: Theology in the "Daily Life" Context

Theology in conversation with the concrete socio-cultural and political matrix is dominated by moral conversion and its mode of mediation is essentially, though not exclusively, existential. Existential mediation is especially concerned with the final functional speciality, communication. It seeks to bring the implication of foundations to bear on concrete life situations. Existential mediation strives to act out and incarnate the meaning of what may be affirmed abstractly by critical or dogmatic mediation. Existential mediation is also the primary mode of mediation operative within the internal religious integration process of individuals whether they are laypersons, bishops, theologians, women religious, or parish pastors.

Under existential mediation, therefore, is included what is often termed "pastoral theology." This of course encompasses the ever increasing range of skills and competencies of the caring professions that must be cultivated for effectiveness in the pastoral ministry. The pastoral theologian may be not as concerned about the cogency of arguments of critical mediation or the venerable tradition of dogmatic mediation as he is concerned about the urgencies of the lived situation of the people to whom he seeks to bring the tangible reality of the good news. Because of his accumulated experiences and insights he develops various pastoral instincts that refine his ministry. While there may be less interest in academic speculation, and dogmatic assertions, the pastoral theologian is no less professional. The disciplines of psychology and sociology are frequently engaged to provide techniques and frameworks.[19]

Also included under existential mediation is that process that goes on within every person who, as a living document, works out an implicit or explicit personal synthesis or religious world view. This is constituted to varying degrees by conclusions gleaned from critical and dogmatic mediation. But most people do not wait for scholars or authorities to resolve theological questions that are real for them. Instead, a kind of existential discernment is operative in their lives by means of which they meet the more pressing theological questions that actually emerge in their concrete life situation. Hence many issues that preoccupy the academic or Church theologian seem of little relevance to the daily lives of many persons. Other questions, however, are burning ones and require an answer. Many of these questions are the same ones that scholars debate. Individuals with the most minimal knowledge of various speculations and theories work out within their own minds and hearts in a commonsense fashion solutions to questions concerning the truth of Scripture, the fate of the dead, sexual morality, the compatibility of world religions.

Even those skilled in theological discipline and those whose very office makes them defenders of the tradition find that, when they advert to their inner world, there is a personal "editing" process at work that accepts this teaching and rejects or holds at bay that one. This process produces a personal agenda of what is firmly believed, believed with some reservations, doubted, denied, or ignored. Some persons may not advert to it, others may feel guilty about it, others may try to correct it, and still others may boast of it. Yet, this editing, integrating, and synthesizing activity is inescapable because of our condition as thinking human beings living in history.[20]

A particular person or community may reach some of the same conclusions by means of existential mediation that are reached by critical or dogmatic mediation, but the convincing factor is not so much evidence, argument, or the weight of tradition. It is rather a kind of existential discernment of the "fitting." That such an existential mediation is operative, is obvious when we acknowledge that most people do not follow the subtle arguments of critical mediation any more than they fully give up their thinking and deciding about crucial matters to an outside authority. Yet they come to some kind of conclusion that is personally satisfying even though it may in part be formed by a hunch, "gut feeling," instinct, as well as the breath of the Spirit sustaining an upright life. For good or ill this is practical theology in the literal sense. For it is by means of these sometimes self-authenticating and self-transforming convictions that men and women *actually* live in their concrete times and circumstances. Most everyone knows this to be the case, but it is rarely mentioned by either theologian, Church leaders, or the people in the pews.

Most importantly, we wish to discuss *praxis theology* as a somewhat novel contemporary instance of existential mediation. Praxis relates theology to particular social, cultural, and political situations because of their radically religious implications. These situations may be social change such as the overcoming of racial, sexual, economic, class, or religious oppression. Praxis theology addresses these concrete realities with less explicit concern for the theoretical and disputed questions of critical and dogmatic mediation. It will rather stress "practice" as the more important criteria of theology especially when

this practice is informed by critical and dogmatic mediation and at
the same time transforms theory and doctrine. In praxis theology,
truth is affirmed not so much as coherence (critical mediation) or
from legitimate authority (dogmatic mediation), but as transformation of a concrete situation (existential mediation) in which the real
and practical implications of the radical and liberating message of religion are operative. For this reason praxis theology demands the embodiment of moral conversion that moves one from words to deeds.
Authentic praxis theology is not content with intellectual consent. It
requires that the theologian and those who share his conclusions be
actively involved in activities that will help to correct the oppression
or alienation of the reality in question. And he does this *qua* theologian and not merely as one getting on the bandwagon of social activism. As a matter of fact much of the writings in the various liberation
theologies come forth from those who have been reflecting theologically in a praxis situation.[21]

Clearly, to be effective, existential mediation must engage some
specific situation with the transformative power of religion. This is a
most important point. In an earlier time it might be argued that theology reflects upon God as related to "human nature." This was the
essential human condition shared by all. Other "accidental" factors
were less important. Existential mediation reflects upon "human nature" as related to the divine. However, the "accidentals" of being
poor and oppressed, handicapped, old, Hispanic, middle class, female,
lesbian, or Afro-American are now seen to have *theological* significance in relation to the gospel. Of course the Church always recognized the value of the particular by fostering ethnic traditions, folk
ways, and even folk religion in Europe. But this was thought to have
no effect upon the essential unity of doctrine.

Therefore, while the number of emerging praxis theologies are
many (e.g., feminist theology, liberation theology, black theology), we
can only gain an understanding of this mode of theologizing by considering a specific instance. Because of the particular social urgencies
involved, and the social situation of the Catholic Church in America,
black theology will be explored as an example of existential mediation.[22]

Liberation theologies in some form are an inevitable consequence of the new key of contemporary theology. But to some they
may appear to be barely theology at all. It is argued that with the cultural breakdown described in Chapter One and the advent of radical
pluralism, the prevailing understanding of theology that had once
been grounded in the unquestioned authority of the revelation of

God mediated through Scripture and tradition, began to be questioned. Theology was once thought of as disciplined and intelligent reflection upon truths whose certitude was known by faith. In the last two decades, however, a host of unanswered questions about the meaning and end of religion emerged. Some concluded that analytic philosophy had definitely dethroned metaphysical theology as at best bad poetry and at worst meaningless. Theology seemed to lose hold on its own principles and integrity. Somewhat nervously it went to the social sciences and secular movements in search of an identity. As a result there poured forth a theology of everything—hope, play, suffering, liberation, womanhood, and yes, a theology of blackness. These "new theologies," it is argued, are simply social and cultural movements appropriating the Christian symbol system in order to enhance and legitimate their partisan concerns. So she who had once been the aloof queen of the sciences, having lost her sense of inner direction, had become a common prostitute.[23]

Without denying the presence of faddism in current theology, it is more correct to argue that the various liberation theologies result from the cultural shift, the turn to interiority, and the consciousness raising that these changes made inevitable. Praxis theology, therefore, seeks to uncover the intrinsic relationship between powerful Christian symbols and the transformation of the social order. Hence in confronting the scandal of oppressed minorities in a supposedly "Christian" society, there develops a theology of the oppressed or black theology. Because of its existential urgency such a theology will not be a fully worked-out conceptual system. It will tend to favor those elements of critical and dogmatic mediation which can effectively transform the larger culture. In the case of black theology the biblical themes of exodus, liberation, and election are particularly prominent.

Despite its relatively recent appearance on the theological scene as a formal corpus, black theology's origins are as ancient as the rich religious culture of Africa, and its roots are found in the pre- and post-Civil War experience of slaves. It has found eloquent expression in spirituals, sermons, blues, and stories of an oppressed people.[24] Its contemporary spokesmen are largely a group of creative Protestant scholars.

Since black theology tends neither to affirm nor to deny the official "doctrines" of Roman Catholicism, it has met with little official reaction in the Catholic Church.[25] It would be wrong, however, to conclude that black theology is, therefore, having no influence within the Catholic Church. Pastorally and liturgically its influence

abounds. More and more priests and sisters ministering to black congregations are turning to black theology for a meaningful idiom for
their ministry. Many have transformed the interiors of their churches
from their original ethnic Italian, Polish, German, or Irish motifs to
the red, green, and black of Liberation Theology. This includes images of Jesus and Mary as black (rather than western European) and
"shrines" for Martin Luther King and Malcom X. And the pioneering
liturgical music of Clarence Rivers and Grayson Brown are further
translations of black theology.

Taking a deliberately offensive tone, black theology rejects the
theologies of what it considers the racist attitudes of white suburban
Christianity. Black theology declares itself to be the reflection of
black religious people on the black religious experience, for the enrichment of black people. Whether or not white theologians read it,
understand it, agree with it, dispute or ignore it, is of little importance.

While Martin Luther King, Jr., might be the admired patriarch
of the present generation of black theologians, his tempered views are
not dominant in the writings of Joseph Washington, Albert Cleage, J.
De Otis Roberts, Eulalio Baltazar, Major Jones, William Jones, and
James Cone.[26]

Since he is the most influential, a brief introduction to James
Cone's understanding of black theology will fill out this example of
praxis theology.[27] Cone's central concern is the uniting of his concept
of Black Power with the biblical depiction of the God of Exodus, and
the New Testament Jesus who proclaims good news to the poor and
release to captives, in order to construct a radical black theology of
liberation.

For Cone, Black Power means the complete emancipation of
black people from white oppression by the means black people deem
necessary. What is more, he contends that Black Power is nothing less
than authentic Christianity. To understand this perhaps startling assertion, we must appreciate the stress Cone places upon personal biography and social context for theology. In the introduction to *God of
the Oppressed*, Cone provides a great deal of personal biography. He
grew up in Bearden, Arkansas, where his perception was shaped by
two main realities: the Black Church experience and the sociopolitical
significance of the white majority. At the Macedonia African Meth-
odist Episcopal Church (A.M.E.), Cone became aware of the presence
of the divine spirit. He was convinced that a reassuring, loving, and
liberating God visited the black community of Bearden as they
prayed, sang, and heard the good news from the preacher. The

Church gave Cone a context for dealing with the many contradictions he found in his life situation. By the grace of God he learned the art of survival and held his own in the face of eight hundred white people who made him acutely aware of the contingency of black existence.

Because his theological reflections are inseparable from the Bearden experience, Cone states that his theology will differ in perspective, content, and style from the Western theological tradition as transmitted from Augustine to Barth. Therefore, while respecting Nicea, Chalcedon, and the Church Fathers, Cone does not hold the *homoousia* controversy to be a black question. Blacks do not speculate as to whether or not Jesus was of "one substance" with the Father or is constituted by two natures in one person. These questions spring from the perspective of white experience and Greek categories of thought that dichotomizes religion and theology. Those who operate from this perspective, Cone states, like to think that theirs is a universal viewpoint, while in fact it is narrowed by a particular culture and experience. And this was an experience that gave white Christians the luxury to theorize about Christ while completely ignoring millions of fellow Christians who were the outcasts of a racist society.

Black theology, therefore, finds its heresy and orthodoxy in the present. Its central doctrine, if you will, is that Jesus Christ is the real and active liberator of the oppressed. Therefore, theological interpretations of the Gospel narratives that do not actively proclaim Jesus as liberator must be declared heretical. Any ecclesiology that fails to see the Church community as missioned to set captives free is anti-Christian.

To explain the social context of theology, Cone turns to Marx's argument that thought has no existence independent of social context. Sociologists of knowledge clarify this point when they stress the reciprocity between ideas and social realities. Thus, there is a "social *a priori*" or "social determination" for all thinking. In Cone's view, theologians must revise their naive assumptions that *their* ideas of God are all completely objective and universal. For these ideas are very much influenced by reflections on specific social conditions. Hence, Cone argues, the reason why Paul Tillich could assert that theology's basic goal is the statement and interpretation of the truth of the Christian message, without mention of implementing that message on behalf of the oppressed, is that Tillich was in no way politically threatened as he lived and wrote in America. By entering into the accepted framework or perspective of American culture, Tillich could work out his theological views with no regard for the widespread, unjust suffering of black Americans. But, asks Cone, is the "new being" purely spiritual? Can those who embrace the new freedom in Christ be blinded to the implications of that freedom in the concrete social context? For Cone it is impossible to do theology in the contemporary American context while being indifferent to the strong hand of God delivering blacks from oppression as he delivered the Jews from Egypt.

Black theology like liberation theology, feminist theology, or any praxis theology that employs existential mediation can easily be criticized from the frameworks of critical or dogmatic mediation.

One of the most persistent questions concerning black theology is precisely what constitutes the "black experience." When Cone indicates that certain questions are not on the black agenda, he is obviously correct if he means those who are struggling for their very livelihood. But the same is true for whites similarly destitute. But who constitues the accrediting agency for the "authentic black experience"? In America it is certainly a multidimensional reality. Even the common history of slavery has more or less impact on different people. Much as one may applaud Alex Haley's brilliant achievement in *Roots*, it remains that in most cases the contemporary black American is a unique hybrid of both African and European cultures. While a good case can be made that the former must be reappropriated, must it be equally argued that the latter must be cast off? Is the "black experience" determined by sharing in a common color, culture, and consciousness no matter what one's educational and economic status may be? In America we have black people who think of themselves as Negroes, colored people, Africans, and Afro-Americans. Who is the final arbiter? This is a question that will not go away. It is because of this very pluralism that many black Catholics in America know nothing of black theology and would be uncomfortable if exposed to it.[28]

Whatever its weaknesses, however, black theology may portend something very good on the theological horizon. Ethnocentric theology need not be a retreat to a privatized, navel-gazing brand of theology. As a matter of fact, the rejection of the negative connotations of the "melting pot" American paradigm, and the retrieval of ethnicity can only enrich our understanding "tradition" and allow for possible new "classics" in religious expression.

It is evident that great "classics" in our secular as well as our religious traditions are at once deeply personal and particular in their origins and expression while at the same time are public and universal in their power to transform the attentive human spirit. In a paradoxical manner the profound penetration of a specific cultural, social, or religious heritage may result in expressions that are universal in their power to illuminate. Hence Louis Armstrong and Billy Holiday created very particularized musical idioms in American jazz and blues. Yet their works have classic power to touch and transform the attentive spirit from whatever culture and context.

In our culture we have a great need to be enriched by new classic expressions. One of the unfortunate by-products of "modern culture" is the fact that over-choice can lead to superficiality. It is possible to have a whole generation of people who know nothing of Melville's *Moby Dick*—the classic story of the menacing and seductive presence of evil that can be symbolized by the sea and by a great sea beast—thinking that Peter Benchley's *Jaws* is the greatest sea story ever.

Remarkably, one need not have had the experience portrayed to be arrested by the illuminating insights presented in a classic work of art. A wealthy suburbanite, having no immediate experience of the special pains and tragedies that befall black urban tenement dwellers, but who has an attentive spirit, is able to participate fully in the catharsis of Lorraine Hansberry's classic play, *A Raisin in the Sun*, in contrast with the vulgar, exploitive, sensationalism that characterizes so much of the so-called Black Cinema.

In an analogous way the emergence of ethnocentric theologies may pave the way for singular contemporary theological classics. The continued effort of black Christians to record their reflections on the meaning of God, Jesus, Church, worship, community, and social responsibility would enrich the whole Church with what Pope Paul VI has termed the valuable and unique gift of "negritude" which the Church needs in a special way at this moment in history. Over time, these reflections on the part of the sons and daughters of former slaves on the meaning of the good news of Jesus, could well produce theological expressions that so profoundly grasped the implications of Christian and moral conversion in a situation of suffering, injustice, and social transformation that they will focus anew the attention of the larger Church upon themes, values, and attitudes of universal significance. In doing so, they cannot fail to address important concrete issues with telling urgency.

Existential mediation in all its forms has as its irreducible starting point the authority and truth that is manifest when relevant religious insights mediated in the critical, dogmatic, or existential mode are penetrated at such a depth that their concrete and practical implications are grasped and actively sought. As pastoral theology it may engage the skills of the caring professions to find apt ways to celebrate the religious dimension of crucial life junctures or to minister to those in various conditions of material, emotional, or spiritual want. As the dynamic that holds together the life world of the individual Christian, existential mediation makes it possible for one not to be paralyzed by the disputes, confusion, and doubts at the critical and dogmatic level. The potent symbols of liturgy as well as an individual's native intelligence, prudence, and prayerfulness are all at play here in what has traditionally been called the *sensus fidelium*.

As praxis theology, existential mediation confronts the multiple social and cultural conditions of peoples, and, where they are malignant, seeks not only to care for them but to struggle for their cure as the only authentic way of doing the truth of one's religious convictions. (See Figure 6.)

6. Conclusion

When thinking about the three modes of mediation or styles of theology as typified by the academy, the Church, and the socio-cultural situation, different individuals no doubt find that they identify more with one than another. Some may even completely reject one of the three contexts of theology as being invalid. But the approach taken here has been to reflect upon the concrete state of affairs. It is an empirical fact that all three modes of mediation are "out there." It is these three conversation partners or various combinations of them that facilitate the move from dialectic to foundations.

It is obvious that few theologians, bishops, priests, or laypeople (if any) can be equally interested, competent, and comfortable in all three of these distinct styles of thought. Different horizons prompt different questions and different degrees of confidence in what are affirmed as irreducible starting points. Dogmatic mediation may be dismayed when critical mediation examines the question of the divinity of Jesus as if this were a matter open to question. Critical mediation may have little patience with the seeming narrowness of a dogmatic tradition which seems to canonize particular linguistic formulations as if they were impregnable. Dogmatic mediation will, at times, make its affirmations in a somewhat undifferentiated and wide-sweeping manner. At other times, it may be very reflective, seeking to rid itself of the dross of what may be subsequently viewed as pious practices and mythological views of reality. In any form, dogmatic mediation seeks to preserve a core of religious meaning and truth for subsequent generations. Critical mediation in turn appears to doubt more and believe less. Meanwhile existential mediation, weary of the debate, turns away somewhat from hypotheses and isolated doctrine in order to engage concrete situations in a prophetic and pragmatic manner or to come to working personal conclusions in the face of pluralism and doubt.

If one has grown to maturity primarily aware of only one mode of mediation, a certain amount of dis-ease or disequilibrium is caused by the encounter with either of the other two. The simplest way to deal with this disequilibrium is the elimination or rejection of one or even two of the three contexts of theological thinking. Paradoxically even if people declare that only one framework or model is valid for them, they will still be influenced in subtle ways by elements of the other two.

In ordinary life, of course, we recognize and accept the complex interplay of all three forms of mediation. When people have need of dental work, for example, they do not go off to dental school to master dental science (critical mediation). Rather, they trust and accept the competence and authority of the dentist (dogmatic mediation). If, however, after costly dental work they still have great discomfort, they may judge, without the technical proficiency of a dentist, that the work done was inadequate or wrong (existential mediation). From circumstance to circumstance the diverse modes of mediation complement, check, or correct one another. In the theological and religious world an individual or a community will arrive at foundations of very diverse sorts depending upon how they meet the tension caused by the encounter between these three distinct but related contexts of theology.[29]

NOTES

1. For a good introduction to theology and its relationship to religion as well as to the natural and human sciences, see Maurice Wiles, *What Is Theology* (London: Oxford University Press, 1976).

2. See Lonergan, *Method in Theology*, Part Two: Foreground. By focusing upon the eight functional specialities here, I do not mean to imply that they alone constitute Lonergan's method. For a full appreciation of all of the interrelated elements of Lonergan's work the reader must also examine Part One: Background. Some parts of Background have been employed in the previous chapters.

3. Ibid., p. 4.

4. For the general description of these "conversation partners" I am following David Tracy. See *Blessed Rage for Order*, Chapter I, "The Pluralist Context," and *Christianity and Crisis*, "Whatever Happened to Theology?"

May 12, 1975, pp. 119–120, and his unpublished paper "The Public Nature of Theology."

5. Like modern science, critical mediation acknowledges that its conclusions are necessarily open to revision because of the recurrent scrutiny of its method. As Lonergan puts it, "Let us consider the foundation of a modern science. It does not consist in any part of the science itself, in any of its conclusions, in any of its laws, in any of its principles. All of these are open to revision, and it is in the light of the foundation that the revision would take place. What, then, is the foundation? It is the method that will generate the revision of conclusions, laws, principles that are accepted today. It is the method that will generate the revision of conclusions, laws, principles of tomorrow. What the scientist relies ultimately on is his method." "Theology in Its New Context," op. cit., p. 64.

6. For a harsh attack upon the importation of the findings of "critical mediation" into the Catholic Church, see George A. Kelly, "An Uncertain Church: The New Catholic Problem," *The Critic*, Fall 1976, pp. 14–26.

7. For a non-technical, if one-sided, reading of the confounding impact of popularized fragments of "critical mediation" upon ordinary church life, see James Hitchcock, *The Decline and Fall of Radical Catholicism* (New York: Herder and Herder, 1971); note especially the appendix, "26 Heretical Attitudes." See also Avery Dulles, "The Critique of Modernity and the Hartford Appeal," *The Resilient Church*, op. cit., pp. 63–91.

8. This is what I judge to be the basis of the conflict between Avery Dulles and David Tracy. "Tracy-Dulles Dialogue," *National Catholic Reporter*, November 1977, pp. 10ff. Dulles seems to find Tracy's "foundations" (in *Blessed Rage for Order*) to be a brilliant achievement. However, in his judgment they are not adequate for a fundamental theology of the Catholic faith. Such "critical" foundations may seem to implicitly rule out or even deny the "fundamentals" of creedal traditions. Tracy, in turn, rejects conclusions that Dulles or others might draw from his first step in an extended project, since these are not conclusions that he himself has drawn.

9. Cf. Van A. Harvey, *The Historian and the Believer: The Morality of Historical Knowledge and Christian Belief* (New York: Macmillan, 1966), and idem, "Whatever Happened to Theology?" *Christianity and Crisis*, May 12, 1975, pp. 108–109.

10. See Gregory Baum, *Faith and Doctrine: A Contemporary View* (Paramus, N.J.: Newman Press, 1969).

11. This in no way intends to imply that critical mediation is one unanimous voice of scholarly progress. Similar problems of pluralism and fragmentation are present. From region to region, for example, one or another school of thought is dominant. At a particular university the pioneering achievements of scholars of recognized genius take on a normative or even "dogmatic" authority. To depart from these "authorities" is the equivalent of a lack of "orthodoxy." Yet, over time the reigning theories and schools of thought are often eclipsed by new ones.

The history of both university theology and ecclesial theology shows an affinity to the history of science and the role of new "paradigms." See Paul M. Quay, "A Distinction in Search of a Difference: The Psycho-Social Distinction between Science and Theology," *The Modern Schoolman*, Vol. 51, May 1974, pp. 345–59; Paul K. Feyerabend, "Problems of Empiricism," *Beyond the Edge of Certainty: Essays on Contemporary Science and Philosophy*, University of Pittsburgh Series in the Philosophy of Science, Vol. 2, edited by Robert G. Colodny (Englewood Cliffs, N.J.: Prentice-Hall, Inc., 1965); Thomas S. Kuhn, "The Structure of Scientific Revolutions," *Foundations of the Unity of Science: Toward an International Encyclopedia of Unified Science*, Vol. 2, edited by Otto Neurath, Rudolf Carnap, and Charles Morris (Chicago: University of Chicago Press, 1970), pp. 53–272.

12. See Paul Ricoeur, *The Symbolism of Evil* (Boston: Beacon Press, 1967), Chapter III, "The Adamic Myth and the Eschatological Vision of History," pp. 232–305.

13. This dialectical tension is exacerbated when the example is shifted from Old to New Testament. Küng's *On Being a Christian*, op. cit., is a case in point. This work is an instance of both dogmatic and critical mediation. In spite of the sympathetic and progressive reading that Küng gives to the other great world religions he does not come to the "uniqueness" of Christianity on critical grounds. This is dogmatically mediated by means of tradition and Küng's established agenda. However, once he is within the horizon of Christian conversion, he employs critical mediation in a dialectic with the dogmatically mediated particulars that have come forth over the centuries from the horizon of ecclesial conversion and have specified the universal meaning of Christ by means of specific theological interpretations as well as normative linguistic creedal formulae. It is this method that explicitly questions, reinterprets, or challenges what was thought to be a cumulative and irreversible tradition that is at the core of the statement issued by the German bishops. Cf. "Declaration of the German Bishops on Hans Küng's Book "On Being a Christian,'" *L'Osservatore Romano*, Feb. 16, 1978, pp. 6–7 (English edition).

14. Hans-George Gadamer, *Truth and Method* (New York: Seabury Press, 1975), pp. 239–40. Here I shall be essentially following Gadamer's philosophical and explicitly non-theological arguments for the truth and meaning conveying power of tradition, pp. 240–56.

15. Ibid., p. 255.

16. Ibid., p. 257.

17. Individuals under the full sway of critical mediation may face a special dilemma here. To the degree that they have made the methods of the university their "tradition" they may have a great difficulty affirming particular beliefs as true which their "tradition" brands as "fantastic" or incompatible with the contemporary world view. Yet they may feel a certain Sartrean forlornness when they see the exceptional forms of life possible for those who do believe what they deem unbelievable, or who do take literally what they are sure can only be symbolic. They can never regain their pre-critical naiveté and they perhaps have not been able to attain what Ricoeur terms a "post-critical second naiveté." If they are somewhat removed from a worshipping

church community, they may feel like Barabbas in the novel of the same name by Par Lagerkvist: drawn by the spirit of love which animates the community but repelled by what they are certain to be the false beliefs that sustain that love.

18. Cf. Michael Polanyi, *The Tacit Dimension* (Garden City, N.Y.: Anchor Books, 1967).

19. Helpful resources in this area include: Seward Hiltner, *Preface to Pastoral Theology* (Nashville: Abingdon, 1958), William Oglesley (Editor); idem, *The New Shape of Pastoral Theology* (Nashville: Abingdon, 1969). Karl Rahner, "New Claims Which Pastoral Theology Makes upon Theology as a Whole," *Theological Investigations*, Vol. XI (New York: Seabury Press, 1974), pp. 115–36; idem., "Practical Theology and Social Work in the Church," *Theological Investigations*, Vol. X (New York: Herder and Herder, 1973), pp. 349–370; Heinz Schuster, "The Nature and Function of Pastoral Theology," *The Pastoral Mission of the Church* (Glen Rock, N.J.: Paulist Press, 1965), pp. 4–14; Robert Evans and Thomas Parker, editors, *Christian Theology: A Case Study Method* (New York: Harper and Row, 1976); Henri Nouwen, "Anton Boisen and Theology through Living Human Documents," *Pastoral Psychology*, 19:186 (1968), pp. 48–63.

20. Karl Rahner examines this inevitable situation in "The Faith of the Christian and the Doctrines of the Church," *Theological Investigations*, Vol. 19, translated by David Bourke (London: Longman and Todd, 1976), pp. 24–46.

21. The challenging and often radical teachings of papal social encyclicals in recent decades are not unrelated to "praxis" theology. However, though they reject every form of oppression, racism, and social injustice, the measured exhortations of these documents are derived from a "deductive anthropology" that draws certain general conclusions concerning the freedom and dignity of all people from generic reflection upon human nature or the human condition. These reflections have powerful implications for the many concrete situations where this dignity is not recognized. Praxis theology, however, begins its reflection in the concrete, suffering-laden, and blood-stained situation of particular people. From this "inductive anthropology" liberation theologies issue a fierce call to active emancipation under a divine imperative. For the key encyclicals and Vatican II documents, see *The Gospel of Peace and Justice*, op. cit. Blanket condemnations of liberation theologies are obviously ill-advised. The fact that some liberation theologians incorporate elements of Marxist ideology does not make liberation theology intrinsically atheistic. The measured words of Pope John Paul II at the Latin American Bishops Conference at Puebla and the subsequent positive and negative responses to his remarks highlight a tension that can exist between "official" Church theology and praxis theology.

22. Note that in Chapter One the discussion of "What Happened?" did not necessitate any particular examination of the black Catholic experience because the relationships between the Catholic Church and the American black population were minimal and to some degree strained. Black Christians migrating from the rural South to the large Northern cities were usually Bap-

tists. They found Catholic ritual and practice strange. Those who became
interested were not quickly welcomed. When neighborhoods changed racial-
ly, the local parishes were often given over to religious orders who had a special commitment to "minister to colored people." Even vocations to the
priesthood were not welcomed in every case. Candidates were "directed" to
the Josephites and the Society for the Divine Word. Today, a larger number
of black Catholics, the existence of such organizations as the National Office
for Black Catholics and the Black Catholic Clergy Caucus, and a gradual
openness to liturgical pluralism are signs of a more vital and more vocal presence of black people in the Catholic Church. However, the present situation
is far from ideal. See Joseph R. Nearon, "A Challenge to Theology: The Situation of American Blacks," *Proceedings of the Catholic Theological Society of
America*, Vol. 30, 1975, Luke Salm, F.S.C., editor, pp. 177–202. For a less
technical but alarming indicator of the situation, see the remarks of sociolo-
gist and population trends expert Philip Hauser, in which he notes that in
Chicago the black-white conflict is very much a black-Roman Catholic conflict. Cf. Sean Toolan, "Population Expert Predicts Trouble Ahead for Two
Cities of Chicago," *Chicago Tribune*, Sunday, March 12, 1978, pp. 1ff.

23. See Gordon Kaufman, "Whatever Happened to Theology?" *Christianity and Crisis*, May 12, 1975, pp. 110–111.

24. Perhaps W. E. B. DuBois gave black theology its most eloquent early
voice when he wrote, "Oh God? How long shall the mounting flood of inno-
cent blood roar in Thine ears and pound in our hearts for vengeance? Forgive
us, good Lord, we know not what we say! Bewildered we are passion tossed,
mad with the madness of a mobbed and mocked and murdered people; strain-
ing at the armposts of Thy throne, we raise our shackled hands and charge
thee, God, by the bones of our stolen fathers, by the tears of our dead moth-
ers, by the very blood of thy crucified Christ: What meaneth this? Tell us the
plan, give us the sign!" "Litany at Atlanta," in *Darkwater, Voices from within
the Veil* (New York: Harcourt, Brace and Howe, 1920), pp. 25ff.

25. Some Catholic criticism has suggested that black theology is marked by
its own bias of "black racism" and was, therefore, unacceptable to the
Church. In spite of the fierce rhetoric of black theology such criticisms, in
my judgment, represent a misreading of the general argument of the literature. Clearly any theology that was racist would be incompatible with a
Church that was genuinely Catholic and reverenced the name of Christ. Gion
Battista Monden's harsh judgment of black theology points out how difficult
it is for one of another culture to sympathetically enter into the horizon of
this uniquely American literature. See "Black Theology," *L'Osservatore Romano*, July 18, 1978.

26. Representative works are: Joseph R. Washington, Jr., *The Politics of God*
(Boston: Beacon Press, 1967); Albert B. Cleage, Jr., *The Black Messiah* (New
York: Sheed and Ward, 1968); J. De Otis Roberts, *A Black Political Theology*
(Philadelphia; The Westminster Press, 1974); Eulalio Baltazar, *The Dark Cen-
ter: A Process Theology of Blackness* (New York: Paulist Press, 1973); Major J.
Jones, *Christian Ethics for Black Theology* (Nashville: Abingdon Press, 1974);

William R. Jones, *Is God A White Racist? A Preamble to Black Theology* (Garden City, N.Y.: Anchor Press, 1973); James H. Cone, *God of the Oppressed* (New York: Seabury, 1975). Baltazar is the only Catholic listed above. Of course there cannot be a significant literature of indigenous black Catholic theology until there are more black Catholics. When the community is larger and there are black Catholics in positions of leadership in the Church, this literature shall no doubt increase in volume. See my articles: "The Church and Black Theology" in Vol. 17 of *The New Catholic Encyclopedia*; "Toward a Black Catholic Theology," *Freeing the Spirit*, Vol. 5, no. 2, pp. 2–6. In October of 1978 a Black Catholic Theology Symposium was held in Baltimore, Maryland. It was a unique gathering. A wide range of papers was presented from both academic and pastoral perspectives. At this writing there are plans for the publication of those papers as well as a subsequent symposium. In this American context it is clearly not possible to touch on the exciting possibility of a true Black *African* Catholic theology. Nevertheless the existence of native African cardinals, archbishops, bishops, priests, and sisters as well as creative forms of adaptation and catechesis in a relatively young African Catholic Church suggests that the universal church may be much enriched by their practices and theological reflections.

27. These remarks are drawn from *God of the Oppressed*, op. cit.

28. See my article "What Is Black Theology Anyway?" *The Critic*, Winter, 1977, pp. 64–70.

29. The range of foundations is illustrated by the five models of contemporary theology as formulated by David Tracy: (1) The orthodox theologian is the firm believer reflecting upon and defending the beliefs of the Church tradition, giving little attention to the questions, challenges, and counter-arguments of the secular scientific and philosophical worlds. (2) The liberal theologian recognizes and accepts the presuppositions of modernity and seeks to reformulate the generic faith of Christianity in a compatible manner. This model may tend to be uncritical in its acceptance of Enlightenment ideals of rationality and progress. (3) The neo-orthodox theologian is a reaction to liberalism. He offers what may be an essentially correct criticism of some of the attacks upon religion by the Enlightenment. Neo-orthodoxy affirms a radical faith in the God of Jesus, but tends not to be critical in evaluating the key doctrines of its tradition. (4) The radical theologian is perhaps typified by the "death of God" theologians in that like the liberal he incorporates the secular world view with a commitment to life and liberation. Jesus is embraced as the paradigm of the human condition. However, the radical model ultimately rejects the reality of God and thereby all but eliminates itself from theological discourse. (5) The revisionist theologian is firm in his commitment to the modern critical enterprise and embraces meaning as disclosed in common human experience as well as in the central motifs of the Christian tradition. The revisionist is not afraid to challenge the inadequacies of the secular and scientific mind-set anymore than he fears employing the best resources of that mind-set for the rearticulation and reformulation of central elements of the

Christian world view. Cf. Tracy, *Blessed Rage for Order*, Chapter 2; and William M. Shea, "The Stance and Task of the Foundational Theologian. Critical or Dogmatic?" *Hethrop Journal*, July 1976, pp. 273–92.

Chapter Five
Theology in a New Key: II. The Question of Authority and Certitude

Introduction

The analysis in the previous chapter of the primary ways by which a move can be made from disputed questions to firm foundations has deliberately not addressed the question of who has the right, the responsibility, the competence, and the authority to adjudicate the obvious differences that are the inescapable consequence of the fact of cultural and theological pluralism. Beyond the question of who is to meet this dilemma is the question in what manner it is to be met for the commonweal of the whole Church.

This raises the question of office and teaching authority. This issue has been separated from our discussion thus far in order to emphasize the fact that in reality all three modes of mediation are operative in our lives in varying degrees according to the issue and circumstances involved. It would be a false caricature to suggest that critical mediation is the exclusive preserve of the scholar, dogmatic mediation that of the bishop, and existential mediation that of the laity. Still the three contexts of theology cannot be discussed in the Catholic tradition without addressing the question of office and authority. This chapter will be in four parts: (1) Teaching Authority and Office; (2) The Question of Certitude; (3) An Example: Christology; (4) Conclusion.

1. Teaching Authority and Office

What is the relationship between the bishops of the Church in their teaching office (magisterium) and the community of theologians? In the light of all that has transpired in the past decades, this has become a real question that is asked by laypeople, bishops, theologians, parish priests, and sisters, as well as by authors in popular journals. To many, the question of office and authority, and certain related questions, constitutes what is potentially the most crucial issue facing the future internal harmony and external credibility of the Church. The potential magnitude of this problem as it is expressed in an apparent gulf and aura of suspicion between many bishops and theologians is a central reason why there is a need to encourage more and more collaboration between bishops and theologians. This book seeks to support that activity.

In preparing this section, the author found it most helpful to consult individual bishops and theologians. The result of these informal interviews and of a study of what has been written on the subject was the realization that the range of opinions and feelings on this issue is in fact even wider than one might think.

One bishop said in effect that whenever he is in the company of a theology faculty, he is there to learn, for he is not a theologian. And he would never author a theological statement without seeking the counsel of capable theologians. Another observed that as the chief shepherd of his diocese he is also the chief theologian. Hence his theological judgment is definitive even though time does not allow him to remain abreast of current theological developments. Yet another said that he avoided theological controversies and concentrated on the "care of souls" as an auxiliary bishop and pastor. Finally, one bishop said that on theological matters his policy was to follow the spirit and the letter of the pronouncements of the Second Vatican Council and statements of the Pope and the Holy See. Where no statements had been made, he followed his own prudent judgment.

Theologians offered equally diverse views. One theologian stated that since so many bishops are not theologically informed, they were not very helpful for him in addressing questions of genuine theological importance. Another offered that he was not at all sure that the consensus of theologians would be a better approximation of the truth than the consensus of bishops. Yet another said that he wished that some structure or forum could be established that would be nonthreatening to bishops and theologians alike, so that they could get to know each other as faithful persons and discuss differences in an ami-

cable atmosphere. Finally, it was suggested that many theologians today have lost sight of their true vocation. A real theologian is at the
service of the Church and hence at the service of the bishops and the
magisterium.

What follows does not pretend to resolve the many obvious differences. The goal is rather to outline some of the key elements of the
situation and to raise some questions for reflection. Frank and honest
conversations with bishops and theologians have been as helpful in
thinking about this question as the documents cited. Nevertheless,
the selection, arrangement, and interpretation of material offered
here is my own. We must begin with three statements from official
documents. The first statement is from the Second Vatican Council's
Dogmatic Constitution on the Church, *Lumen Gentium* (1964):

> Among the principal duties of bishops, the preaching of the gospel
> occupies an eminent place. For bishops are preachers of the faith
> who lead new disciples to Christ. They are authentic teachers, that
> is, teachers endowed with the authority of Christ, who preach to
> the people committed to them the faith they must believe and put
> into practice. By the light of the Holy Spirit, they make that faith
> clear, bringing forth from the treasure of revelation new things and
> old (cf. Mt. 13:52), making faith bear fruit and vigilantly warding
> off any errors which threaten their flock (cf. 2 Tim 4:1–4).
>
> Bishops, teaching in communion with the Roman Pontiff, are
> to be respected by all as witnesses to divine and Catholic truth. In
> matters of faith and morals, the bishops speak in the name of Christ
> and the faithful are to accept their teaching and adhere to it with
> religious assent of soul.[1]

The second statement is from a statement of Pope Paul VI to the
Rector of the Catholic University of Louvain in Belgium (1975):

> The attempt to make the Christian message more accessible to the
> modern mentality has led certain people to question the very con-
> tent of the message! Not that the theologian must be denied the
> rightful freedom indispensable for his work, but theology is not a
> private affair; what is not in the Church and for the Church is no
> longer theology. The theologian's responsibility lies within the
> "*communio ecclesiae.*" Now theology today is sometimes tempted to
> think that its rights to academic freedom are the same as those of
> profane sciences. As a matter of fact the definition of the rights of
> the theologian is derived from principles that are peculiar to this
> science: The theologian's function is exercised with a view to the
> building up of the ecclesial communion. . . .

Theology can never be conceived as an independent authority within the Church or as an alternative to the magisterium.[2]

The third statement is an excerpt from the "Twelve Theses on the Relationship between the Ecclesial Magisterium and Theology" of the International Theological Commission (1976):

1. The magisterium and theology have distinct roles in the Church and function with different methodologies but they are interdependent also.
2. Both share a common task though in analogous fashion. The common task is "preserve the sacred deposit of revelation, to examine it more deeply, to explain, teach and defend it for the service of the people of God and for the whole world's salvation."
3. "The magisterium and theologians differ in the quality of the authority with which they carry out their tasks."
   a. The authority of the magisterium derives from sacramental ordination.
   b. Theologians derive their specifically theological authority from their scientific qualifications.
4. The difference between the magisterium and theology also calls for special consideration of the freedom proper to each.
   a. "By its nature and institution, the magisterium is clearly free in carrying out its task. And while it is often difficult, it is nonetheless necessary that the magisterium use its proper freedom in such a way that it not appear to theologians or to the faithful at large to be arbitrary or excessive."
   b. "To the freedom of the magisterium there corresponds, in its own way, the freedom that derives from the true scientific responsibility of theologians. It is not an unlimited freedom, for besides being bound to truth, it is also true of theology that 'in the use of any freedom, the moral principle of personal and social responsibility must be observed.'"
9. "The exercise of their tasks by the magisterium and theologians often gives rise to a certain tension. But this is not surprising nor should one expect that such tension will ever be resolved here on earth. On the contrary, whenever there is genuine life, tension also exists. Such tension need not be interpreted as hostility or real opposition, but can be seen as a vital force and an incentive to a common carrying out of the respective tasks by way of dialogue."[3]

These passages clearly present the teaching as it has been commonly understood, that it is the bishops who are the final authoritative teachers of the Church. In the language of the previous chapter these passages give the final weight to *ex officio* dogmatic mediation over critical or existential mediation. A healthy tension between theologians and bishops is recognized, but the bishops clearly have the final word. Of particular significance is the statement of the International Theological Commission that the authority of the magisterium derives from ordination to the episcopacy, while that of theologians comes from their technical academic qualifications. In distinguishing these two sources of authority, the commission does not elaborate the precise manner in which these two distinct groups collaborate in the service of the Church. But even if the relationship between theologians and the magisterium as given in the cited documents was agreed upon, there would remain the question of how it is to be worked out in the concrete contemporary situation.

In recent years, some theologians themselves have advanced the argument (sometimes cautiously, other times boldly) that the strictly hierarchical interpretation of teaching authority in the Church does not do justice to the evidence of Scripture, the developments of history, and the needs of the present context.

Avery Dulles' recent writings have been especially helpful in this regard because of their irenic tone and because of his personal involvement in advancing the conversation between theologians and bishops. Dulles, himself an accomplished Church theologian, argues that in the Christian tradition there are a plurality of authorities variously weighed. So besides the judgments of theologians and the teachings of bishops, there are the Scriptures, the sense of the faithful, and the witness of those gifted with special prophetic charisms.

Dulles calls attention to certain historical developments. In the early centuries many of the most remarkable bishops were also theologians of high stature. Irenaeus, Cyprian, Augustine, Leo, Athanasius, Chrysostom, Cyril of Jerusalem, Cyril of Alexandria, Gregory of Nyssa, and Gregory of Nazianzus were among them.[4]

In the medieval Church, when most bishops were no longer theologians, there seems to have been a distinction between the manner in which bishops and theologians were teachers. Thomas Aquinas argued that professional university theologians were teachers (doctors) in the Church whose authority rested upon learning, argument, and evidence, and not upon office. In some circumstances, however, these Church theologians were called upon to approve documents of councils and judge the orthodoxy of those branded as heretics. Aquinas states that the pastoral magisterium of the bishops primarily concerns the maintenance of good order in the Church and overseeing the authentic public preaching of the gospel. The intricacies of speculative theology were left to the competent scholar.

By the nineteenth and twentieth centuries a neo-scholastic understanding of the magisterium had all but eliminated the dialectic between the competence of bishops and theologians, giving all teaching authority to the bishops. It would seem that many bishops today follow this view, which Dulles considers a somewhat recent development. According to this position, the "episcopoi" as successors of the apostles[5] have the "sure charism of truth" and the responsibility to teach definitively in matters of faith and morals. Theologians on the other hand serve to clarify and provide supportive evidence for official teachings. While they may advise or inform bishops as to the result of their scholarship, they are not to be considered official teachers in the Church.

If we draw out the implications of this position, the responsibility of the bishop is an immense one. Within this framework, it could be argued that the bishop is expected to resolve highly nuanced and debated theological issues even if, through no fault of his own, he does not have the necessary background to do so.[6] Unfortunately this may lead to conflict and a loss of credibility.[7] But even if the bishop consults a theologian, he is forced to select from a wide range of positions held by theologians.

Karl Rahner has observed that if bishops are not themselves theologians, they obtain their theological views *from* theologians and not from some special reserve available only to them. Rahner suggests that in the concrete situation bishops tend to follow the views they mastered when they studied theology, or the conclusion of theologians they regard as loyal to the Church. In practice the bishop is not so much teaching in the manner of an original theorist as he is making the important prudential discernment concerning which theologians' theories may be aptly followed.[8]

These historical developments have resulted in an understanding of the teaching authority of bishops that may not be altogether clear as to how they are to learn what they are to teach. While teaching clearly embraces a whole complex of activities, the teaching function of bishops can be conceived essentially as the activity of pronouncing judgment on particular theological opinions. The simplest way to make this judgment is to compare the theologian's statement with official Church statements on a particular question. In the manner of what has been termed a "hard apologetic," the emphasis is not placed upon the cogency of the evidence and arguments, but upon the authority of authentic teachers and tradition. The theologian is remind-

ed of the docile and obedient posture that should be his as he mediates
the judgments of the magisterium to the people. But the bishops
know well that they must be knowledgeable if they are to make such
judgments.

In the years since the Second Vatican Council there have been
more and more signs that bishops and theologians can find ways of
collaborating for the good of the whole Church community. Many individual bishops in their dioceses have established structures that
make the counsel of competent theologians available to them. There
is evidence that a number of bishops agree in practice with the conclusions of Richard McCormick, that if bishops are to be apt teachers
they must be diligent students. This is why we have more and more
continuing theological education programs specifically for bishops.
In the pastoral context, it is obvious that the prudent judgment of the
bishop is one important element in the overall ministry of teaching.
In practice, many individuals other than the local bishop or college of
bishops have gifts and charisms that are essential for the effective
ministry of teaching.[9] To the degree that this is not recognized, various forms of dissent on the part of theologians and laypeople appear
unavoidable.[10]

In the midst of so much discussion of the relationship between
bishops and theologians and the larger Church, it is not surprising
that pastorally sensitive bishops would express serious concern about
the welfare of their people. Archbishop John R. Quinn (the present
President of the National Conference of Catholic Bishops), for example, has expressed the concern that the people will be without direction if the teaching authority of the Church becomes "an undifferentiated or oligarchical magisterium of bishops, theologians and
saints." If a multidimensional model of bishops, theologians, and holy
people as teachers is embraced, Quinn wonders "how there could be
any point of real certitude for the faithful if the magisterium is conceived as a fugue of frequently dissonant voices forming a choir with
no director."[11]

While applauding the efforts of Avery Dulles in general, the
Archbishop suggests that it is too limiting to view the pastoral office
of bishops as primarily that of an administrator looking out for the
practical needs of the people. He argues that the biblical and patristic
description of pastor is one who feeds the flock by teaching sound
doctrine. The bishop as pastor, therefore, is of necessity teacher and
judge of faith.

Archbishop Quinn suggests that the whole controversy over who
holds the magisterial office in the Church is the result of larger cul-

tural and ideological developments that have been discussed earlier in this work. He notes especially the post-Enlightenment conviction that the scientific method is the only valid way of reaching truth. He also notes the contemporary concern for the dignity, freedom, and rights of every person and an emphasis upon personalism which stresses self-determination while tending to reject external authority. Not wishing to reject either the scientific method or personalism, Quinn argues that if either is carried beyond its proper sphere, they easily contribute to the present confusion over the teaching office in the Church.

While he is clearly concerned about the "style" and "tone' of magisterial statements that may at times seem to be insensitive to the achievements of the scholarly community, as well as the diverse and particular situations of the faithful, Quinn concludes that the mind of the Church, following the Scriptures, the Councils of Florence, Trent, Vatican I, Clement of Rome, Ignatius of Antioch, Tertullian, and Irenaeus, is that it does not now nor has it in the past considered anyone other than the college of bishops and the Roman Pontiff to constitute the Church's magisterium or definitive teaching office.[12]

At the outset of this discussion on the relationship between theologians and bishops, it was stressed that there are no easy answers. What has been offered here is simply an outline of the problematic for the benefit of those who are unfamiliar with certain historical developments. This outline also provides a locus for common reflection.

From this brief analysis three points emerge: (1) In its official statements (from the Popes and bishops) the Catholic Church, while respecting the special competence and singular contributions of theologians, does not consider them to share in the formal authoritative teaching office. (2) A growing number of theologians in examining the genesis of the present understanding of the magisterium, are suggesting a greater interdependence between bishops and theologians. As a result, it is argued that it is more the competence of the theologian to resolve complex speculative and theoretical questions, while it is the competence of bishops to make the practical pastoral decision of what is compatible with the tradition and palpable and helpful for the local Church community. (3) Because of the impact of the media, the communication skills of some bishops and some theologians, the sometimes incomprehensible language of magisterial documents and the writings of theologians, and the emergence of a more educated Catholic laity with urgent personal questions, there exists *de facto* two important teaching voices for many Catholic people (bishops and theologians). Neither, however, is a definitive voice in every case.

From the bishops laypeople hear authoritative teachings which they are asked to accept because of the charism of the episcopal office (various degrees of dogmatic mediation). And from the theologians they hear seemingly equally authoritative statements which they are asked to accept due to the cogency of the arguments and evidence (various degrees of critical mediation). As a result many laypeople, with neither the charism of office nor the credentials of scholars, cannot turn a deaf ear to either voice, and must finally make a decision if they are to have inner peace and anything like an integration of their religious world view (various degrees of existential mediation).

It will be useful to examine and reflect upon the first of these conclusions: The pope and bishops alone constitute the teaching office of the Church. Two important historical points must be noted at the outset. The first is the crucial early history of the Church during which the charism of the episcopal office and the skills of the theologian were often embodied in one person. Clearly, if that situation existed today, the conflict would not be so acute. For, then, the tension between scholarly findings and loyalty to tradition would reside in the same persons.

The other historical factor is the dialectical relationship that has existed through the centuries between the teaching of the magisterium and the theologians. Many of the departures from neo-scholastic philosophy and theology that appeared in the Second Vatican Council are the results of the pioneering labors of such theologians as De Lubac, Chenu, Congar, Teilhard de Chardin, Murray, Schillebeeckx, and Rahner. However, in the past, a number of them were "warned," "silenced," or even "condemned" for their writings.

A more dramatic example is that of the position taken by biblical scholars decades ago on the possibly non-literal nature of the creation narrative (hence the possible compatibility of Scripture and evolution theory). This position, once rejected by the magisterium, now appears to be at least tacitly approved. Is there some sense in which the conclusions of theologians can be premature, and hence "errors," when they are novel and not sufficiently mature for general acceptance and understanding? The question does not mean to deny the fact that history reveals that within theology there is a dialectic that makes it possible for the reigning theory of one period to be eclipsed or reversed by a subsequent generation of scholars. It is also true that some theological positions which have been rejected by the magisterium have never gained subsequent acceptance. But the process by which the magisterium gradually incorporates and accepts elements of once unacceptable theological views suggests a more subtle and more nuanced process than simply declaring the eternally true and the eternally false. The question of the timely, the appropriate, and the palpable seems to be of equal, if not greater, importance.

In the light of the distinction we have drawn between generic faith and specific beliefs a further question arises. When it is affirmed that the college of bishops in communion with the bishop of Rome are the definitive teachers, does that affirmation refer only to the content of generic "faith," or does it equally embrace "beliefs" as they are spelled out in specific doctrines and organized in systematics? The verbal expressions of religious meaning have a long history that takes on many differentiations. There is, as we have noted, the biblical proclamation, "Jesus is Lord," made possible by the transforming existential experience that the apostolic community had of Jesus. There are the subsequent conciliar decrees that seek to preserve the authentic interpretation of that foundational biblical experience and witness. But with the Councils a technical, philosophical language is employed instead of the complex imagery and descriptions of the scriptural texts. Subsequently even more specific theoretical elaborations of the inner meaning of the creedal statements are developed by individual theologians and schools of systematic theology. Put another way:

> Behind the datum-discourse of doctrine is the datum-discourse of scripture. Behind the datum-discourse of scripture is the datum-discourse of the apostolic preaching. Behind the apostolic preaching is the apostolic experience of Christ and the language that brought this experience to speech: Behind the apostolic experience and language is the human history and human language of Christ.[13]

Does the "charism of truth" enable the bishop to interpret and judge with equal ease every stage in this process? Or does he judge the compatibility of more recent stages with earlier ones? Or is it the bishop's charism and ministry to protect and mediate some "deeper" reality that exists independent of the vicissitudes of ongoing history and changing cultures?

John Cardinal Wright, in his published lectures, *The Church: Hope of the World*, suggested that the "faith" preserved and taught by the magisterium has little to do with the developments and findings of theology. He declared:

> . . . theology is not faith and all the "theologians" combined do not add up to faith. . . . "Theologies" are influenced by human condi-

tionings (cultural, political, subjective), but the faith is from God and its content is from his revelation through Christ Jesus.... God's revelations are the object of the faith. His Church authoritatively sets forth God's revelation. The Church is not a forum nor a school of theologians and theologies.... Only what the Church teaches authoritatively as the mind and will of Christ the Lord is the object of faith: all theologies, even those which most she welcomes as helpful in understanding the faith or blesses as most consistent with the contents of the faith are secondary and marginal, related to the faith, perhaps, but not to be confused with it.[14]

From this view it appears that there exists a transcultural, transhistorical datum-discourse that gives expression to the "propositions of faith" that is completely independent of any form of theology or the theological process. And it is precisely this perennial living faith that the bishops are charged to guard, interpret, and proclaim. But where is this "faith" without any admixture of theology to be found? The impression is had that a certain moment in the theological process, such as the definitions of Ecumenical Councils, has been selected and enshrined as somehow immune to historical and cultural variables. But this manner of thinking can lead to a kind of doctrinal fundamentalism or positivism in the Catholic Church that is no less intransigent than the biblical fundamentalism of some Protestant traditions.

If the bishops do not have a kind of private access to "the faith" in its transcultural form, it is equally obvious that admission into the episcopal college does not automatically provide bishops with the specialized skills of theological science if that discipline is not actually mastered and regularly exercised. It is not surprising that, in the modern context, where democratic models of life are seen as an ideal and the scientific method has played such a crucial role, many people can become somewhat dissatisfied when there can be given no adequate account of precisely how the episcopal charism for truth functions. It may even be implied that self-serving ideology is at work when bishops place great stress upon the unique prerogative of their office, an uncritical understanding of apostolic succession, divine right, and special graces.[14a]

In spite of that caution, however, it remains a fact that the good faith and diligence of the majority of bishops is real. Every reality that cannot be proclaimed unambiguously is not necessarily false. It should not be surprising that a religious community which proclaims the mystery of God cannot give a fully scientific account of how the protecting gifts of the Spirit work. Through its long history there are many instances of "tacit knowing" in the Church. The community knows more than it can say. The many questions and difficulties of recent years will perhaps occasion a greater articulation of *how* the various members learn and teach. In practice it is certain that at the center of the charism of the episcopal teaching office is not a kind of gnostic grasp of the irreducible starting points of religion and theology, but rather the very real virtue of prudence and discernment. An example will illustrate this.

Let us say that a university theologian publishes a scholarly study entitled *There Are No Angels*.[15] The author uses the historical-critical method of the university. He employs arguments and evidence from the best in current Scripture studies, comparative religion, psycology, and history of religion and anthropology. On hearing of the work a bishop may judge that the widespread circulation of such a book would be pastorally harmful, because it would stir confusion and doubt among some of his people. He may reflect that some of his people have a lively devotion to angels while others never think about them. He may reflect upon how little or how much angels have meant to him personally and he may think that over and above the scriptural testimony concerning angels, the Church has constantly taught that there were angels. But he may wonder how central is the belief in angels to the faith he is charged to preserve.

Next he may consult his fellow bishops and they may decide to establish a committee of theologians and bishops to examine the question and draft a statement for the bishops' consideration. Then the bishops make the further important decision to include certain theologians and to exclude others from the committee. The theological commission may report that yes, there is a long-standing authentic teaching of the Church on the reality of angels as pure created spirits, though this teaching has been much overlaid by devotional practices, artistic renderings, and religious imagination. These encrustations, the committee argues, have all but obscured the original biblical meaning of angels. Further the committee may concede that the evidence and arguments advanced by the book, *There Are No Angels*, are quite persuasive and seemingly irrefutable within the work's own methodology. This is so much the case that a number of members of the committee suggest that *in spite* of long-standing teaching and tradition, they themselves conclude that, as a matter of fact, angels probably do not exist.

In response to this the bishop may, on the one hand, seek to revive devotion to angels, and, on the other hand, seek to overcome aberrations in popular piety in his diocese. Based upon existential mediation (his own experiences and devotions that convince him of the existence of angels) and dogmatic mediation (the constant teaching of the Church), the bishop may judge that the methodology (critical mediation) of the work in question is not adequate for the issue in question and hence it has come to conclusions beyond its competence. After reflecting and praying over the whole matter, he may conclude that the results of the theological commission should or should not be published.

If, however, the bishop wishes to dispute the accumulated evidence and arguments in a particular area such as biblical interpretation, then, it would seem, he could not do this automatically and *ex officio* independent of the skills and diligent and objective research that should characterize a good theologian. For if the theologian's biblical research is simply rejected out of hand, there arises the question on what grounds and by what methods, other than explicitly theological investigation, can such a rejection be made.

Finally, the bishop may reflect upon the distinction made by the committee between the constant teaching of the Church and what is *de facto* the case. He may ask are these not, in every case, the same. Or he may think that perhaps angels do not exist in exactly the way that they were thought to exist as a result of Church teaching mixed with popular devotion. He might conclude that his charism and responsibility is to proclaim the authentic teaching of the Church, the presumption being that such teaching coincides with reality. Such a bishop may hope that the day never comes that he is forced to conclude, in the face of inescapable evidence, that something is or is not the case in spite of Church teaching to the contrary. Were he to entertain such conclusions, what would have become of his loyalty to the Church?

This example does not propose to explain how the ministry of episcopal magisterium works. What it does point out is that even when a fundamentalist or agnostic interpretation of the bishops' theological capacities is rejected, real and true responsibilities and charisms remain. One of the most important among them is a remarkable amount of discernment and prudence and consummate skill in exercising them.

The theologian who authors *There Are No Angels* lives in a special tension. He rightly distinguishes between theology and religion, between giving a theoretical account of faith, hope, and love and incarnating these virtues. However, his life-world may not only distinguish theology from religion, it may separate them altogether.

Caught up in the exacting activity of critical investigation, the theologian may have few occasions to be a part of "ordinary parish life." He may not often celebrate the liturgy or preach in a regular parish setting. Hence his ideas are not tested in the ecclesial community. He may very well be somewhat uncomfortable with certain devotional practices which his historical and theological knowledge call into serious question.

If it is true that in earlier centuries many of the leading bishops were also influential theologians, it is equally true that many of those influential theologians were also leading saints. If theologians today are to make a credible witness and have a lasting impact upon the shape of the Church to come, then, it seems, they must be striving for sanctity. If one's goal is to be a theologian in and for the Church, religious, theistic, Christian, ecclesial, moral, and intellectual conversion shall all be manifest in the ongoing transformation of one's life. This does not deny the important function of the secular university theologian who hypothetically or actually brackets his religious convictions in order to establish common ground with his secular academic community. But he would be the first to admit that he is not primarily speaking to the Church, for the Church, or from within the Church. But such a university theologian should understand more than anyone else why the Church does not, perhaps cannot, always embrace his findings even though he is convinced that they are true.

To borrow from Ezra Pound's description of the poet—theologians are at times the "antennae of the race." And this is precisely why it may be difficult for a theologian to be saintly. Paradoxically he knows too much and never leaves off questioning. His studies may have forced him to leave behind the pre-critical naiveté of earlier years during which the great symbols of Christianity engaged him in a literal and undifferentiated way. It may be a very real struggle for him to be engaged anew by religious realities in a post-critical naiveté. Deep down in his soul-space the theologian knows that his considerable intellectual activity is no more the cultivation of the interior life than is the exhausting schedule of a bishop's ceremonial and administrative duties.

If the theologian is going to speak effectively to the parish priest, the people in the pews, and the bishops, a genuine modesty must moderate his acumen. This modesty and humility should not be the misplaced humility of subservience to those who may misuse their authority, but it must be a humility that recognizes the limitations of all human discourse, the historicity of the human race, and the permanence of mystery. While he should never concede mystery where there is only misinformation and mystification, at the limit, the theologian, like Job, knows that he is holding forth upon marvels beyond his wit and his understanding. (See Job, 42:3.)

The praxis or existential theologian may marvel over the amount of energy expended over such a question. As far as he is concerned, there may or may not be angels in the sense of pure spirits as understood by the medieval theologians. But for him the only angel of relevance might be an angel of *justice* who would liberate the socially and economically oppressed and feed the hungry.

Meanwhile, the "average Catholic" may respond in a number of ways to *There Are No Angels*. One may declare that there certainly *are* angels and continue his personal devotion and prayers to angels. Another may reflect on the fact that he has heard less and less about angels in recent years. Since angels were never very significant to him, it is just as well to acknowledge that "angel" is a symbolic way of describing a special awareness of God's guiding presence in one's life. Finally, another type of Catholic may think that we should not be so quick to dismiss angels. Perhaps contemporary experiences of UFOs and psychic visions are akin to what were once interpreted as angelic visitations.

2. The Question of Certitude

The whole discussion of teaching office deals with the complex question of who has the last word in disputed theological matters. And this in turn is related to a concern for the people of God who might be left insecure, confused, and without direction if they could not be sure of whom to look to as the final word. As has already been indicated, existential mediation is the operative solution in the concrete situation for many people. It might be helpful to conclude this section with a consideration of the question of certitude in its relationship to the ultimate purpose of religion.

When it is said that unless someone is clearly in charge, uncertainty will result, we must ask, with regard to what will uncertainty arise? Obviously there will be uncertainty about the organizational structure of the Church. But the question goes deeper than that. There is the further uncertainty that asks what exactly is the Church's self-understanding or teaching on particular central religious questions such as God, sin, Jesus, Church, ministry, salvation. This is the matter of common meaning and community, as it was elaborated in Chapter One. A cacophony of voices surely played a part in the decline of common meaning. But beyond the question of certitude concerning who the Church teachers are, is the question of certitude regarding what is taught.

When the Church community proclaims, for example, that it is certain that the Christian community believes in God, this is not the same as proclaiming that there is a God in such a way that all will become certain of that fact because of the proclamation. For if what is certainly believed could be proclaimed as certain in this latter sense, then there would be no need of belief. Religious beliefs are clearly affirmed as more than subjective states. They mean to refer to how things are. But this need not mean that religious assertions are all "facts" in the ordinary sense of the term. They may indeed point to a reality, but that reality is never fully apprehended. This is why even dogmatic statements must be reflected upon if one is to grasp the realities to which they refer.[16] But one's certain affirmation of what is certainly a dogma of the Church does not give one certitude about the objective status of a particular world view or metaphysical system. An example will help.

While preparing this text, word has come of the death of the father of a good friend. Through the "knowledge" born of religious faith, I may proclaim that I am certain that with death "life is not ended but merely changed." But this genuine faith stance does not command belief in, or give me certitude concerning, a particular theory of the human soul as the spiritual and immortal "form" of the material body. This becomes especially clear when I reflect upon the fact that the biblical notion of the resurrection of the dead and the philosophical speculation concerning the existence and immortality of the human soul are related but clearly distinct questions.[17]

Therefore, while the Christian may be certain in his belief that the fate of the dead is not extinction, he does not have certain knowledge of precisely what metaphysical structures exist that make his belief correct. This is so even if one or another theory seems particularly apt. An important reason for this is the multidimensional nature of all religious language. This is not intended to suggest that normative religious discourse does not intend to point toward reality structures. Clearly it does. Such language has what Rahner has termed an "ethos of truth."[18] But insofar as all dogmatic expressions point ultimately to God, the referent of all such language remains more concealed than disclosed.

Over and above the question of certitude there is the question of the relationship between normative religious language and the ultimate purpose of religion which, at least generically, is union with God. We have been discussing the expressive development of religion in its discursive and theoretical form. Let us suppose that there are ten central formulations (dogmas) that constitute the core of the Catholic world view. What precisely is accomplished when one believes unreservedly in the orthodox formulations of these dogmas? Does such an assent of its own advance the union of an individual with God? Or does such an affirmation attempt to bring one into closer contact with the radical, inner, experiential element that eludes conceptual formulations? If we argue that the acceptance of dogmas of itself advances our union with God, what are we to make of the obvious fact that Catholic people affirm those dogmas with an incalculably wide range of understanding and differentiation?

Consider, for example, the dogma of Trinity: God is one in three divine persons. It may be diversely affirmed as: profound and disclosive symbolic language that illuminates the mystery of divine dynamism; metaphysical language that provides an actual and accurate description of the inner life of God; the definitive rendering of the meaning of the biblical references of Jesus to the Father and to the Spirit; the high achievement of the early Councils but now so hopelessly entangled in Hellenic thought as to have no contemporary relevance save as a "symbol" of continuity with an ancient tradition; the fiery center of a lively faith that enkindles all of one's hope of human community and world progress; or finally, remote and meaningless yet affirmed in obedience to the Church.

Do the diverse modes of affirmation of this dogma in some way affect the spiritual significance it has in the interior life of the believer? The issue is complicated when we reflect upon the fact that with the Second Vatican Council the Catholic Church has acknowledged that union with God or salvation is truly possible not only for Christians of other traditions (who would dispute, reject, or nuance one or another dogmatic Catholic formula) but also for members of other world religions which might not embrace any of the ten hypothetical dogmas in their particular formulation.

This would seem to suggest that the inner conversion process is of far greater importance for one's ultimate union with God than is the outer expression. Religious transformation or salvation is, therefore, not accomplished *ipso facto* by the affirmation of orthodox formulations of religious formations. Rather, adherence to these expressions or formulations gives witness to an individual's commitment to his particular concrete, historical tradition as the avenue to God. But we must acknowledge, with Rahner, that the Church is, in a paradoxical sense, the extraordinary means of salvation, since most of the peoples of history do not become members of the family of the

Church though they may be pure of heart and in communion with God. Therefore, while doubting, questioning, or even denying dogmatic formulations of particular beliefs which specify generic faith may well be indicative of tension in an individual's relationship to his faith tradition and its explicit self-understanding, it is not necessarily an indiction of the state of one's interior relationship with the mystery of God. There really is nothing particularly startling about this save the fact that we tend to forget it. It seems well in force when we are engaged in serious ecumenical and interreligious discussion. But there is a tendency to overlook it when trying to evaluate differences of opinion within our own Catholic tradition.

Surely, when we collaborate with Christians of other traditions and peoples of other religions, we are not being facetious when we confirm that God's saving presence is in them. Yet when we encounter diversity of understanding and interpretation among priests, theologians, bishops, and laity in our own tradition, we sometimes act as if we have a window into another's soul. We seem as sure that those Catholics who differ from us are damned, as Catholics and Protestants were once sure of each other's fate.

3. An Example: Christology

This discussion of theology in a new key has been a necessarily generic account of dogmatic, existential, and critical mediation. Hopefully, in following the general outline of each of the modes of mediation, each person has been able to supply examples from his particular perspective. Perhaps it happened that you were able to note the greater or lesser impact of each mode of mediation upon your personal convictions and beliefs. If this is the case, you have probably become aware of the fact on some specific issues you actually moved from existential, to critical, to dogmatic mediation or from critical, to existential, to dogmatic mediation, or some other sequence. The lack of examples has lessened the likelihood of premature judgment in favor of one mode over another based upon a positive or negative response to an example. However, it might be helpful to conclude this chapter with an example.

I will use the study of Jesus, or Christology, as my example. In using such a profound and complex example, we will not be able to examine the full texture of the theological and doctrinal statements involved. This is not a short tract on Christology, the defense of classical Christological theories, or the tentative putting forth of new ideas. It is only a descriptive account of the dialectic between the three contexts of theology. Inevitably as a summary description the material is much simplified.

We will begin with classical Christology as it has been dogmatically mediated. That will be followed by some of the questions, problematics, and challenges from critical and existential mediation that classical dogmatic Christology has gradually faced, challenged, accepted, rejected, ignored, or by adaptation integrated and subsumed into itself.

Classical, dogmatically mediated Christology may be termed "high Christology." That is, it "begins" from "above" with a divine reality. From all eternity before the world began God dwelled in unapproachable light in the mystery of the Trinity. As we used to chant:

> Domine, sancte Pater, omnipotens aeterne Deus: Qui cum unigenito Filio tuo, et Spiritu Sancto, unus es Deus, unus es Dominus: non in unius singularitate personae, sed in unius Trinitate substantiae. Quod enim de tua gloria, revelante te credimus, hoc de Filio tuo, hoc de Spiritu Sancto, sine differentia discretionis sentimus. Ut in confessione verae sempiternae que Deitatis, et in personis proprietas, et in essentia unitas, et in majestate adoretur aequalitas.[19]

This eternal triune God[20] created the world, and humankind was the apex of that creation. The first humans, Adam and Eve, lived in paradisal bliss with the benefit of special preternatural gifts. By eating of the tree of knowledge, they shattered their relationship with God. Cast from the garden, they passed on the stain and the pain of their original sin to their descendants by biological generation.

God resolved to be reconciled with his people and salvation history began. He elected the Jewish people as his chosen ones. Through the prophets he taught them to hope for salvation and revealed himself as Yahweh, Lord, and Father. In the fullness of time, the eternal Logos, the Word of the Father, the second person of the Trinity entered the womb of a young Jewish virgin named Mary. By the overshadowing of the Holy Spirit and the miracle of the hypostatic union, the divine person and the divine nature were united with a human nature. This constitutes the Incarnation by which the Son of God came into the world to save the human race from Adam's sin and its own.

The mission of Jesus Christ, therefore, was the salvation of the world. By his life, teachings, and wondrous signs he revealed that he was a divine legate, the fulfillment of all the Old Testament expectations for a coming prophet, suffering servant, high priest, and even more, the very Son of God.[21] He called to himself a small band of disciples who were to be both his witnesses to his message of repentance and the kingdom of God, and the core of the Church he founded. In fulfillment of his Father's will, Christ died on the cross for the forgiveness of sins. For since by man came death, so by man comes the resurrection. Three days after his death, Jesus rose from the dead, definitively validating his claim to be God's only Son. Having completed the salvific work, forty days later he ascended into heaven to be seated in glory at the right hand of the Father. But he left behind not only his Spirit to teach and guide but also his Church, his mystical body on earth.

This Christology was often defended by means of a hard apologetic. Jesus provided the motives of credibility by his marvelous works and deeds. The gospel writers were credible eyewitnesses to the key events of salvation history. Jesus established his Church with the seven-fold means of grace (sacraments) and its essential structure including that of Peter and twelve as the college of bishops with the mandate to teach in his name. The Church (protected by the Spirit), in turn seeking to clarify what might appear ambiguous or only implicit in Scripture, made definitive pronouncements about the ontological and metaphysical condition of Jesus' being in precisely the language of the trinitarian preface with which we began. The same high "Logos" Christology was mediated through the solemn stateliness and multiple symbols of the liturgy.

This Christology, dogmatically mediated through the authority of witness, and the authority of the magisterium of the Church, clearly proclaimed the divinity of Christ (against adoptionists) and defended his humanity (against docetists). It further grounded the divine origins of the Church and the divine destiny of the human race. The four gospels with their significant discrepancies were almost thought to be integratable somewhat like the chapters of a novel. So the portions of the Lucan nativity narrative that are not found in the other gospels, and the prologue of John's gospel also not found in the other three, were seen as complementary elements of a larger whole. While the best theologians of every age, whether bishops or not, knew that analogy, symbol, metaphor, legend, philosophical speculations, and indirect discourse all played a part in this Christological synthesis, many of these distinctions, however, were unknown or inaccessible to the vast majority.

This classical dogmatic Christology affirms that Jesus Christ is a divine being and the exclusive way to salvation. The fullness of God's saving grace and love is all but limited to Christians who are explicitly members of the Church. The secular non-Christian world is judged as the locus of sin and error, and other religions seen as human efforts with no real saving value. Hence there should be a strong missionary zeal to bring all people to Christ in the Church. Recognizing one's sinfulness, the individual is saved by orthodox belief in the paschal mystery of the incarnate Son of God.[22]

When Protestant scholars[23] began to examine this dogmatic Christology in the light of the critical methodologies of the post-Enlightenment period, Catholic biblical scholars were strictly charged not to accommodate Catholic teaching to Protestant methods and theories. However, with the emergence of "historical consciousness" and under the impetus of Pius XII's pioneering encyclical on biblical studies, *Divino Afflante Spiritu*,[24] Catholic biblical scholars engaged more actively in critical biblical scholarship. Over time, a growing collaboration developed between Protestant and Catholic biblical scholars because of an increasing awareness that the functional specialities of research and interpretation (to recall Lonergan's usage) should not be denominationally different because they employ the same scholarly methodologies.[25]

Once the critical method took hold, nothing was outside of its range. For example, when the literal nature of the Adamic narrative was questioned, the traditional understanding of original sin was questioned. When that was questioned, the traditional understanding of the need for a savior and the mission of Christ was questioned. As Rudolf Bultmann is said to have remarked, once one entertains the possibility that the "last trumpet" that is to accompany the resurrection of the dead might be metaphorical, then one's religious world view will never be the same again.

By means of literary criticism, it became possible to uncover the complex compositional structure of the Scriptures with its various strata.[26] Gradually scholars came to a number of startling conclusions. The Scriptures are not eyewitness accounts as was once thought. They are rather a proclamation of faith, a kerygma that employs many different forms of literature including myth.[27] They were composed "backwards" from the perspective of the resurrection event. And the resurrection event itself is as problematic as it is pivotal.

First of all, there is no account of the resurrection in the gospels. What is present are three distinct proclamations. The first is the proclamation, "He is risen!"; the second, "We have seen him"; and the third, "The tomb is empty." Many questions emerged. Among them, did the disciples come to believe that Jesus was the Christ because of the resurrection as a definitive miracle or did they believe the resurrection because they had gradually come to believe him to be the Christ?[28] Of equal consequence was the critical conclusion that few, if any, of the words "spoken" by Jesus in the gospel are his in the literal sense of "ipssisima verba."[29] An immediate consequent question, of course, is what becomes of the authority of the statements of Jesus about himself especially as found in St. John?[30] Are these mere interpretations or valid extrapolations under the guidance of Easter faith?

Working backwards through the gospel accounts, some scholars questioned the literal nature of the more wondrous miracles as well as the more explicit testimonies of Jesus and others about his divinity. The legendary and symbolic nature of much of the nativity narrative was recognized as well as points of similarity between the narratives of Jesus' origins and accounts of virginal conception of mythical heroes.

With all of this it was a logical step to ask whether the idea of Jesus as the pre-existent logos was a metaphysical fact or mytho-poetic language to convey the unique significance of Jesus.[31] Finally there arises the question: Is the Trinity a metaphysical given before the foundation of the world, or a symbolic construct of the early Christian community to meet the problem of the unique relationship they believed existed between Jesus and God in the light of their resurrection faith? The press of these and so many other questions leads to a new point of departure for Christology: the humanity of Jesus. This is Christology "from below," an ascending model. Taking seriously the humanity of Jesus, such an approach allows for real development, discernment, emotions, needs, uncertainties, and a gradual realization of mission, vocation, and identity.

If it ends embracing many of the affirmations of a high or descending Christology, a low Christology accomplishes this only after a painstaking exploration and with a much more controlled and exact use of language that carefully differentiates the multiple ways in which religious meaning is conveyed.[32]

Specialized contemporary critical questions press dogmatically mediated Christology even further. Two of the most challenging of those questions concern the relationship between Christology and the

overwhelming evidence in favor of the evolution of the human species, and the more recent Christian recognition of the value, validity,
and truth dimension of other religions.

Jesuit theologian and paleontologist Teilhard de Chardin's view
of reality is passionately Christological, yet because of his inability to
reconcile certain interpretations of "the Fall" with the reality of evolution and his sense of the future of the race, he proposed a bold vision of a Christic Omega point—with Christ at the summit of the
evolving process.[33] Paradoxically Teilhard's speculations revived the
minority position of a never resolved medieval debate. Aquinas argued that in the original divine "plan" (the order of creation) there
was no provision made for the Incarnation. It was only after Adam's
sin that the Incarnation was "decreed," establishing the order of redemption by which the Son of God would restore the primal harmony. For Duns Scotus, however, Christ is seen as the goal and
crowning point not only of the supernatural but also of the natural
order. From the start, independent of the Fall, the whole creation was
"planned" with the Incarnation in view. If there had been no sin, Jesus would still have come as the supreme revelation of God in this
world. Sin added another dimension to his coming. The Christ would
not only disclose the goal and zenith of creation, but he would also
die a redemptive death.

Teilhard, more akin to Scotus than to Thomas, envisions the redemption as an important moment in the dynamic fullness of "Christ
the evolver," the vitalizer, the super-creator of an unfathomable
future, Christogenesis.[34]

Living and teaching in a multireligious setting forced new questions upon theologian John Hick, and prompted him to try to reformulate Christology in a manner that takes other religious traditions
seriously.[35] He examines the long sequence of re-interpretations of
the phrase "outside the Church there is no salvation" to that of "outside of Christ there is no salvation," to that of the "anonymous Christian." He argues that there is needed in theology an equivalent of the
Copernican revolution that overturned the Ptolemaic world view.

Just as the Ptolemaic world view sees the earth as central and sta-
tionary while the sun and other heavenly bodies move about it, so
Ptolemaic theology locates one's own religion in the center of reality.
The Copernican world view located the sun in the center and the
earth moves about. So too, a Copernican revolution in theology
would be radically God-centered, rather than Christ-centered.

Hick suggests that the Johannine formula, "Anyone who has

seen me has seen the Father," expresses the significance of Jesus in Christian circles at the end of the first century. Gradually the language of divine Sonship floated away from its Jewish context developing a new meaning and taking root once more in Graeco-Roman culture. In this context the early Christians accounted for Jesus as an absolute encounter with God by re-interpreting the Old Testament language concerning God's Messiah. They developed expressions making use of the Greek philosophical categories that were available to them. Hence Jesus, the beloved son of the Father (in a Jewish context), becomes of one substance with the Father, the second person of the Trinity and God incarnate in a Greek context.

Hick asks: What if Christianity had expanded eastwards? Speculative Christology would have developed in an Asian, rather than European, culture. Would not the conceptual explanation of the Christ-event have taken a very different form? Had it moved into India, where Buddhism was becoming a powerful influence and the Mahayana doctrines were being developed, most likely Jesus would have been identified not as the divine Logos but as a Bodhisattva, who like Gotomoa had attained Buddhahood, the perfect relationship with reality.

Had this happened, would the Eastern interpretation of Christianity have been wrong or merely different? Hick argues that it would be different only because of a radically different context. Theology, in Hick's view, is but the human attempt to articulate the ineffable meaning of revelatory events experienced in faith. As a human, culturally conditioned reality, even "orthodox" theology is but one aspect of the interaction between the Christ-event and the human race in the past nineteen centuries.

Hick takes great pains to argue that he is not in favor of absolute relativism in order to come to terms with world religions. He staunchly defends Christ as the absolute encounter with God for Christians, but he argues that the absolute center of religion is not Christ but the one God whom he reveals. Hence the Copernican revolution constitutes a shift from a Christo-centric to a theo-centric religious world view.

In order to come to terms with classical Christology and contemporary discussions, Karl Rahner indicates six different types of Christology which differ according to language, context, the problems they address, and the way in which they move beyond the original Christ event to theological reflection and development sparked by that event. Hence the first two, the salvation-historical (from his humanity) and the metaphysical (from his divinity), seem most closely related to the biblical account. The next two are termed "ontic" and "ontological" because of their philosophical reflection upon the identity and nature of Christ independent of the ministry of Jesus. They are closest to the teachings of the Council of Chalcedon. Finally there is Christology in a scientific and evolving world view and an inquiring Christology. These two deal with the contemporary questions such as those touched upon in the above discussion of Teilhard and Hick. But even under the skillful orchestration of a master theologian such as Rahner, a real tension is manifest in the effort to hold such diverse themes together.[36]

Dogmatically mediated Christology has by no means appropriated all of the developments and speculations of critically mediated Christology. Conflicts flare up between dogmatic theologians and Scripture scholars when the critical work of the exegete seems to undermine long-standing dogmatic views.[37] Many speculative theories have been clearly and firmly rejected, others have been set aside for further reflection, while others have been implicitly accepted. Nevertheless there is such collaboration between the two approaches that most leading dogmatic theologians in the Catholic tradition would not only employ various critical methods, but they would also affirm that such critical tools have enhanced their scholarship and deepened, rather than undermined, their faith in and understanding of the presence of God in Jesus Christ.

Because dogmatically mediated Christology understands itself to be charged with the preservation, interpretation, and proclamation of the received doctrine of the Church which it may not alter for any reason, it is to be expected that at certain points it will challenge, counter-argue, reject, or even ignore some of the claims of critically mediated Christology as being no longer compatible with authentic and constant tradition.

The line may be drawn over a question of generic faith, particular beliefs, or even over such a distinction as that. The challenge or response may come from the dogmatic theologian himself, the magisterium, or the people in the pews writing "letters to the editor." Through diversity expressed and ranging from highly sophisticated to completely unnuanced understandings of the issue involved, the point will be the same. There is more here than scholarship can uncover. Here is an irreducible starting point, a foundational affirmation, a crucial link with the earliest experience and understanding of the Church community. This foundational reality is grounded in faith and, while acknowledging that it is paradoxical, full of mystery, and a seeming affront to critical intelligence, dogmatic mediation declares that humility, prudence, and most of all obedience to the word of God demands that it hold with the tradition and its classic affirmations rather than the new "findings" of the ever changing theological schools and esoteric methodologies. The point on which the line is drawn will more likely be one which is believed to be essential to an orthodox interpretation of the divinity of Jesus.

Perhaps not all but clearly *some* of the wondrous miracles must be fact.[38] Perhaps not all but clearly *some* of the authoritative sayings of Jesus must be his exact words. On the question of the resurrection of Jesus, dogmatic mediation may defend a resuscitation of the body of Jesus in a literal and uncritical manner,[39] or it may offer a highly refined and critically informed defense of the resurrection as a trans-historical "event," a wondrous glorification of the body of Jesus that would make it unthinkable that his body could somehow be found by archeologists.[40] And this "event," apprehended by faith, can neither be validated nor invalidated by critical mediations.

Existential mediation is also a part of the development of Christology. While dogmatic and critical mediation may be in a state of unresolved conflict over a question of fact or theory, existential mediation has its own secure hold upon an error, a truth, or a partial truth. This allows one person to nurture a devotional life centering on the divinity of Christ that in effect denies, rejects, or ignores the fact and implications of his humanity. Another person, baffled by trinitarian language and suspecting tri-theism of many Catholics, comes to terms with God and Jesus in a rather Unitarian manner though he has never studied Unitarian theology. Another gives utter intellectual assent to orthodox trinitarian theology and official Church positions on disputed issues, but experientially God and Jesus are encountered only in their devotions to the Sacred Heart.

Furthermore, because of its praxis and pastoral orientation, existential mediation may employ various elements of classical or contemporary Christological theory in order to elaborate bold visions of human growth and potential. Existential mediation may espouse a Christology that favors political, social, economic, racial, and sexual liberation in a manner that was not foreseen by the proponents of dogmatic or critical Christology. Such an existential Christology may be challenged or rejected by critical and dogmatic mediation for coming to inappropriate and ungrounded conclusions. Yet the wide appeal and practical success of these existential interpretations will give them a life of their own that will be all but impervious to the scholarly challenges and official rejections of critical and dogmatic mediation.

4. Conclusion

This extended example has not been a study in Christology. As a descriptive summary, it is necessarily incomplete. But the intention of the example was to bring out in greater relief the differences between critical, dogmatic, and existential mediation discussed in the previous chapter as well as questions relating to authority, office, and certitude discussed in this chapter.

The example has underscored a key difficulty in the interaction between critical, dogmatic, and existential mediation. The difficulty is this: Each style of thought or mode of mediation is more or less coherent within itself. But no one "lives" exclusively in one context of academy, Church, or practical daily life. One moves from one to the other even if it is unwittingly. And this is as it must be, since each can gain from the other.

But for that gain to be long-term and systematic, structures must continue to be developed so that individuals who are primarily in one context may become familiar with the presuppositions and canons of thought of the other. This will certainly require reading and, more importantly, "experiencing" outside of one's primary context. Without such opportunities for exchange laypersons will continue to take their stand on a particular issue, the theologian will take another, and the parish priest or bishop will take yet another—each one with varying degrees of personal confidence and technical competence. Without such structures for collaboration, the university scholar can become indifferent to the Church, the Church leader can become skeptical about secular scholarship,[41] and the people in the pews may feel forced to further "privatize" their religious convictions since they may not agree with either of the other two. The result, of course, is that communities of meaning which may in *fact* be complementary and pointing toward a common meaning, in *practice* become more fragmented.

If there are a few, however, who are willing and able to enter such bridge-building efforts, then a host of religious issues could be addressed with a wealth of resources, lived experiences, scholarly findings, and a vital tradition. In such an exchange implicit, irreducible starting points would be made explicit. This would make seemingly irreconcilable differences more comprehensible. Diverse foundations or interpretations of common foundations would be surfaced, shared, and dicussed. Because of a unique level of involvement that comes about only when people are present to one another, rather than simply reading another's ideas, some particular differences would become less significant. Others would loom large and invite serious and honest examination.

It is the goal of "the wisdom community" to support, sustain, and facilitate just such examination, recognition, and perhaps eventual reconciliation. In the concluding chapters we will elaborate upon the metaphor "wisdom community" that has been mentioned throughout these pages. And we will fill out the program that the image invites.

NOTES

1. *The Documents of Vatican II*, Walter M. Abbott, S.J., general editor (New York: The American Press, 1966), "Lumen Gentium," paragraph 25, pp. 47–48. I am not examining the related but separable question of papal infallibility. Some key references are: The Sacred Congregation for the Doctrine of the Faith's "Declaration in Defense of the Catholic Doctrine on the Church against Certain Errors of the Present Day (*Mysterium Ecclesiae*)" (Washington: USCC 1973); *Infallibility in the Church: An Anglican-Catholic Dialogue* (London: Darton, Longman and Todd Ltd., 1968); Peter Chirico, *Infallibility: The Crossroads of Doctrine* (Kansas City: Sheed Andrews & McMeel, Inc., 1977). Hans Küng, *Infallible? An Inquiry* (Garden City, N.Y.: Doubleday and Co., Inc., 1971); *The Infallibility Debate*, edited by John J. Kirvan (New York; Paulist Press, 1971); Samuel D. Femiano, *Infallibility of the Laity: The Legacy of Newman* (New York: Herder and Herder, 1967).

2. Quoted by George A. Kelly, "Uncertain Church: The New Catholic Problem," op.cit., p. 22.

3. I am quoting the summary given by Archbishop John Quinn, "The Magisterium and the Field of Theology," *Origins*, Nov. 17, 1977, Vol. 7, N. 22, p. 343.

4. See Dulles, *The Resilient Church*, op. cit., pp. 95, 104. For this brief sketch of the historical developments I am following Chapter 5, "Doctrinal Authority for a Pilgrim Church."

5. For a discussion on apostolic succession, see Raymond Brown, "Are the Bishops the Successors of the Apostles?" Chapter 2, in *Priest and Bishop: Biblical Reflections* (New York: Paulist Press, 1970); and Lawrence Cardinal Shehan, "Apostles and Bishops: Still Another Point of View," *Homiletic and Pastoral Review*, January 1976, pp. 8–23.

6. This is especially true in medical moral issues which are immensely complex. The United States Bishops in 1971 issued a set of *Ethical Directives for Catholic Health Facilities* that put so much responsibility upon the local

bishop that it could be interpreted to suggest that a bishop can resolve such issues by the charism of his office. See John Dedek, *Contemporary Medical Ethics* (New York: Sheed and Ward, 1975), p. 208. It should be noted that, in many cases, theologians do participate in the drafting of such documents as the *Ethical Directives*. This raises an issue. Perhaps the question is not "Why do bishops not consult theologians?" but rather, "How are the theologians who *are* consulted selected?" What spectrum of the theological community do they represent?

7. As Dulles observes: "It may be sufficient . . . to note that certain official statements seem to evade in a calculated way the findings of modern scholarship. They are drawn up without broad consultation with the theological community. Indeed, a few carefully selected theologians are asked to defend a pre-established position, making use of whatever support they can glean from the scholarly publications." "The Theologian and the Magisterium," *Catholic Mind*, February 1977, p. 9. See also T. Howland Sanks, *Authority in the Church: A Study in Changing Paradigms*, A. A. R. Dissertation Series No. 2 (Missoula, Mont.: Scholars' Press, 1974).

8. See Rahner's exchange with Joseph Cardinal Höffner in *The Month*, April 1971, "Documentation: Cardinal vs. Theologian," p. 106, and Dulles, "The Theologian and the Magisterium," p. 10.

9. See Richard A. McCormick, "Conscience, Theologians and the Magisterium," *New Catholic World*, Nov./Dec. 1977, pp. 268–71, and idem, "The Teaching Magisterium and Theologians," *Proceedings of the Catholic Theological Society of America*, 1969, Vol. 24, pp. 239–254.

10. See Dulles, *The Resilient Church*, pp. 110–112, for helpful suggestions that would overcome some of the negative consequences of dissent. For a careful study of dissent in relationship to a specific teaching, see Karl Rahner, "On the Encyclical *Humanae Vitae*," *Theological Investigations*, Vol. 11, Confrontations (New York: The Seabury Press, 1974), pp. 265–287.

11. See Quinn, op. cit., p. 342, and idem, "The Magisterium and Theology," *Proceedings CTSA*, 1969, Vol. 24, pp. 255–261. Bishops are not alone in their concern in this regard. See, for example, Francis E. King, "Avery Dulles on the Magisterium," *Homiletic and Pastoral Review*, October 1977, pp. 9–17.

12. Quinn, op. cit., pp. 341–342.

13. See John Connelly, "The Task of Theology," *Proceedings of the Catholic Theological Society of America*, 1974, Vol. 29, p. 27. This article provides an excellent overview of the classical Catholic understanding of theology as a Church-related discipline that can be performed only by one who is an explicit Christian believer (dogmatic mediation). The two responses in the same volume by Schubert Ogden (pp. 59–66) and David Tracy (pp. 67–75) provide incisive criticism from the point of view of university theologians and argue that in principle, at least, the theologian need not profess explicit Christian belief (critical mediation).

14. John Cardinal Wright, *The Church: Hope of the World*, Donald Wuerl,

editor (Kenosha, Wis.: PROW Books, 1972), pp. 43, 45, cited in the above-mentioned Connelly article, p. 17.

14a. See Dulles, *The Resilient Church*, pp. 108–109.

15. I have deliberately chosen an example that is not in the center of contemporary controversy so as to more easily illustrate some of the prudential judgments that are operative. The general responses indicated are not intended to be a set form but rather an indication of why prudence must be placed at the heart of the episcopal charism. This by no means exhausts the virtues that must be operative in such discernment. It is difficult to see how these or similar activities are not present when pastoral decisions are made concerning disputed theological questions. The question of angels is not an altogether neutral one. See Edouard Dhanis, S.J., and Jan Visser, C.SS.R., "The Supplement to a New Catechism," *A New Catechism* (New York: Herder and Herder, 1970), p. 517; and Rob Van der Hart, *The Theology of Angels and Devils* (Notre Dame, Ind.: Fides Publishers, 1971).

16. The significance, strengths, and weaknesses of dogmatic discourse in the Church are examined in Avery Dulles, *The Survival of Dogma* (Garden City, N.Y.: Doubleday, 1971), and Gerald O'Collins, *The Case against Dogma* (New York: Paulist Press, 1975).

17. What we say of certitude concerning theological assertions about the human condition are *a fortiori* the case when we speak of God. Classical theism proclaims that God is unchanging by virtue of his perfection. Some contemporary theologians influenced by Blondel, Whitehead, Teilhard, and various biblical scholars suggest that it is precisely because of his perfection that real change must be attributed to God. See *Process Theology*, edited by Ewert Cousins (New York: Paulist Press, 1971); Eugene Fontinell, "Religious Truth in a Relational and Processive World View," *Cross Currents*, Summer 1967, pp. 283–315; Tracy, *Blessed Rage for Order*, op. cit. "The Meaning, Meaningfulness and Truth of God Language," pp. 172–203. The theologian may argue that a process understanding of God is more coherent in the present context. The magisterium may counter that the classical understanding of God would seem more compatible with its teaching. But can it be said that either is providing certitude on how God is God?

18. A number of essays by Karl Rahner are instructive on the "ethos of truth" in religious discourse in relation to its symbolic nature. Cf. "What Is a Dogmatic Statement?" and "What Is Heresy?" *Theological Investigations*, Vol. 5 (Baltimore: Helicon Press, 1966), pp. 42–66; 468–512; "The Development of Dogma," *Theological Investigations*, Vol. 1 (Baltimore: Helicon Press, 1965), pp. 39–78; "Considerations on the Development of Dogma," "The Concept of Mystery in Catholic Theology," and "The Theology of Symbol," *Theological Investigations*, Vol. 4 (Baltimore: Helicon Press, 1966), pp. 3–35; 36–76; 221–252.

19. From the now no longer used preface of the Trinity. "Holy Father, almighty and eternal God: for with your only-begotten Son and the Holy Spirit, you are one God, one Lord. Not in the unity of a single person, but in the

Trinity of one substance. For what we believe of your glory, through your revelation, that we also believe of your Son and of the Holy Spirit, without difference or distinction. So that in confessing the true and eternal Godhead, we adore the distinction of persons, oneness in being, and equality in majesty."

20. For a brilliant and readable attempt to rescue trinitarian theology from obscurantism and picture thinking that suggests that any one of the "persons" in God "could have become human," see Karl Rahner, *The Trinity* (New York: Herder and Herder, 1970).

21. For a complete study of the biblical Christological titles, see Oscar Cullmann, *The Christology of the New Testament* (revised edition), translated by Shirley C. Guthrie and Charles A. M. Hall (Philadelphia: The Westminister Press, 1963).

22. See J. Peter Schineller, S.J., *Christ and Church: A Spectrum of Views*, *Theological Studies*, Vol. 36, No. 4, December 1976, pp. 545–566. This is a most helpful article. It would be a useful point of departure in a wisdom community discussion of one's operative Christology. Note especially the analysis of Christ as exclusive, constitutive, normative, or one of many mediators of salvation. This article has been used in many continuing education sessions with priests, sisters, and laypeople to facilitate their self-location and self-understanding.

23. Perhaps the most important of the earlier works was D. F. Strauss, *The Life of Jesus Critically Examined* (London: S.C.M. Press, 1973) (first published in 1835).

24. Pope Pius XII, *Divino Afflante Spiritu* (Washington: National Catholic Welfare Conference, 1943).

25. This collaboration has borne fruit in such important ecumenical projects as The Anchor Bible translation and commentaries.

26. See Reginald Fuller, *The Foundations of New Testament Christology* (New York: Charles Scribner's Sons, 1965).

27. The work of Rudolf Bultmann was most influential in this area. See *Kerygma and Myth*, edited by H. W. Bartsch, translated by R. H. Fuller (London: S.P.C.K., 1953); *Theology of the New Testament*, 2 vols. (London: S.C.M. Press, 1952). See also Karl Jaspers' fascinating debate with Bultmann, *Myth and Christianity: An Inquiry into the Possibility of Religion without Myth*, translated by Norbert Guterman (New York: The Noonday Press, 1971).

28. See Raymond E. Brown, *The Virginal Conception and Bodily Resurrection of Jesus* (New York: Paulist Press, 1973), Chapter 2, "The Problem of the Bodily Resurrection of Jesus." See also the articles under "Resurrection" by Karl Rahner, Joseph Schmitt, and Werner Bulst in *Sacramentum Mundi: An Encyclopedia of Theology*, Vol. 5, pp. 323–333, edited by Karl Rahner et al. (New York: Herder and Herder, 1970). In lecturing on Christology I find that audiences continue to be surprised when asked to point out the actual account of the resurrection in the gospel. What they find, of course, is a clear proclamation that "He is risen!" but no description of the resurrection itself. Many then realize that they have extrapolated their "image" of the resurrec-

tion from the account of the resurrection of Lazarus (John 11: 1–45) or more likely from nineteenth-century devotional paintings.

29. See Norman Perrin, *Rediscovering the Teaching of Jesus* (New York: Harper and Row, 1967).

30. See Ernst Käsemann, *The Testament of Jesus According to John 17*, translated by Gerhard Krodel (Philadelphia: Fortress Press, 1968).

31. See Karl Rahner, "Current Problems in Christology," *Theological Investigations*, Vol. 1, op. cit., pp. 149–200.

32. From the viewpoint of dogmatic mediation, one of the frequent criticisms of Küng's *On Being a Christian* is that his "low Christology" stops short of affirming the divinity of Jesus at least as it has been traditionally understood. Piet Schoonenberg also starts with a "low Christology" in his efforts to re-interpret the Calcedonian doctrine of one person and two natures in Christ. See *The Christ*, translated by Della Couling (London: Sheed and Ward, 1969). While past theological works and liturgical expressions may have all but ignored the full meaning of the humanity of Jesus, questions concerning his divinity spark volatile dicussion in all sectors of the Church. See Avery Dulles, *The Resilient Church*, pp. 78–79, where he suggests that David Tracy's provocative metaphor "supreme fiction" disastrously weakens the Christian message. For Tracy's position, see *Blessed Rage for Order*, "Christological Language as Representative Limit-Language," pp. 218–236; *The Myth of God Incarnate*, edited by John Hick (Philadelphia: The Wesminister Press, 1977); *The Truth of God Incarnate*, edited by Michael Green (Grand Rapids, Mi.: The William B. Eerdmans Publishing Co., 1977). Even the popular media are aware of the problem. See *Time*, February 27, 1978, pp. 49–54, "New Debate over Jesus' Divinity."

33. See Pierre Teilhard de Chardin, *Christianity and Evolution*, translated by Rene Hague (New York: Harcourt Brace Jovanovich, Inc., 1971); and *The Phenomena of Man* (New York: Harper Torchbooks, 1961).

34. See N. M. Wildiers, "Cosmology and Christology," in *Process Theology*, op. cit., pp. 283–298, and *Process Philosophy and Christian Thought*, edited by Delwin Brown, Ralph S. James, Jr., and Gene Reeves (New York: The Bobbs-Merrill Co., Inc., 1971); John B. Cobb, Jr., *Christ in a Pluralistic Age* (Philadelphia: The Westminster Press, 1975).

35. See John Hick, *God and the Universe of Faith* (London: The Macmillan Press, 1973).

36. See Karl Rahner, *Sacramentum Mundi*, op. cit., Vol. 3, "Incarnation," "Jesus Christ," pp. 111–118; 174–208; *Theological Investigations*, Vol. 4, "On the Theology of the Incarnation," pp. 105–120; Vol. 5, "Christology within an Evolutionary View of the World," "Dogmatic Reflections on the Knowledge and Self-Consciousness of Christ." "Christianity and the non-Christian Religions," pp. 157–192; 192–218; 115–134; Vol. 11, "Christology in the Setting of Modern Man's Understanding of Himself and of His World," pp. 215–229; Vol. 13, "The Quest for Approaches Leading to an Understanding of the Mystery of the God-Man Jesus," "The Two Basic Types of Christology," pp. 195–200, 213–223.

37. Karl Rahner, *Theological Investigations*, Vol. 5, "Exegesis and Dogmatic Theology," pp. 67–96.

38. See Walter Kasper, *Jesus the Christ* (New York: Paulist Press, 1977). Note his treatment of miracles (pp. 88–99) in contrast to that of Küng, *On Being a Christian*, pp. 226–237.

39. Consider, for example, novelist John Updike's statement in his Sermon at Easter:

> Make no mistake: if he rose at all
> it was as his body!
> if the cells; dissolution did not reverse, the molecules
> reknit, the amino acids rekindle,
> the church will fall.

40. See Wolfhart Pannenberg, *Jesus: God and Man* (London: S.C.M. Press, 1973).

41. In a letter to the editor after the above-mentioned *Time* article, Bishop Stanislaus Brzana wrote, "In this age and in ages to come many things will be said about Jesus Christ, but the faithful, united with their shepherds and guided by the Spirit, will continue to believe and profess that Jesus Christ is true God and true man in one divine person, and that he is the Lord who will come again" (*Time*, March 20, 1978, p. 4). This may be a good example of a bishop prudentially recalling a classical formulation as a touchstone or guidepost for religious meaning. The problem, of course, is this. Such reaffirmations of tradition by means of dogmatic mediation are reassuring to those who are well within the tradition. They may not be so helpful for those on the edge of the tradition or for those who raise new questions for which the past has no ready answers. See John Robinson, *The Human Face of God* (London: S.C.M. Press, 1972); Gerald O'Collins, *The Calvary Christ* (Philadelphia: The Westminster Press, 1977); Karl Rahner, *Theological Investigations*, Vol. 3, "The Eternal Significance of the Humanity of Jesus for Our Relationship with God," pp. 35–46.

Chapter Six
The Wisdom Community: I. The Metaphor

Introduction

The wisdom community is both a metaphor and a program. As a metaphor it describes an attitude of mind, a style of thought, that should be helpful to an individual's efforts to understand himself and others at this crucial juncture in the Church. When the attitudes that aid and enhance individual growth in a personal way are made explicit and developed into a structured activity for a group, you have the foundations for the program. The advantage of this "style of thought" is that it enables a person to understand or "read" the story of his religious journey in a new light. Each person comes to a better appreciation of the implications of the fact that he and everyone else are "living documents."

The goal of this process is the uncovering of "zones" of common meaning as well as "zones" where common meaning has broken down. The attitude suggested by the metaphor "wisdom community" is a possible as well as a desirable achievement for many, whereas the program that is implicit in the metaphor is perhaps possible and desirable only for a smaller number. In every case the wisdom community serves as a corrective of the tendency within us all to yield to the flight from understanding that allows us to lose contact with our deepest selves, the interiority of others, and the central issues of difficult theoretical or practical questions.

171

These final two chapters will make explicit the relationship between the material in the first five chapters and the individual in his own personal journey into religious meaning. The attitudes implied by the wisdom community as a metaphor will be elaborated. The structure of the wisdom community as a program will be explained. And finally, some of the pastoral implications will be examined. This chapter then will be in six sections: (1) The Wisdom Community as Metaphor; (2) Living Human Documents; (3) Paulo Freire on Dialogue; (4) Pope Paul VI on Dialogue; (5) Bernard Lonergan on Transcendental Method; (6) Conclusion.

1. The Wisdom Community as Metaphor

The wisdom community as a metaphor suggests a descriptive image of certain internal attitudes and ways of thinking that facilitate growth in understanding oneself as a living document. Furthermore, this attitude or style of thought makes it possible for one to read and understand the stories written in the lives of those committed to very divergent viewpoints. Therefore, a person whose attitude towards others is marked by an appreciation of the Church as a wisdom community is able to really hear what is genuine in the statements of the passionate reader of *The Wanderer* or *The National Catholic Reporter*. For, unlike a certain type of unreflective conservative or unreflective liberal, one who has a sense of the wisdom community grasps a radical unity. For both readers proclaim that Jesus is the sacrament of God, that the Church is the sacrament of Jesus, and that each of them is called to be a sacrament of the Church. Hence, no matter what is disputed (and a great deal is), what is affirmed is more important because it is foundational.

The attitude of heart and the style of thought desired for the wisdom community can be characterized by a certain understanding of human communication or dialogue, and an appreciation of, and a fidelity to, the dictates of authentic human knowing, loving, and doing. To elaborate upon the important attitude of openness to dialogue, we will turn to the thought of Paulo Freire in *Pedagogy of the Oppressed* and Pope Paul VI in his much overlooked first encyclical, *Ecclesiam Suam*. To specify the imperatives that carry forward human knowing, we will look to Bernard Lonergan's *Method in Theology*. First, however, we must turn our attention to the fact that each of us is a living human document and recall key questions from the previous chapters that must now be engaged and answered by each reader.

2. Living Human Documents

The expression, "we learn more from experience than we can ever learn from books," is as common as it is fallacious. Experience alone teaches us very little. It is *reflection* upon experience that is instructive. Books of quality, like films, paintings, and other works of art, are, among other things, the distilled reflections of an author upon his experience. In the serious reading of a book of value or the appreciation of an art work, the attentive person encounters some aspect of the world as it has been interpreted and transformed by the creator of the work. In such an encounter one not only sees a vision of reality through another's eyes, but one also encounters the interior world of the creative artist himself. To some extent, then, the artist becomes a living human document.

Unfortunately, it is possible to go through a great part of our lives vicariously living off of the experiences of other persons whether renowned or insignificant. Meanwhile, our own experiences go unreflected upon, and they remain a random series of events or happenings with no center of unity or point of integration. In this matter, we can tend to view the sequence of our personal experiences as a series of discrete phenomena rather than as a history from which we can learn a great deal about ourselves, our past, and our future. We are inclined to say that this is obvious and that we realize this, but that protest is not always supported by the reflection that is of such great importance.

The first five chapters of this book contain a series of descriptive models and frameworks that suggest a way of looking at the present state of ferment and change in the Catholic Church in America. It is possible to read them and simply agree and disagree with this or that point of their content. But that is not their purpose. Their purpose is to facilitate a process of self-location on the part of the individual reader. For the most part, the earlier chapters have not been intended as a defense of certain positions, but rather, as the laying out of the context of why there are conflicting positions and suggesting some of the broad lines of what these positions might be. Too great an emphasis upon agreement or disagreement with a specific point of content may distract one from the self-discovery that the book seeks to bring about.

As individuals, we have very different horizons and hence very different questions. One's religious questions may be, for the most part, questions of the heart, of the feet, or of the mind. Questions of the heart concern our feelings, affections, and emotions. These embrace our religious sentiments, interior dispositions, and commitments. Questions of the feet concern our involvements, actions, and doing. These embrace our desire to see the commitment to values that we cherish in our hearts bear fruit in our active involvement in the transformation of the individual and of the larger social order. Finally, questions of the mind concern our understandings, interpretations, and theories. These embrace our examination, organization, and evaluation of ideas, speculations, and opinions concerning the foundations of our religious sentiments and actions.

For this reason, one person finds in the story of Jesus an inspiration that challenges him to holiness; another finds an urgent cluster of values that challenges him to active involvement; and a third finds a religious world view that challenges him to overcome his intellectual skepticism. The very fact that *The Wisdom Community* is in book format may suggest that its essential concern is with questions of the mind. But in truth, questions of the heart and feet are equally urgent. The life story that we are each seeking to read is the story of the whole person: heart, feet, and mind.

Every reader should have some relationship to the interpretative schemes and descriptive models developed in the earlier chapters of this book. That relationship may be profound or superficial, explicit or implicit, reflected upon or ignored, comprehended or confounding, sympathetic or opposing. Still, as a living document, each reader, whether bishop, layperson, religious, parish priest, or theologian, should find that his or her religious life story touches and is touched by these basic realities.

Chapter One explored the decline of common meaning. At the foundation of religion there is a paradigmatic "event" or "experience" that is disclosive or revelatory of "the sacred." The meaning of this experience is preserved and prolonged in community by means of signs, symbols, narratives, rituals, sacred texts, norms, and rules for community order, and theoretical reflections upon religious meaning that take the form of more or less sophisticated theology. With the shift from a classical to a modern notion of culture there emerged a pluralism so acute that for many people a once secure and familiar religious framework in which their parents lived and died began to give way, resulting in the decline of common meaning. Diverse and seemingly incompatible views emerged in every quarter of the Church on almost every conceivable topic. In the face of this, various forms of alienation and estrangement emerged.

This was manifest in various forms of doubt. Operational doubt is apparent when there is a notable change in performance, such as a diminishing participation in Sunday Eucharist. Ideological doubt is apparent when practices which were once accepted require defense, or new ones are hastily embraced. Ethical doubt is apparent when individuals feel that they have been hurt, let down, or even deceived by those whom they trusted as having similar commitments. Intellectual doubt is apparent when members of a religious tradition feel forced to reconsider the meaning, meaningfulness, and truth of their tradition. Absolute doubt is manifest in apathetic withdrawal of the individual from the community. One may respond to this situation in many ways, as a conservative, rehabilitator, revolutionary, or reactionary.

You must now review Chapter One, reflecting upon the material and your own life so as to surface the broad lines of your personal story. Minimally, this process will include a scrutiny of the various mediators of religious meaning in your life. Do religious symbols, rituals, and stories serve as the core of your religious self-concept, or is that core formed around norms and rules or theoretical theology? What specifically are the elements of this personal "core"? What have been your personal experiences and observations independent of religion that underscore the shift from classical to modern culture?

Is the decline of common meaning real for you or is it an overstatement? Do you view it essentially as a positive or a negative development? How has this development and your reaction to it affected your relationship with your peers? those older than yourself? your children? If you are a university student, a seminarian, or in your twenties, your only memories may be those of a changing, developing Church. How well do you listen to and understand those who are older? Where in your life or in the life of your friends or colleagues have there been instances of operational, ideological, ethical, intellectual, and absolute doubt as well as responses that may be termed conservative, rehabilitative, revolutionary, or reactionary? If you have judged the entire account in Chapter One to be inaccurate, still something has happened. What would be your account of what has happened? One way or another, the position advanced in Chapter One should provide a framework for the start of an articulate grasp and understanding of your religious self-concept.

Chapters Two and Three explored the turn to interiority. In the wake of staggering change in the world of religious meaning, there are many possible responses. One person may cling to past devotions and expressions of belief and find genuine comfort in this continuity. Another may attempt to do this, but gradually find the earlier practices somewhat hollow. Many others may begin to participate in support groups or prayer groups of various kinds which serve to ground anew the foundations of religious meaning in a self-authenticating manner. Whether long-term or short-term in their effects, such activities clearly serve to refocus the interior religious world for many who experienced a painful disorientation.

More systematically, the turn to interiority recognizes the primacy of the questions in many people's lives that may signal an awareness of, or openness to, the divine. To locate the horizon of the questions of ultimate meaning, Chapter Two examined the compenetrating patterns of human experience. In the biological pattern we encounter the vast potential and painful limits of our enfleshed condition. In the psychological pattern we encounter the great range of effects, feelings, moods, passions, images, symbols, dreams, and fantasies that constitute the complex network of our personal, internal communication systems. In the aesthetic pattern we encounter color, form, and tone when we are caught up in the elemental sweep of wonder in the face of beauty in the natural world or in the arts. In the social pattern we encounter the other now as the "it" to be used, the "you" to be acknowledged, and the "thou" to be cherished as the beloved, and paradoxically we also encounter the existential void deep within our soul space. In the dramatic pattern, we encounter significant "stories" that have the power to illuminate our individual and collective lives as meaningful and of value or to underscore them as tales told by an idiot. In the mystical pattern we encounter the wholeness and holiness of reality through infrequent experiences of "ecstasy" that disclose what is ordinarily not seen or seen only "through a glass darkly." In the intellectual pattern we encounter the advance of our understanding and its inability to satisfy our appetite to know ever more.

Amid this complex of human experience there is the possibility of self-transcendence or conversion which can utterly change our horizon. Chapter Three examined conversion. Religious conversion, marked by a sense of awe and mystery, is an affirmation that existence is not random but gracious and meaningful. Theistic conversion is the affirmation that the foundational ground of graciousness and meaning is the reality intended by the word "God." Christian conversion is the experience of Jesus as the Christ of God. Ecclesial conversion is the turn to community, a sense of peoplehood, history, and tradition. Moral conversion is the struggle for self-consistency between the values one affirms and the deeds one incarnates. Intellectual conversion is the liberation of mind that recognizes that in spite of the permanence of mystery, the limits of language, and the historicity of the human race truth is one and at least partially attainable.

Finally, generic faith in God, Jesus, and the Christian community must be distinguished from particular beliefs concerning how God is God, how Jesus is the Christ of God, and how the Church is the body of Christ. In light of the above, it was possible to distinguish a hard apologetic which stresses obedience and authority from a soft apologetic which stresses experience and authenticity.

Again, you must now review Chapters Two and Three, reflecting upon the material and your own life so as to bring to consciousness your personal history. Minimally, this process will include a careful scrutiny of your own interior world, your spiritual or devotional life. How have you been affected by recent momentous changes in the Church? Do you experience yourself as more or less a part of a community? What modes of prayer have been abandoned and what new ones have been embraced? Have your judgments been harsh, sympathetic, or indifferent as "novel" forms of religious expression appeared? How attentive are you to the multiple patterns of human experience and the questions of meaning they raise and the dimensions of meaning they disclose? Do you advert to one pattern of experience in your life, such as the social patter, with regularity, while remaining indifferent to another, such as the psychological? Are all six modes of conversion truly operative in your life? How are they interrelated? Which ones have priority? How do you deal with conflict or tension between them? How would you go about intensifying one of the patterns of experience or modes of conversion in your life? Are you more comfortable with generic faith or specific belief? Do you lean toward a hard or a soft apologetic?

Chapters Four and Five explored the question of theological method and three distinct modes of mediation that are at play when one moves from the disputed questions of dialectics to the relatively secure horizons of foundations. The eight functional specialities of research, interpretation, history, dialectic, foundations, doctrine, systematics, and communication are relevant to each of us whether we are engaged in scholarship or not.

Each one of us moves through an abbreviated, non-technical version of the specializations in commonsense routine conversations and exchanges concerning religion or any other topic. For example, a woman at a party enters a discussion of the difficult question of women and ministry. She is convinced that women should not be priests for what she considers to be theological reasons (foundations). That conviction has crystalized after heated discussion with others (dialectics). Her convictions, as well as those of the ones who differ with her, developed and took different turns over a period of time (history).

The woman's position is a combination of feelings, information, opinions, teachings, convictions, and beliefs, all of which can only be understood by means of reflection and analysis (interpretation). In order to get in touch with every significant factor to be interpreted, the woman would have to surface all of her sources of input on the issue in point (research). Over and above her convictions, the woman in question has specific beliefs about women, ministry, magisterium, and the like (doctrines). After the heated discussion she thinks more about the questions and tries to see the compatibility of her belief with her other convictions concerning the Equal Rights Amendment, married priests, the nature of the Church (systematics). As a result of this thinking process she gains a clearer grasp of her position and is more confident that she will be understood and agreed with in future conversations (communications). Obviously, the activities of those defending women in ministry also fit into the eight "specialities."

In spelling out the "new key" of theology, we elaborated three modes of mediation. Critical mediation, or university theology, tends to bracket or suspend explicit beliefs and focus upon the authority and truth-finding powers of its scientific methodology as its irreducible starting point. While it may employ some of the skills of critical mediation, dogmatic mediation, or Church theology, focuses upon the authority and truth-bearing power of a privileged religious tradition as its irreducible starting point. Existential mediation, or *praxis* theology, is anxious to relate the visions of religion to concrete socio-cultural situations. For this reason, the authentic engagement of the theologian in the process of liberation functions as the irreducible starting point, rather than critical method or a specific ecclesial tradition. Existential mediation also embraces the individual working out a personal synthesis amid the currents of diversity and change. This whole discussion raises the questions of teaching authority, office, and certitude.

You must now review Chapters Four and Five reflecting upon the material and your own life so as to gain an overview of your personal thinking and development. Minimally, this process will include a careful scrutiny of your core religious convictions and the manner in which they are formulated. This would necessitate an evaluation of your relationship to the eight functional specialities with regard to religion and theology. Is your primary approach to religion essentially technical or commonsensical? In religious and theological matters, do you tend to favor critical, dogmatic, or existential mediation? Why is one more worthy of trust to you than another? Do you find that the achievements of one mode of mediation support or undermine the achievements of another? So long as most theologians are not bishops and most bishops are not theologians, do you see any solution to the seeming conflicts that are emerging between some members of the theological community and some members of the hierarchy? Or is this a natural tension? What is the relevance of the question of religious certitude for you? In what sense are your religious beliefs certain? In what way would you distinguish religious meaning from religious truth?

The aim of the self-analysis intended by these questions is to facilitate a process by which you may become aware of the realities that are deepest within yourself. In this way you can bring to the level of articulate consciousness your actual *operative* horizons and the specific convictions, beliefs, and uncertainties that fill out those horizons. In order to accomplish this, each person has to reactivate a practice that was common in childhood. Namely, you must talk to yourself—*really* talk to yourself. Concern for the opinion of others may be the reason why we do not always risk speaking honestly to others. But why do we fear speaking honestly to ourselves? Unwillingness to come to terms with ourselves and what we actually think, believe, and do in contrast with what we think we are supposed to believe or do, because of our office or function or because of common opinion, is a most dangerous form of the flight from understanding. Clearly, we must meet ourselves in naked knowing before we can share any of the major truths of our interiority with others in a wisdom community.

As you learn to read yourself as a living human document, you must do more than come to terms with your convictions, ideologies, and theories. You must read your actions and your abstaining from action as well. You must examine your non-committal silence on one issue and your outspoken activism on another. Such a thorough self-scrutiny can be accomplished only by an attitude of self-monitoring that will heighten your awareness of yourself and your responses that you often take for granted. As a result, you can gain a glimpse, as it were, of yourself in action. You can gain an overview of your irreducible starting points.

In this manner you can begin to see the sequence of your personal development, your spiritual pilgrimage, the influence of a seemingly insignificant past experience, a pivotal book, a certain teacher, a timely retreat, a cluster of emotions, a once cogent argument, or the inspiring example of a certain parishioner, sister, brother, bishop, or priest. No doubt, you will discover that in spite of important areas of continuity your journey has been marked by much change. Where you were once unbending, you have been mellowed by experience. Where you were once open to many possibilities, you have now taken a firm stand. Just as you moved from earlier positions to your present stance by a complex interaction with many others, so too you are likely to move again toward an as yet unknown horizon.

3. Paulo Freire on Dialogue

In the view of many, "dialogue" is a holdover word from the sixties. During that time some people thought that if you put a group of Protestants and Catholics or black and white people in a room together and brought in a facilitator, you could bring about instant intimacy between the participants, and then centuries-old barriers would be broken down by the coffee-break time. Dialogue need not be idle chatter or the artificial and unprepared-for revelation of one's interiority to strangers. Clearly this is not what is meant by the term when it is employed by Paulo Freire or the Roman Pontiff.

In *Pedagogy of the Oppressed* Freire proposed an enabling activity which he terms *"conscientização."* This "conscientization" is the achievement of critical consciousness that allows individuals to perceive social, political, and economic contradictions. This heightened consciousness is enabling and liberating because it allows individuals to see social and political realities with a new honesty. And it moves them to take action against oppressive elements in the social context.

The socially and economically oppressed are not the only people who would benefit from *conscientização*. In a manner that is less traumatic, but no less real, priests, sisters, brothers, bishops, theologians, and laypeople can each be "oppressed" by narrow horizons and parochialism. As a result, some members of each group tend to affirm their particular identity and authenticity while questioning or even undermining that of others. But in each of these divergent groups we have instances of conscientization. So the priests of a diocese may come to recognize the good faith of the bishop in spite of their many disputes with him. Meanwhile, the bishop may recognize that his distrust of his seminary faculty is inordinate and try to renew channels of communication.

In each case there is a new freedom, a new risk taking, and a new effort to overcome once accepted tensions. The sensitivities and sensibilities of those who allow themselves to be liberated from their oppression and desire to oppress are such that they are able to participate in dialogue. Freire argues that people exist *humanly* when they engage in naming or transforming the world. No one can speak another's word for them. Nor can anyone say a completely true word in isolation. Dialogue is the way by which people name the world and make it their own. Dialogue is not possible between those who would deny others their right to speak their word and those whose right to speak has been denied them. Freire considers this mode of transformative dialogue to be essential if individuals are to attain their true significance as human beings. In his own words:

> And since dialogue is the encounter in which the united reflection and action of the dialoguers are addressed to the world which is to be transformed and humanized, this dialogue cannot be reduced to the act of one person's "depositing" ideas in another, nor can it be a simple exchange of ideas to be "consumed" by the discussants. Nor yet is it a hostile, polemical argument between men who are committed neither to the naming of the world, nor to the search for truth, but rather to the imposition of their own truth. Because dialogue is an encounter among men who name the world, it must not be a situation where some men name on behalf of others. It is an act of creation; it must not serve as a crafty instrument for the domination of one man by another.[1]

The attitude of one who enters into dialogue as Freire defines it must be marked by a love for the world and humankind and by humility. Each participant must have faith in the birthright of all people to create, re-create, and be more fully human. Mutual trust, hope, and critical thinking are also required.

One who is capable of dialogue is loving when he neither dominates nor allows himself to be dominated. Such love is courageous and not sentimental. It is an act of freedom that commits one person to another. Dialogue requires more than a loving regard for the other. It requires humility. For the link between the two speakers is severed if one person sees the other as of a lower rank or as ignorant with no real contribution to make. Total self-sufficiency is incompatible with dialogue. Such a person presupposes that they have nothing to gain; hence they never genuinely enter into the dialogue.

An *a priori* requirement for dialogue is a basic faith in other people. This faith in the genuineness of others is not naive. For it is obvious that the same power that we each have to create, transform, and communicate may be used in a negative way in a concrete situation. But this knowledge is a challenge to all who would seek honest communication. The only way to meet this challenge is by acknowledging impediments to communication and working to overcome them.

If those who are seeking to communicate are marked by a vigilant effort to be loving, humble, and faithful, a climate of mutual trust should be born and hypocrisy will have no place. Where conflicts exist, full trust cannot be established prior to dialogue. It is the interchange between differing parties in a humble, caring, faithful manner that actually creates the trust that is hoped for at the outset.

Hope flows from the very nature of dialogue. As was seen in the study of the patterns of experience, all people experience a certain incompleteness and continue to search for meaning. Ultimately, this search cannot be carried out alone. Meaning is found and recognized in communion with others. For this reason, people of good faith can approach the most severe differences with the real hope that areas of mutual agreement will be found. Hopelessness is the sure way to turn dialogue into empty, tedious, *pro forma* routine for the sake of appearance with no sincere expectation of progress.

Critical thinking advances dialogue because it constantly requires that each person immerse himself in the particular situation where he is in spite of the risk that may be involved. This is not a blind immersion. Critical thinking does not seek to accommodate all differences into an artificial stability even when serious differences remain. If critical thinking is absent, it is very possible for individuals to naively stand firm on their position expecting others to concede that all of the difficulties rest with themselves and not with both sides.[2]

4. *Pope Paul VI on Dialogue*

In *Ecclesiam Suam* Pope Paul VI writes at length of the dialogue in which he wishes to participate with the world, with all who acknowledge God, with Christians, and with members of the Catholic Church. Clearly, the concern of the Pope was for an open style that would characterize his pontificate. Fifteen years have passed since he published the encyclical and yet his very specific account of what he means by dialogue complements the points already enunciated from Freire, and further elaborates the attitudes that are necessary if one is to benefit from the wisdom community.

Reflecting upon his ministry and the dialogue of salvation in a general way, Pope Paul states that this mission cannot be accomplished by force. In order to communicate his teaching, he wishes to employ the means of human education, interior persuasion, and ordinary conversation, always respecting the rights and freedom of others. Dialogue must be free of *a priori* condemnations of those with whom we differ. There is nothing gained either by empty and time-worn polemics.[3] Furthermore, dialogue should not cling to hard and fast forms that no longer have the power to address or move people. Since true communication is desired, participants in dialogue must seek to overcome unintelligible terminology and enter into the mind-set of each other if they hope to be listened to and understood.[4] Pope Paul stresses that if dialogue is truly authentic, participants will be willing to listen to others *before* they themselves speak. And this listening is not simply to another's voice, words, and ideas, but to his heart so that he may truly be understood.

In paragraphs 81–83 the Pontiff elaborates the specific characteristics of dialogue:

> Clearness above all; the dialogue supposes and demands comprehensibility. It is an outpouring of thought; it is an invitation to the exercise of the highest powers which man possesses. This very claim would be enough to classify the dialogue among the best manifestations of human activity and culture. This fundamental requirement is enough to enlist our apostolic care to review every angle of our language to guarantee that it be understandable, acceptable, and well chosen.
>
> A second characteristic of the dialogue is meekness, the virtue which Christ sets before us to be learned from Him: "Learn from me, because I am meek and humble of heart." The dialogue is not proud, it is not bitter, it is not offensive. Its authority is intrinsic to the truth it explains, to the charity it communicates, to the example it proposes, it is not a command, it is not an imposition, it is peaceful: it avoids violent methods, it is patient; it is generous.
>
> Trust, not only in the power of one's words, but also in an attitude of welcoming the trust of the interlocutor. Trust promotes confidence and friendship. It binds hearts in mutual adherence to the good which excludes all self-seeking.
>
> Finally, pedagogical prudence, which esteems highly the psychological and moral circumstances of the listener, whether he be a child, uneducated, unprepared, diffident, hostile. Prudence strives to learn the sensitivities of the hearer and requires that we adapt ourselves and the manner of our presentation in a reasonable way lest we be displeasing and incomprehensible to him. In a dialogue conducted in this manner, the union of truth and charity, of understanding and love is achieved.
>
> In the dialogue one discovers how different are the ways which lead to the light of faith, and how it is possible to make them converge on the same goal. Even if these ways are divergent, they can

become complementary by forcing our reasoning process out of the
worn paths and by obliging it to deepen its research, to find fresh
expressions.

The dialectic of this exercise of thought and patience will make
us discover elements of truth also in the opinions of others, it will
force us to express our teaching with great fairness, and it will reward us for the work of having explained it in accordance with the
objections of another or despite his slow assimilation of our teaching. The dialogue will make us wise.[5]

The primary intent of Pope Paul's reflection upon dialogue was
to indicate the style and tone that he wanted to be manifest in the
Church's contemporary dialogue with Christians of other traditions
and more importantly with those who are not Christians at all. However, at the present juncture the degree of estrangement and alienation that exists among some of those who are *within* the Church is
such that the attitudes of dialogue suggested by the Pope and Freire
are precisely those that must be self-consciously cultivated by priests,
bishops, nuns, brothers, laity, and theologians if there is to be any advance over the gulfs that presently separate many from a common
conversation.

5. Bernard Lonergan on Transcendental Method

A crucial attitude that must be present in the dialogue of a wisdom community is a process of self-monitoring that is obliquely re-
ferred to in Freire's call for "critical thinking" and the papal exhortation that we force our reasoning process out of worn paths,
deepen our investigation, and find fresh expressions. Bernard Lonergan has spelled out the critical dynamics of effective self-monitoring
by calling our attention to the almost obvious fact that we all have experiences, seek to understand those experiences, make judgments
about our understandings, and commit ourselves to act in accord with
those judgments. These recurrent processes are termed "self-transcendence." This self-transcendence is no more and no less than the
activities by which we daily encounter the world as a whole, ask questions about the network of realities we encounter, judge their worth
or value, and manifest our judgments in our deeds and actions.

Every person performs operations that can be termed "empirical,
intellectual, rational, and responsible." Self-monitoring makes it possible for us to become aware of these operations, their interconnec-
tedness, and the implications they have for understanding and
resolving the disputes that at times turn what should be the collabora-

tion of different members of the Church family into the raised voices of a quarrel or the silent rejection of condemning judgment. Lonergan describes the four successive, related, but qualitatively different levels of conscience in this way:

> There is the *empirical* level on which we sense, perceive, imagine, feel, speak, move. There is an *intellectual* level on which we inquire, come to understand, express what we have understood, work out the presuppositions and implications of our expression. There is the *rational* level on which we reflect, marshal the evidence, pass judgment on the truth or falsity, certainty or probability, of a statement. There is the *responsible* level on which we are concerned with ourselves, our own operations, our goals, and so we deliberate about possible courses of action, evaluate them, decide and carry out our decisions.[6]

In other words, the experiences we have nudge us to ask questions about the meaning of those experiences. But our understandings can be just bright ideas or incorrect opinions borrowed from another person or context. This is why rational reflection seeks to evaluate and judge that what is so, is so; and what is not, is not. In many cases, judgments of fact and value demand some mode of response on our part that compels responsible involvement. Each person can validate this description as the objectification of their personal experience by reflection upon their actions prior to taking up this book, or better, by attending to themselves and their conscious activities after they put these pages aside.

These fourfold dynamics are brought to consciousness by a shift of focus that makes it possible to attend to the activity of knowing rather than the object known. As Lonergan puts it, it becomes the fourfold matter of: (1) experiencing one's experiencing, understanding, judging, and deciding; (2) understanding the unity and relations of one's experienced experiencing, understanding, judging, deciding; (3) affirming the reality of one's experienced and understood experience, understanding, judging, and deciding; (4) deciding to operate in accord with the norms immanent in the spontaneous relatedness of one's experienced, understood, affirmed experiencing, understanding, judging, and deciding.[7]

The fruit of such a shift of focus is that it becomes possible to express in words what Lonergan terms "transcendental imperatives" that are the very structure and dynamism of human consciousness. These transcendental precepts are: Be attentive. Be intelligent. Be reasonable. Be responsible. In order to be faithful to these seemingly simple precepts one must ponder and make one's own the difference between attention and inattention, intelligence and stupidity, reasonableness and unreasonableness, responsibility and irresponsibility.

Fidelity to these imperatives involves a person in an ongoing, never-ending, self-correcting process of learning. No one is content with the mass of experiences that are theirs as living human documents. For this reason intelligence prompts us to inquire beyond the empirical data of experience to ask what the experience might mean. How and why and what for? But we are not content here. Reasonableness takes us beyond the answers of intelligence and demands that we decide whether the answers are true or false. What, as a matter of fact, is the case? Nor is this all. For human dynamism does not cease with detached judgments of fact. Responsibility and involvement demand that we distinguish the truly good from the apparently good and take our stand on judgments of value and commitment. Throughout the advances and regressions in our knowing, loving, and doing, the successive and recurrent advertence to the transcendental precepts provides a constant pattern.

Awareness of these patterns is a particular asset to the wisdom community. They provide a clear framework for interpreting the dynamics by which an individual as well as others come to what they consider their irreducible starting points. More importantly, it also equips one to evaluate that stance in order to assess what may be premature conclusions, insufficiently nuanced or undifferentiated positions. Once one has appropriated the implications of the transcendental precepts, it is possible to appreciate and understand more sympathetically not only the positions that are opposed to one's own, but also, and more importantly, the individual persons who hold such positions and how and why they could have come to their conflicting point of view in good faith.

6. Conclusion

The breakdown in common meaning between the people in the pews, the parish priests, the university theologians, and the bishops takes a great deal of its impetus precisely from the fact that more and more, these groups no longer have the same shared base experience of religious, theistic, Christian, ecclesial, moral, and intellectual conversion. Nor do they have the same understanding of those conversions, or make the same judgments in their regard. It goes without saying, then, that they will not make the same commitments, and common meaning cannot be maintained.

A particular bishop and a particular theologian, however, could enter in good faith the kind of dialogue we have been describing. They could do so by striving to embody the attitudes called for by Paulo Freire and Pope Paul, exploring their separate journeys as living human documents, trying to remain faithful to the transcendental precepts and uncovering the significant areas where experience, understanding, judgment, and commitment are no longer shared. They could also uncover significant areas where communality endured. The goal of such a dialogue would not be for one to bend the other to his position. Some of the differences will be necessary. Others will be complementary; others may simply be non-essential. Still others may result from different irreducible starting points. But in such a dialectic process these various possibilities would be clarified while the individuals are engaged in human encounters that ultimately cannot be controlled or manipulated, and the result of these ongoing encounters could be the gradual discernment of broad lines of convergence and agreement, as well as a deeper appreciation of the lines of divergence and disagreement.

And if such is possible between bishop and theologian, in a similar manner it might be possible between pastor and associate pastor, a sister who prefers the older traditions and one who is exploring new styles and modes of ministry, the parishioner who thinks the parish should be on the cutting edge of innovation and the parish priest who thinks the Church has gone far enough, the parent who upholds traditional morality and the collegian who challenges it.

This in brief is what is meant by the wisdom community as a metaphor. It is a cast of mind, a style of thought, a cluster of attitudes, and an openness that make it possible for one to attain a high level of self-knowledge by means of self-reflection, a scrutiny of one's self as a living document. *Conscientização*, a love for others, humility, faith in human potential, trust, hope, critical thinking, clearness, prudence, a radical openness to new ways of thought, and a willingness to really listen to another are all attitudes that can be developed and brought to every encounter with those of differing horizons, thus allowing for dialogue. Add to that a conscientious effort to be attentive, intelligent, rational, responsible, and willing to change, and then the kind of communion that authentic dialogue intends might be possible.

Obviously no single individual can easily embody all of these qualities to the fullest. But they can be adverted to, worked at, cultivated. The wisdom community is a process, not an accomplishment.

Still it is easy to conceive that many might appreciate what would be gained by bringing such attitudes as these to play in their specific situations and, at the same time, be disposed only to do so in an informal manner. While a greater awareness of these factors might be deemed quite helpful by many for their self-understanding, as well as their understanding of others, many more might be inclined to shy away from any sustained or systematic efforts at such an activity. For those who would actually commit themselves to a systematic and prolonged effort at such a dialogue, only the wisdom community as a program will do.

NOTES

1. Paulo Freire, *Pedagogy of the Oppressed*, translated by Myra Bergman Ramos (New York: Herder and Herder, 1972), p. 77.
2. For a fuller elaboration of these points, see Freire, op. cit., pp. 77–87.
3. Pope Paul VI, *Paths of the Church (Ecclesiam Suam)* (Washington, D.C.: NCWC), par. 75–79.
4. *Ibid.*, par. 87.
5. *Ibid.*, par. 81–83, pp. 34–35.
6. Lonergan, *Method in Theology*, p. 9.
7. Ibid., pp. 14–15.

Chapter Seven

The Wisdom Community:
II. The Program

Introduction

There are a number of reasons why many who might applaud the general openness to understanding oneself and others more deeply, as suggested by the metaphor "wisdom community," might still be unenthusiastic about the systematic and prolonged pursuit of that understanding in a program. Priests, theologians, bishops, sisters, brothers, and laypeople might raise any of the following objections.

The wisdom community is too idealistic. It would simply be one more weekly or monthly meeting and there is not enough time as it is. If people were brought together representing the diverse concerns and beliefs that exist in the Church today, the participants simply would not be fully honest with each other. Or, if they were honest, temperament and emotion would get in the way and raised voices and hurt feelings and self-righteous condemnations would only widen the gulf between differing groups.

The laity should not be exposed to differences that may exist between some outspoken bishops and some outspoken theologians. Such exposure gives them the impression that there is disunity in the Church and this disturbs their faith. Some theologians seem to care less and less about the Church. What value could their views have? Many participants will use such an activity in order to confirm their suspicions and stereotypes of others. What is gained by surfacing problems and issues that cannot be solved? Most people would be emotionally uncomfortable with this kind of process. The result could be an instant replay of the traumatic experiences that accompanied the "sensitivity sessions" of the 1960's when they were not directed by professionals.

The kind of sharing and mutual involvement suggested by the wisdom community gives people a sense of participation and ownership. Their views gain in value and significance. False hopes and expectations may be raised with no tangible results. Distrust and indifference may widen. Finally, those who most need to participate in the ongoing dialogue of a wisdom community would be the very ones who would have no interest in it.

Each of these observations contains a partial truth. Certainly no program is a panacea that will meet all objections. Any imaginative initiative will necessarily be marked by risk and have no guarantee of success. Nevertheless, we must do something. Or at least *some* must. At parish adult education programs, at institutes for continuing education for clergy and religious, at professional gatherings of theologians, and at meetings of bishops there is more and more discussion of the need and desirability to establish structures and programs that will increase communication and collaboration between all sectors of the Church.

The reason for such a growing need has been well expressed by Bernard Lonergan in a statement that could well serve as the "preamble" of the wisdom community as a program:

> The crisis, then, that I have been attempting to depict is a crisis not of faith but of culture. There has been no new revelation from on high to replace the revelation given through Christ Jesus. There has been written no new Bible and there has been founded no new Church to link us with him. But Catholic philosophy and Catholic theology are matters, not merely of revelation and faith, but also of culture. Both have been fully and deeply involved in classical culture. The breakdown of classical culture and, at least in our day, the manifest comprehensiveness and exclusiveness of modern culture confront Catholic philosophy and Catholic theology with the gravest problems, impose upon them mountainous tasks, invite them to Herculean labors. Indeed, once philosophy becomes existential and historical, once it asks about man, not in the abstract, not as he would be in some state of pure nature, but as in fact he is here and now in all the concreteness of his living and dying, the very possibility of the old distinction between philosophy and theology vanishes.
>
> What is true of that distinction is true of others. What is true of distinctions, also is true of each of the other techniques that mark

our cultural heritage: classical culture cannot be jettisoned without being replaced; and what replaces it, cannot run counter to classical expectations. There is bound to be formed a solid right that is determined to live in a world that no longer exists. There is bound to be formed a scattered left, captivated by now this, now that new development, exploring now this and now that new possibility.

BUT WHAT WILL COUNT IS A PERHAPS NOT TOO NUMEROUS CENTER, BIG ENOUGH TO BE AT HOME IN BOTH THE OLD AND THE NEW, PAINSTAKING ENOUGH TO WORK OUT ONE BY ONE THE TRANSITIONS TO BE MADE, STRONG ENOUGH TO REFUSE HALF MEASURES AND INSIST ON COMPLETE SOLUTIONS EVEN THOUGH THEY HAVE TO WAIT.[1] [Emphasis added.]

This "not too numerous center" is not intended as a "middle of the road" compromise position. While its efforts will be marked by prudence, it is a prudence that must discern not the safest course but the best one. Nor is it an elitist center sure that its participants are in the know. Such a group must be ever aware that its members are not the only ones seeking to avoid the flight from understanding. Nor does the shape of the Church to come depend upon their lone labors. It is evident at this time that many and divergent activities are each contributing to the configuration of the unknown future.

The attentiveness to ourselves and others as living human documents, the attitude of other-centered openness to dialogue, and the fidelity to the transcendental precepts that constitute the wisdom community as a metaphor are the foundation of the wisdom community as a program. To that foundation, however, must be added a pattern of activities and a structure so that the dynamics of communication and understanding will advance in a systematic manner. Over time this structured activity should yield cumulative and progressive results.

As a program, the wisdom community envisions two to ten persons meeting on a regular basis in order to engage in a form of dialectical communications that goes beyond differing theologies to embrace the whole person. In this manner, deeply held convictions, commonsense opinions, "gut feelings," suppressed emotions, as well as reasoned arguments, theoretical and technical findings, and official positions are all acknowledged.

The wisdom community as a program can be developed in different ways according to the needs and goals of the participants. However, it must be marked by personal commitment, prayer, methods to insure honest sharing, focused issues, and a supportive structure. This chapter, then, will be in nine sections: (1) Commitment; (2) Prayerful Reflection; (3) Horizon Analysis; (4) A Personal Journal; (5) Dialogue Partners; (6) Common Reading; (7) A Specific Structure; (8) Who Is the Wisdom Community For?; (9) Conclusion: Pastoral Implications.

1. Commitment

The wisdom community will have no chance of success as a program without commitment. This includes commitment to the Church as it is, as well as it can and should be. The participants in the wisdom community must be committed to the group and its gatherings as a top priority. Once the meetings are fixed, absence should be rare and yet attendance should not spring from feelings of obligation but a genuine desire to be part of the experience. This commitment must extend to *each* member of the group. Only in this way can the appropriate atmosphere of trust, support, and confidentiality develop.

This commitment to the individual participants presumes that one shares with Pope John XXIII the ability to distinguish between a person whom one can love and respect and positions which that person may hold with which one finds oneself in strong disagreement. While the group will be enhanced by participants representing divergent horizons, self-righteous individuals intent on condemning and rejecting those with whom they disagree will only be destructive. In some cases there may be a need to include such persons, but then a professional facilitator may be needed to bring about the necessary openness of those involved.

This commitment to the group should be marked by genuine, no-nonsense, aggressive honesty, but bearing in mind the attitudes that Freire and Pope Paul stress as conditions for dialogue. Every effort must be made to correct and overcome stereotyping, categorizing, and name-calling. Nothing will be gained by branding those with whom one differs as conservative or liberal, intellectual or anti-intellectual, heretical or orthodox. For this can easily degenerate to the level of a childish game of "good guys" versus "bad guys."

This commitment to the members of the wisdom community is not based upon a relativistic disregard for truth, but rather upon an appreciation of the prior world of interiority. An interior genuineness, authenticity, good faith, and orthopraxis will be present in various degrees in all participants no matter how startlingly different their formulations, expressions, and points of emphasis may be.

Therefore, the distinction between generic faith and specific beliefs must be borne in mind. In an atmosphere of commitment and other acceptance, it will be possible for individuals to speak as persons rather than as positions or offices. Laypeople should not be intimidated by clerics. Those without technical training should experience as much respect for their "lived theology" as scholars experience for their technical findings. Theologians, bishops, and all others should feel comfortable enough to share thoughts and feelings with the group that they would be more guarded about before the general public.

2. Prayerful Reflection

If the wisdom community is to be more than a lively discussion group, the individual participants as well as the group must find and share something of the "pool of their hearts." This is why reflective prayer is so important. In it is the overflow from the world of interiority. In order for the participants to surface, thematize, and articulate the key moments of their religious journey and to share stories of their conversion, each must set aside times of silent reflection and prayer in anticipation of the gathering.

Each person will have his own unique style of prayer: silent meditation; reading the Scripture; prayerful reflection upon the common reading of the group. All of these are possibilities. Karl Rahner's *Encounters with Silence*, Henri Nouwen's *With Open Hands*, or James Carroll's *Contemplation* might be helpful catalysts for this interior exploration. For some, discipline of posture and place, as well as fasting, might enrich the efforts to pray in a reflective manner. In this way, amid the now turbulent, now serene waves of the pool of their hearts, each person gains snatches of his most honest affirmations and convictions about the world, God, Jesus, the Church, morality, truth, and ministry.

This attitude of prayerful reflection must be an integral part of the wisdom community as a group. This may mean times of silent prayer, readings from Scripture or other appropriate texts, informal prayers of praise, thanksgiving, and hope, para-liturgies, traditional prayer forms, and, of course, the Eucharist itself. In some groups the sacrament of reconciliation might be discerned as fitting after a certain stage in the process.

A note of special frankness is in order here. The place of prayers in a wisdom community cannot be superficial or cosmetic. Prayer cannot be used to conceal differences or to suggest that "well no matter what our differences are, we are all one in prayer." This can be a serious act of self-deception on the part of individuals or the entire group. It may well be that before some groups can meaningfully and authentically pray together, or perhaps simultaneously with their efforts, it will be necessary for the members to come to terms with what may be a breakdown in common meaning with regard to prayer. Certainly no particular mode of prayer (e.g., traditional, charismatic) can be imposed upon the group. A genuine appreciation of another's journey will support, rather than depreciate, the reticent or those lacking in eloquence. For some groups, questions concerning the meaning and nature of prayer will not be real or urgent. In others, it surely will be, and the issue should be addressed rather than awkwardly ignored.

3. Horizon Analysis

The term "horizon" was introduced in the earlier chapters on interiority to describe the framework, perspective, or vantage point from which a person encounters and interprets reality. Conversion is marked by a thoroughgoing shift or transformation of an individual's vision or horizon. Within a particular horizon certain realities are adverted to, while others are overlooked or ignored. There are also questions for which an individual has a ready answer, and other questions which never emerge, or if they do, they are dismissed. Reflecting upon these differing questions and points of view in a disciplined manner is what is meant by horizon analysis.

Participants in the wisdom community must each employ the self-knowledge that they have gained from attentiveness to their personal stories or examining themselves as living documents in order to determine the explicit content and preoccupations of their present horizon in comparison to their past horizons and those of others. Honesty and thoroughness of self-examination will increase the possibility of self-understanding and the appreciation of another's horizon, even if it is radically different from one's own. This reflective activity should be employed for examining oneself and the group as related to the various forms of conversion, as well as the other questions raised by this book and by the group process itself.

Horizon analysis, then, is simply the process by which people consciously advert to and monitor the dynamic of raising and answering questions that relate them to realities with which they have varying degrees of familiarity. Each of us has to deal with what we know, what we know we do not know, and what we do not even think about (thus we do not know that we do not know it). Thus we may speak of the worlds of the "known," the "known unknown," and the "unknown unknown."

The world of the "known" is the wide or narrow range of questions that you are capable of raising, do in fact raise, and consider to be of significance. You are in the process of answering these questions, have correctly answered them, or at least you think you have. The questions involved could address any area of religion. Your confidence of knowledge could be based upon common sense, theory, trusted authority, or personal conviction.

The world of the "known unknown" is constituted by the range of questions that you are capable of raising, find to be meaningful, significant, and worthwhile; yet for diverse reasons you do not raise them or do not explore them in a consistent manner. If you do raise them, you have only partial clues as to how they might be answered. You feel you could answer them if you "worked at it." You may know the answers given by others. They are authorities or specialists and so you feel you can trust them. But, at the present time, you honestly know that you cannot answer such questions in a conclusive manner for yourself or others. Knowledge of this limitation may or may not distress you depending upon the urgency or import of the question in relation to your concrete practical situation. Because of diverse backgrounds, the question that is gnawingly urgent for you has long since been answered to another's satisfaction. While for someone else, it is a question that has never occurred.

The world of the "unknown unknown" is constituted by the broad or narrow range of questions that you simply never raise. For the most part you do not respond to these questions in any way at all. They are beyond you, and hence utterly outside of your horizon. And since the questions are completely unknown, they cause no notable distress.

When someone else raises a question that was outside of your horizon, you may find it difficult to believe that the question had not previously occurred to you. Other questions will be put aside while you investigate this new and pressing one. However, other novel questions will be raised and you will find them obscure or of no consequence. Finally, questions may strike you as unanswerable or an odd sort of "mental exercise." They may be unnerving, the kind of questions that one simply should not ask. While you may not be sure how to answer these new questions that emerge, it is possible to overcome the tension of inquiry. You may seek out trusted conclusions of those who have already considered the question. You may begin a process of investigation on your own, or, unfortunately, a simplistic answer may be chosen as a stop-gap measure.

Obviously, the social, cultural, educational, and religious factors of one's personal journey will color in a significant manner each person's individual horizon at a particular time. It should be noted that, besides questions and answers, horizon analysis may also be employed to explore the range of symbols, rituals, and devotions in one's life and the process by which they seem to decrease or increase in importance.

Equally open to horizon analysis is the range of social, moral, and political convictions that flow from religious commitments. What is the range of questions and involvement one has with regard to war, poverty, racism, capital punishment, the Equal Rights Amendment, care for the aged, fair housing, and unbiased employment? What is the relationship of commitments, involvement, or non-involvement to the conversion process ongoing in one's life?

This kind of exploration of the present range of what one perceives as meaningful questions and adequate answers is one of the best ways to become concretely and personally aware of historical consciousness. This is so because questions which were once naively thought to be securely answered at one moment in one's life are often radically reopened subsequently. Hence, what was once the known becomes the unknown. Other questions, once thought to be of no account or not even thought of (unknown unknown), now have a pressing urgency. Meanwhile, the very questions and issues that once seemed so urgent recede into the background and are forgotten. Finally, other questions which were unanswerable to you for a long time are now confidently resolved as the "known." To make the process of horizon analysis concrete, you have only to think of your changing attitudes and questions regarding such issues as the development of doctrine, liturgical renewal, or ecumenism.

If the wisdom community is to be effective, the process of horizon analysis must become a regular activity for the individual alone as well as an important activity to share with the group for their support, challenge, and insights. Most groups will benefit from collective horizon analysis. This will bring to conscious awareness the scope of the similarities and differences within the group. The collective awareness of the fact that what is for one the known, is for another the known unknown, and yet for another the unknown unknown will give the participants much to think about and move the process ahead.

4. A Personal Journal

The keeping of a personal journal will be an important and help-ful discipline for the process of horizon analysis and the dialectic of the wisdom community. Those familiar with the writings and work-shops of Ira Progoff will already be accustomed to working with a journal.[2]

In the wisdom community the personal journal should consist of personal reflections upon the whole process as well as a series of com-mon questions to which each participant should make written re-sponses over a period of time. These responses should be completely honest even to the point of writing what you might at first be hesi-tant to share with your dialogue partner or the larger group. The spe-cific questions should be formulated by the participants or at least agreed upon by them. The questions will differ depending on the makeup of the group and the issues focused upon.

The questions are intended to invite reflections and not simple "yes" or "no" responses. Initially, one question might trigger a lengthy response, another only a few sentences, and another nothing at all. Each entry should be dated and the writer should return to the question again and again, answering the question anew without re-gard for consistency or continuity with an earlier response. This is important because over time there is very likely to be nuance, devel-opment, correction, and even retraction of previous responses as the question is mulled over and more and more personal data are allowed to float loose and surface within the individual's memory and con-sciousness. Obviously, fidelity to making entries in the journal is re-quired, if it is to be a helpful activity for personal horizon analysis, communicating with the participants, and sharing with one's dia-logue partner.

The questions addressed in the journal should attempt to encom-pass all three horizons: the known, the known unknown, and the un-known unknown. They could follow the general progression of this book. The questions indicated in the discussion of living human docu-ments might serve as a point of departure. However, original ques-tions that come forth from the particular group will be the most important. Since the question of Christology was used as an example in the discussion of critical, dogmatic, and existential mediation in Chapters Four and Five, "Theology in a New Key," it may be helpful to use that example again to exemplify the range of possible questions on a specific topic. The following questions are taken from those that have emerged in "wisdom community" seminars that I have conducted on the topic "Jesus":

1. Is it correct to say that to be fully human is to be Christian and to be fully Christian is to be human?
2. What is your mental picture of Jesus (e.g., do you think of him as Jewish)?
3. Do you ever dream of Jesus?
4. Where is Jesus most "available" to you? Within your own interiority? In your active life or ministry? In other Christians? At the Sunday Eucharist? In nature? In the reserved sacrament? In the Scriptures? In a priest? In the poor and oppressed? In mystical prayer?
5. What are the most important teachings of the Catholic Church about Jesus? Are they biblically based? Do you understand them? Do you believe them? Do these beliefs make a significant difference in your personal life? Do most Catholics you know believe these teachings? In what sense are they true?
6. What do you understand to be the meaning of the statement that bishops speak in the name of Christ?
7. What does it mean to speak of a priest as "another Christ"?
8. Does Christian conversion necessarily imply a special homage to Mary, the Mother of Jesus?
9. Would your thoughts and beliefs about Jesus Christ change if you became convinced that there was no life after death?
10. Is it possible to you that Jesus did not explicitly establish any religious institution?
11. Would it make any difference to you if Jesus were married or homosexual?
12. Do you have a personal relationship with Jesus? Explain.
13. What does the resurrection of Jesus mean to you?
14. Are the terms "Jesus Christ" and "God" equally inclusive?
15. How strong is your missionary zeal to proclaim Jesus as the Christ of God?
16. Do you think that it is valid to say that the Christian religion is the result of God's divine initiative while the other leading world religions are the result of profound human efforts to reach God?
17. Is it easier for you to think of Jesus as a human being with a unique relationship with God or a divine being with a unique relationship with humankind?
18. Do the questions and findings advanced by biblical scholarship sustain or undermine the more cherished religious sentiments that you associate with feasts such as Christmas and Easter?

19. What *minimally* must be believed or done to constitute one as a follower of Jesus Christ?
20. Is there a distinctively Christian ethic? If so, what would be its general content?

Your initial response to simply reading over these questions might well be the point of departure for your horizon analysis on the question of Christian conversion. The questions are of many different types. It might be thought that some are more aptly answered by the scholar, others by the devout parishioner, others by the bishop. But, in fact, everyone answers these or similar questions to some degree without much regard for the fact that others may dismiss their response as unorthodox, incorrect, or uninformed.

Some of the questions are limit questions. They are not so much questions of fact. They drive one into inner depths, beyond pat answers and formulas. They push one to the limits of one's feelings, understandings, and beliefs. Limit questions force a person out of standardized categories of thought and break open questions in a new way and with a new intensity. They seek to uncover theological presuppositions, cultural influences, and personal biases. Question eleven, for instance, does not intend to ask what if by some method of investigation it was determined that Jesus was in fact married. It intends rather to reveal the inner attitudes of the responder concerning Jesus' humanity, and his relationship to the broader questions of masculinity, femininity, and sexuality.

The questions chosen for the journal will not be equally interesting to each participant. But all should respond to each of the questions. It would even be good to write about why a certain question is uninteresting. Each question addressed will have a particular possibility for bringing participants closer to their interior worlds. For this reason participants should not conceal their genuine and pressing questions. There should be no pre-judgment of the questions that can or cannot be asked. While it may be argued that the Catholic tradition has formulated long-standing responses to certain questions, it cannot be argued that some questions should never even enter a person's thoughts because they are not "Catholic questions."

5. Dialogue Partners

The program of the wisdom community as it has been outlined thus far indicates some of the activities appropriate for the individual as well as the whole group. In order to enrich and deepen those activities, and to distill their benefits, it is necessary to engage in a reflection process that is not possible alone or in a larger group. For this reason dialogue partners are an essential component for the wisdom community. In this way there can be increased communication and greater understanding. Dividing the group into pairs of dialogue partners makes it possible for group members to support and share in each other's efforts at self-understanding in a more intimate manner than the larger group will allow.

Prayer, horizon analysis, and journal responses are obvious areas where dialogue partners should be in communication. During the meetings of the wisdom community there should be ample time allowed for walks and extended conversations between the partners. Furthermore, the participants should spend time together on their own in informal sharing as well as in more structured exchanges.

Dialogue partners need not be friends or foes. In one case it might be helpful for someone to be associated with another who is somewhat like-minded and who can help him to attain an articulate grasp of his basic questions and convictions. In another instance that would not be necessary. It might be better to join with someone with whom one strongly disagrees on a number of basic issues. Individuals who find that their differences lead to bad feelings and hostilities should not avoid becoming dialogue partners. If the wisdom community meets over an extended period, dialogue partners should change from time to time.

It is not necessary to elaborate upon the idea of dialogue partners here. Much of what can or cannot be accomplished by such an activity will be apprehended quite easily by the participants in a concrete situation. Clearly a special candor should characterize such a partnership. Each person would be called upon to strive to communicate honestly and to confront the other when it was judged necessary in order to sustain communication. Obviously, such confrontation should be firm, even aggressive when necessary, without betraying the principles of dialogue that have already been discussed in the previous chapter.

6. Common Reading

If the dynamic process of the wisdom community is to advance in a disciplined manner, there must be not only common journal questions and dialogue partners, but also common reading. Common reading will focus the activity of the wisdom community by providing more fully articulated expressions of various issues. This will enable participants to discuss the positions they favor, reject, or are not sure of, with the help of more developed expressions than they themselves might be able to formulate. Common reading will also aid and stimulate the efforts of personal reflection, prayer, horizon analysis, journal keeping, and dialogue.

However, the wisdom community is not a book "study group." The use of common reading will be destructive if it is employed in such a manner that directs attention away from the participants and focuses completely upon the presumably absent author. The goal is not to heap praise or blame on particular authors or texts or to become bogged down in a minute analysis of a specific work. The reading must serve to help the *readers* to recognize and take possession of their *own* views and positions in order to better appreciate the strengths, weaknesses, and logical or illogical consequences of those views as related to the views of others.

If the participants of the wisdom community choose to follow the progression of this book, then common reading should be chosen that will examine more deeply questions that could only be sketched or outlined here. In many cases the notes at the back of the chapters in this book offer representative works on pertinent topics. The bibliography at the end of the book has also been compiled to help in selecting appropriate reading. Of course, each participant will bring a knowledge of particular books and articles that might be singularly apt for a certain topic or group. Those who are not living or working in an academic context might make a special effort to browse through the current periodicals of a theological library or a quality religious bookstore. In this way it is possible to chance upon the very book or article that will give the wisdom community better direction.

Since each group will have its own personality, degree of sophistication, and agenda, any specific suggestions made here can only serve as indicators or possibilities. Obvious starting points are the Scriptures themselves on specific topics and appropriate commentaries. The decrees and constitutions of the Second Vatican Council are nearly a decade and a half old and yet many people (laity and clergy alike) do not have a deep and clear grasp of these fundamental documents. There are also a number of important statements by various Vatican Congregations or the American bishops that could serve as thought-provoking points of departure on specific topics.

The purpose of common reading is to enhance the active dialectic between the participants. It should not serve as a diversionary tactic that avoids this activity. The reading need not be of an explicitly theological nature. Depending on the agenda of the group, a wide range of other disciplines could and should be explored. The reading need not be of a technical nature either. Works of fiction may be especially illuminating and provocative. Hermann Hesse's *Narcissus and Goldmund* and Nikos Kazantzakis' *Saint Francis* and *The Last Temptation of Christ* have been used in an experimental wisdom community (with university students) with great success. Books and articles of a more explicitly spiritual and devotional nature as well as material from popular journals would also be appropriate. An examination of the relationship between devotional literature, official teaching, and scholarly theology would be of benefit to many.

Since a key function of common reading is to provide the group with common points of departure, exceptional works of cinema, significant television specials, music, and theater should not be excluded as possible sources of "common reading." Many of these often communicate values concerning religion, God, Jesus, and the Church on a very deep, if not always explicit, level.

When the participants of a particular wisdom community are not primarily in the academic world, there may be a temptation to shy away from reading. While such groups should choose reading of a quality and quantity that is appropriate to its concerns, reading should not be avoided altogether. When participants in a wisdom community are of a more academic makeup, there is likely to be a tendency to overemphasize reading and analyzing at the cost of personal sharing and interaction. While such a group obviously has a unique responsibility to meet head-on some of the complex technical and theoretical questions before the Church today, the purpose of the program would be defeated if the meeting of minds completely eclipsed the meeting of hearts.

7. A Specific Structure

The wisdom community gatherings must be sufficiently structured if the program is to yield cumulative results. The structure, however, may be as elaborate or as simple as the needs and goals of the participants require. Whatever structure is chosen, four elements will be involved. These are: (1) the number of participants; (2) the locale of the meetings; (3) the style of leadership; and (4) time and schedule.

It has already been indicated that the wisdom community should ideally consist of two to ten members. If there are only two or three participants, the entire process becomes more concentrated. Hence there is more flexibility and less need to formalize the structure. Even so, small groups should not be allowed to become informal "talk sessions." The following comments envision a larger group. If the group is larger than ten, it easily becomes cumbersome and the cumulative and collective sharing process can be retarded or prevented altogether. If a larger number than ten is involved, then perhaps two groups should be formed.

Ideally, the locale of the wisdom community meetings should be away from the usual distractions of the daily routine. They should be in a reasonably comfortable and non-threatening atmosphere. While undue concern should not be given to the question of locale, everyone has participated in meetings where some of the participants were unwilling or slow to enter into the dialogue because the environment was not marked by an atmosphere of welcome. Often this was due to past associations with the place. Settings such as that must be avoided.

The wisdom community can come about only if someone or a small group takes the initiative and suggests it to friends, associates, or colleagues. In the concrete situation, the convener may be anyone—a parish council leader, a professor, a bishop, a pastor. But the person who initiates the meeting need not be the leader. The leader may be chosen by the group. Each of the members may take turns with the leadership responsibilities. In some cases it might be appropriate for a leader to be invited in who is not a part of the original group of participants. It would be better if the leader was not a person whose office or authority might impede frank discussion.

The role of the leader is to be especially attentive to the dynamics of the process. This is done by being sensitive to the tendency of some to monopolize the discussion and of others to observe silently. The leader also tries to keep the discussion on target by refocusing the issue, acknowledging and articulating breakthroughs, advances, and declines. In this manner the leader is eager to nudge the group out of ruts and to applaud and sustain instances of genuine spirals of understanding. As the wisdom community is envisioned, the leader is always a full participant in the group. He should never become an outsider concerned mainly with logistics and mechanics.

The length, frequency, and schedule of wisdom community meetings will be determined by the goals and intentions of the conveners and the participants. It is possible to work within a very modest schedule. For example, the priests and sisters of a parish staff might be working through *The Wisdom Community* very carefully over several months of meetings in order to articulate a parish plan. In order to share the process with lay leaders of the parish, the pastoral staff might plan an afternoon meeting that would focus upon only a few key topics pertinent to the parish. In this case the lay participants will not have read *The Wisdom Community*. They may not even have heard of it. Nor need the descriptive title "wisdom community" be used if another would be more helpful. All that will be required is that the conveners direct the group in the light of what they learned from working with the program and their desired goals.

In a more academic setting, *The Wisdom Community* could serve as the focal text for a whole semester of study. It would provide the students with an overview and a frame of reference. It would necessarily be augmented with more expanded and more specific content, in order to fill out and exemplify the issues treated. Used in this way, *The Wisdom Community* would encourage the students to "think theologically" and help them articulate their own personal synthesis rather than simply passively learn the opinions and beliefs of others.

Bishops and theologians in a local or regional area might find that working through *The Wisdom Community* in a rather concentrated way over a weekend or an overnight might serve as a good ground-clearing activity to improve their communication and collaboration. After the initial session, periodic meetings over an indefinite period of time could continue to employ whichever dynamics of *The Wisdom Community* that proved to be fruitful. The bishop of a diocese and his immediate staff could employ *The Wisdom Community* in a similar manner in order to better articulate their *theological* vision of their shared ministry.

If any of the high hopes of the wisdom community are to be realized, there must be a real investment of time. In the light of the above examples it is clear that the wisdom community could be structured as a single weekend meeting, a series of evening meetings, a series of weekend meetings, a series of monthly meetings, or a combination of these.

A weekend schedule starting on Friday evening and going to Sunday afternoon would allow sufficient time to introduce participants to the activities described in Chapters Six and Seven, as well as an opportunity to apply them to some of the key issues addressed in the earlier chapters. After such a weekend individuals might continue the program informally with their dialogue partner or they may simply attempt to keep the process operative in their own lives by means of a personal journal and reflection. While a single weekend model would be a useful initiation into the kind of collaboration that *The Wisdom Community* is asking for, it would not be very suitable for attaining the depth and long-term results that are desirable. These are attainable only by an ongoing process.

The weekend structure, however, would be very effective if it were followed up by evening sessions every week for six to ten sessions. In this framework, the structure of the book could be followed allowing appropriate numbers of sessions for discussion-reflection upon the first six chapters. The number of sessions would be determined by the depth of sharing and understanding desired as well as range of topics and readings selected. Between these weekly meetings there should be some time allowed for work on the personal journal as well as conversation between the dialogue partners.

For those groups that plan to follow the text closely, it is important that all participants have copies of *The Wisdom Community* well in advance of the *first* meeting. In that way everyone will have had an opportunity to reflect upon the general movement of the book, the key themes treated, and the requirements of the program. The participants will be able to note topics of special interest, write down initial questions, as well as specify their special concerns not explicitly addressed by the book. In this manner the reflective process envisioned by the program would have begun prior to the first meeting.

The following is a general model for a weekend meeting. This would be for a group that has read *The Wisdom Community* in advance, prepared some initial questions, and intends a separate meeting for each chapter.

Day One: Friday

Evening:
1. Gathering.
2. Convener shares goals and hopes.
3. Sharing of general reactions to the book.
4. Informal sharing of personal and professional background (life journey).
5. Surfacing of questions pertinent to Chapter One: What Happened? for personal journal.
6. Selection of dialogue partners.

Day Two: Saturday

Morning:
1. Time alone for reflection on Chapter One.
2. Group discussion of Sections One, Two, and Three (The Na-

ture of Religion; The Emergence of Theology; The American Context).

3. Dialogue partners discuss same material or questions prompted by prior reading and discussion.
4. Time for journal reflections.

Afternoon:
1. Time alone for reading, reflection, prayer, informal conversation.
2. Group discussion of Section Four (The Shift from Classical to Modern Culture).
3. Dialogue partners discuss Section Four.
4. Journal reflections.

Evening:
1. Group discussion of Section Five (The Decline of Common Meaning).
2. Dialogue partners' discussion of Section Five.
3. Journal reflections.

Day Three: Sunday

Morning:
1. Group reflections, sharing and evaluating; determine structure and time for next meeting.
2. Focusing of areas of concern for subsequent meetings.
3. Selection of topic, common reading.
4. Sharing of initial journal questions.
5. Prayer or liturgy.

With adjustments, a similar schedule could be followed on subsequent weekend or evening meetings. It is not necessary to begin with the first chapter. It is possible to begin with Chapters Six and Seven and work out the specifics of the program. Others might choose to focus upon issues raised in the four key chapters on interiority and theological method (Chapters Two–Five).

The exact structure of the wisdom community in its detail must be the work of the participants or at least of those who call the group into existence. The particulars of that structure will be dictated by the number and diversity of the participants as well as the level of intensity at which it is judged desirable to proceed. In some circumstances, the program of the wisdom community will be judged as being without success unless it bears the fruit of specific and concrete actions. This will be especially true of those who focus upon what has been described as existential mediation. It will be for group members themselves to detemine what those actions should be.

8. Who Is The Wisdom Community For?

The wisdom community as a program is intended as an instrument that will encourage and facilitate continued communication and understanding between members of the Christian community who feel the strain brought about by the decline of common meaning. The program of the wisdom community does not presuppose a uniform state of affairs. There are great differences between the Church in New England and the Church in the Midwest or the Southwest. A large urban diocese and a small rural diocese are as different as inner-city parishes are from those in the suburbs. In some parishes, the members of the pastoral staff have a confident and shared sense of their ministry, while in others there is a great void between pastor, associate pastors, and parishioners. Instances of support and understanding between bishops and theologians can be found as well as instances of mutual harsh judgment. Many laypeople are abreast of, and puzzled by, a host of contemporary theological developments in the Church, while many others "practice their faith" in the same devout and confident manner that has been theirs for years.

In spite of the general flexibility and openness to adaptation built into the program, the wisdom community is not for everyone in every situation.

The wisdom community, therefore, is for a group of adult Christians who are anxious not only to support, and be supported by, the Christian witness and vision of others, but also to come to terms in a straightforward manner with subtle or blatant differences that undermine that support and witness. The wisdom community is for those who are convinced that the whole Church in the United States would be enriched if some concrete and explicit efforts were made to bring about more authentic communication between priests, laity, theologians, and bishops. More specifically, then, the wisdom community is for the priests, sisters, deacons, and laity who make up the pastoral staff of a parish community. It is for the pastoral staff and the parish council. It is for a group of laypeople on their own.

The wisdom community is for a group of parish priests, students in the theologate of a seminary, or members of a seminary faculty. It is for a cluster of men preparing for the permanent diaconate. It is also for a group of religious women who live together or share a common ministry. The wisdom community is for religious brothers as well.

The wisdom community is for a local bishop, a professional theologian, parish priests, sisters, deacons, and laypeople in a diocese. It is equally for a small group of bishops and theologians alone or together. It is for directors of religious education or a group of university students and the campus minister. It is for those engaged in dialogues and activities working for the unity of the separated Christian traditions.

While the wisdom community is a distinct program in itself, the theological background, general overview, and structure that it contains should make the study a valuable resource for existing continuing education programs. Examples of these are the Summer Institutes for Clergy Education sponsored by the American College in Louvain, and the North American College in Rome, in collaboration with the University of Louvain and the Gregorian University, and The Institute for Clergy Education at the University of Notre Dame.

The wisdom community is also intended to support the work of a growing number of spiritual enrichment programs such as "The Genesis Two" program developed by the Center for Human Development at the University of Notre Dame, and the "Emmaus Spirituality Planning Program" developed for the National Organization for Continuing Education of Roman Catholic Clergy.

If the wisdom community is to contribute to the growing dialogue within the Church, then it must reach the lives of laypeople. In some places the laity have attained a high level of knowledge, expertise, responsibility, confidence, and enthusiasm. In other circumstances the laity are only on the verge of coming into their own. In both of these circumstances, the wisdom community could serve as a catalyst for continued adult Christian growth. The wisdom community could be a helpful follow-up of a well thought-out program of adult education, retreat, or parish renewal program. By building upon these activities, the wisdom community would prolong, interiorize, and articulate the benefits and developments of the earlier activities and thereby strengthen bonds of the local church.

It must be admitted that there are circumstances where the introduction of the wisdom community could be harmful unless it is used gradually and under skilled and sensitive leadership.

Ultimately, the only way to find out who the wisdom communi-

ty is for, will be for you not to merely read these pages, but to do
what they suggest.

9. Conclusion: Pastoral Implications

Because of the natural dynamism of the human spirit, each one of
us hopes for and searches for answers to the questions we entertain.
When we read books and articles on religion and theology, particularly those which treat questions that are most pressing to us, we are
somewhat disappointed if we find that no clear and certain answer is
given. We feel a little betrayed if the author states at the end of his
work that all he intended to do was to put questions before the reader
in a new and fresh perspective. At best, the author only hopes to have
made some tentative observations about the diverse directions from
which answers appear to be forthcoming. *The Wisdom Community* has
not intended to mislead. It is true that this book raises many questions and examines the diverse contexts in which responses to those
questions have been given. But it would be contrary to the central intention of this book if it now concluded with the author's version of
"the answers."

The only way possible for stating "the answers" to the kinds of
questions that have been addressed in these chapters is to eliminate
prematurely significant conflicting positions which dissent from "the
answers." It is easy enough to point in a general way to "the answers"
if we attend only to particular groups or individuals. There is no
great difficulty in assessing the answers held by those priests, bishops,
theologians, and laity who take their stand on a "conservative" theology. The same is true of those priests, bishops, theologians, and laity
who take their stand on a "liberal" theology. In other words, while
there is pluralism within dogmatic, critical, or existential mediation,
a certain degree of harmony can be found within each framework
which cannot be easily found if one seeks to integrate that which is of
value in all three. Much of what is written in theology implicitly or
explicitly takes its stand with one while rejecting or criticizing the
other two. And this is precisely what one must do when one judges
that one's own position is completely correct and the others are incorrect.

But it is not easy to do this if it is not so clear that one position
alone is correct and all others are wrong. The majority of bishops are
aware that a new sense of harmony cannot be brought about in the
Church by means of a decree from on high. They are more and more

sensitive to the diverse views among themselves, theologians, and other members of the Church. They are looking for ways to meet that diversity. Yet they rightly declare that truth is not assured by abandoning tradition and taking a show of hands.

Most theologians see clearly that there is no new Aquinas on the horizon. Indeed they know we are at a juncture in the history of ideas and the history of the Church that will not allow for the development of the kind of master synthesis produced by Aquinas. They also know that those who are in the vanguard of new developments rarely find ready acceptance. They are equally aware that not all new ideas have lasting value and merit.

The people in the pews are generally aware that a grass roots commonsense "consensus" over disputed issues is less than what is desired and needed for a tradition respected for centuries for its wisdom. Many laypeople also have a quiet sense that in spite of all the stringent confusion going on "above them," they are a part of a living tradition of lasting value. Not a few of the laity discern that while they are neither scholar nor cleric, they are custodians of that tradition. It is in their bones.

In spite of the immense conflicts that are apparent in the Church over abstract, concrete, and disciplinary issues, we continue to see examples of fierce loyalty, joyful pride, patient concern, and spiritual genuineness within the entire spectrum of the Church. This genuineness and authenticity is in many cases more than individuals with good intentions who happen to be wrong. For many of these individuals are of good faith as well as good intention. For good faith can exist as an abiding reality at the radical depth of a person. This good faith on the part of people who are theologically at odds is manifested by their conduct. Each is seeking to understand and be understood and to live and give expression to the Christian faith as best they know how in their concrete situation.

The wisdom community as program and process intends to move individuals toward the formulation of their own personal synthesis. It also compels a genuine desire to hear and understand fellow human beings and fellow Christians. This personal synthesis does not intend to turn belief into a purely private affair. Rather, it intends to aid each person in the articulation and thematization of his present horizon. This must be done if we are to face the implications of the fact that we are all at different stages in the process of religious, theistic, Christian, ecclesial, moral, and intellectual conversion. It is only after one has articulated and thematized one's own presuppositions, irreducible starting points, generic faith, specific beliefs, and devotional feelings that one is able to participate in a trusting exchange with another as a whole and integrated person.

Encounter, however, is not designed to cultivate indifferentism. The result of the wisdom community will not be a group of people concluding that since they are all caring, honest, and prayerful people, the radical differences that separate them may as well be dismissed as insignificant. The differences must be faced. In some cases they will be shown to be misunderstandings. In others, they will be seen as complementary stages in an ongoing development. In still others, diversified experiences, understandings, judgments, and commitments will be uncovered as the issue. As a result, conflict may hinge upon diverse differentiations of consciousness, the pre-eminence of one mode of mediation over another, or the presence or absence of one or another form of conversion. Only when these differences are known can they be addressed.

This dialogue between persons sharing themselves and their interiority must not lead individuals to the abdication of their specific identity, ministry, and responsibility. The laity will still know that they are not theologians. Bishops will still know that they are not parish priests. Theologians will still know that they are not bishops.

The laity know that they are not "religious professionals" in the sense of priests, sisters, theologians, and bishops. (Happily, a noticeably significant number of laypeople are becoming *professional theologians.*) Even though they usually are not such professionals, they must come to realize more and more that the questions of ultimate meaning—hence the religious questions in life—are truly their own questions. These questions cannot be abdicated to others in the same manner that questions of medicine and law are left to doctors and lawyers. It is not the role of the laity to wait passively for a prescription from the "deposit" of faith as the answer to life's most burning questions and then never to think about those questions, answers, and their implications again. In the long run, of course, it *is* the people in the pews who account for the continuity of religion more than the religious professionals.

Bishops sustain their identity and office in the dialogue of the wisdom community as well. The wisdom community as a program does not undermine even the most traditional interpretation of the teaching office of the bishop. Nothing about this process intends to imply that truth is arrived at by taking a poll. But just as a bishop is free to come to his own conclusions without any form of consultation, he remains free to follow his best judgment even if it differs from the conclusions of his wisdom community. But participation in such a dynamic activity may well enrich his discernment process. Some bishops might even choose to be more active as theologians if their ministry allows the time.[3]

Theologians must also remain committed scholars. They realize that those without their formal training are not likely to ask the same questions they do. And if they do, they will not respond to them in the same manner. Nevertheless, the wisdom community will heighten the theologian's sensitivity to the peculiar theological concerns of the bishop, parish priest, and laity in their life situations. The regular and open exchange with people who are far more occupied by questions of religion than of technical theology might nudge the theologian into facing the easily overlooked tensions between religion and theology that may exist in his own life.

The Wisdom Community is intended as an invitation to an adventure of mind, heart, and spirit. It clamors for an individual as well as for a communal journey. It is certainly not difficult to understand why some, perhaps many, will not wish to embark on this journey. They will lean to the right or to the left in the name of certitude or freedom. And that may be as it should or even must be. And those who do so may well be playing their proper role in a long and complex development in the life of the Church. But it is hoped that some will see the urgency of joining that "not too numerous center" who are enough at home with the old and the new that they are able and willing to work at the complex transitions into an unknown future. It is hoped that there are some who will refuse half measures and insist upon complete solutions even if they must wait and work for them.

Are you such a person? If you are, why not share these pages with another? With that act of sharing you have the foundations of a wisdom community. Now you have only to build upon that foundation.

To do nothing at all is to abdicate to the hands of others your unique part in the shaping of the Church to come.

NOTES

1. Cf. Lonergan, "Dimension of Meaning," *Collection* F. E. Crowe, S.J., editor, (New York: Herder and Herder, 1967), pp. 266–67. Lonergan's assertion that the present crisis is of culture and not of faith might be considered a moot point since faith is everywhere entangled in culture. The distinction, however, remains a helpful one.

2. See Ira Progoff, *At a Journal Workshop* (New York: Dialogue House,

1975). See also George F. Simon, *Keeping Your Personal Journal* (New York: Paulist Press, 1978).

3. Lawrence Cardinal Sheehan's article "Apostles and Bishops: Still Another Point of View" in *Homiletic and Pastoral Review,* January 1976, pp. 8–23, provides an instance of a bishop in dialogue with a theologian (Raymond Brown). Whatever one thinks of either position, the point is that the Cardinal is making his case on theological grounds and in a public and professional context. *The Wisdom Community* is intended to encourage more such interaction and exchanges.

Bibliography

Note: While a cross-section of both popular and technical works are included here, this bibliography is intended only as a point of departure. The best source of appropriate reading material will be known by individual participants in particular wisdom communities. For some groups, a number of these works may be too technical. For others, a chapter or even a few pages of a particular work will be sufficient to focus their activities. This bibliography does not duplicate references to specific topics already included in the notes of the text, located at the end of each chapter.

Documents

Vatican Council II: The Conciliar and Post Conciliar Documents, Austin Flannery, O.P., general editor (Northport, N.Y.: Costello Publishing Co., 1977).

The Documents of Vatican II, Walter M. Abbot, S.J., editor (New York: Angelus Books, 1966).

The Teachings of the Catholic Church (as Contained in Her Documents), Karl Rahner, editor, originally prepared by Josef Neuner and Heinrich Roos (Staten Island, N.Y.: Alba House, 1967).

Note: The National Conference of Catholic Bishops and the United States Catholic Conference publish a wide range of documents on timely theological, social, moral, and liturgical issues facing the Church. The National Catechetical Directory, *Sharing the Light of Faith*, is an important example. A listing of these works may be obtained from the USCC, 1312 Massachusetts Avenue, N.W., Washington, D.C. 20005.

Individual Works

Alves, Ruben. *Theology of Human Hope* (Washington: Corpus Books, 1968).

Arzube, Bishop Juan. "Criteria for Dissent in the Church," *Origins: N.C. Documentary Service*, May 11, 1978, pp. 748–750.

Augustine, Saint. *The Confessions*, translated by John K. Ryan (Garden City, N.Y.: Doubleday & Co., 1960).

Austin, J. L. *How to Do Things with Words* (New York: Oxford University Press, 1965).

Balthasar, Hans Urs, von. *Elucidations* (London: SPCK, 1975).

Becker, Ernst. *The Denial of Death* (New York: The Free Press, 1973).

Becoming a Catholic Christian: A Symposium on Christian Initiation (New York: Sadlier, 1978).

Bellah, Robert. *Beyond Belief* (New York: Harper and Row, 1970).

Bent, Charles. *Interpreting the Doctrine of God* (New York: Paulist Press, 1968).

Block, Ernst. *Man on His Own: Essays in the Philosophy of Religion* (New York: Herder and Herder, 1970).

Boff, Leonardo. *Jesus Christ Liberator* (New York: Orbis Books, 1978).

Boisen, Anton. *The Exploration of the Inner World* (New York: Harper Torchbooks, 1936).

Bok, Sissela. *Lying: Moral Choice in Public and Private Life* (New York: Pantheon Books, 1978).

Bokenkotter, Thomas. *A Concise History of the Catholic Church* (Garden City, N.Y.: Doubleday & Co., Inc., 1977).

Boros, Ladislaus. *The Mystery of Death* (New York: The Seabury Press, 1973).

———. *Open Spirit* (London: Search Press, 1974).

———. *Pain and Providence* (London: Search Press, 1972).

Brown, Raymond E. *An Adult Christ at Christmas: Essays on the Three Biblical Christmas Stories* (Collegeville, Minn.: The Liturgical Press, 1977).

———. *Biblical Reflections on Crises Facing the Church* (New York: Paulist Press, 1975).

———. *Jesus God and Man* (New York: The Macmillan Co., 1967).

Brown, Raymond E., Fitzmyer, Joseph A., Murphy, Roland E. (editors). *The Jerome Biblical Commentary* (Englewood Cliffs, N.J.: Prentice-Hall, Inc., 1968).

Brown, Robert McAfee. *Theology in a New Key* (Philadelphia: The Westminster Press, 1978).

Burghardt, Walter. "A Theologian's Challenge to Liturgy," *Theological Studies* 35 (June 1974): 233–48.

Callahan, Daniel (Editor). *God Jesus Spirit* (New York: Herder and Herder, 1969).

Cassirer, Ernst. *An Essay on Man: An Introduction to a Philosophy of Human Culture* (New Haven, Conn.: Yale University Press, 1969).

———. *Language and Myth*, translated by Susanne Langer. (New York: Dover Publications, 1953).

Catholic Theological Faculty of Tübingen. *Bishops and People*, edited and translated by Leonard Swidler and Arlene Swidler (Philadelphia: The Westminster Press, 1969).

Cirne-Lima, Carlos. *Personal Faith* (New York: Herder and Herder, 1975).

Cobb, John. *The Structure of Christian Existence* (Philadelphia: The Westminster Press, 1967).

Cook, Bernard. *Ministry of Word and Sacrament* (Philadelphia: Fortress Press, 1976).

Cox, Harvey. *The Feast of Fools* (Cambridge, Mass.: Harvard University Press, 1969).

———. *The Secular City* (New York: Macmillan, 1965).

———. *Turning East: The Promise and the Peril of the New Orientalism* (New York: Simon and Schuster, 1977).

Daly, Mary. *Beyond God the Father: Toward a Philosophy of Women's Liberation* (Boston: Beacon Press, 1973).

———. *The Church and the Second Sex* (New York: Harper and Row, 1968).

Davis, Charles. *A Question of Conscience* (New York: Harper and Row, 1967).

DeBecher, Raymond. *The Understanding of Dreams: Or the Machinations of the Night* (London: George Allen and Unwin, Ltd., 1968).

DeUnamuno, Miguel. *Abel Sanchez and Other Stories* (Chicago: Henry Regnery Company, 1965).

———. *Essays and Soliloquies* (London: George G. Harrays & Co., 1963).

Dewart, Leslie. *The Foundations of Belief* (New York: Herder and Herder, 1969).

———. *The Future of Belief* (New York: Herder and Herder, 1966).

Dolan, Jay. *Catholic Revivalism: The American Experience 1830-1900* (Notre Dame, Ind.: University of Notre Dame Press, 1978).

Douglas, Mary. *Natural Symbols: Explorations in Cosmology* (New York: Pantheon, 1970).

Driver, Thomas F. *Patterns of Grace* (San Francisco: Harper and Row, 1977).

Duggan, William. *Myth and Christian Belief* (Notre Dame, Ind.: Fides Publishers, Inc., 1971).

Dunne, John. *Devotions upon Emergent Occasions* (Ann Arbor: University of Michigan Press, 1959).

Dupré, Louis. *The Other Dimension: A Search for the Meaning of Religious Attitudes* (Garden City, N.Y.: Doubleday & Co., Inc., 1972).

Dyer, George (Editor). *An American Catholic Catechism* (New York: The Seabury Press, 1976).

———. (Editor) *Chicago Studies*, Summer 1978, "The Magisterium, The Theologian and The Educator."

Ebner, James H. *God Present as Mystery: A Search for Personal Meaning in Contemporary Theology* (New York: Paulist Press, 1977).

Eliade, Mircea. *Myth & Reality* (New York: Harper Torchbooks, 1963).

Evans, Donald. *The Logic of Self-Involvement* (London: SCM Press, 1963).

Farnsworth, Dona L., and Braceland, Francis J. (Editors). *Psychiatry, The Clergy and Pastoral Counseling* (Collegeville, Minn.: St. John's University Press, 1969).

Feiner, Johannes, and Vischer, Lukas (Editors). *The Common Catechism: A Christian Book of Faith* (New York: The Seabury Press, 1975).

Fontinell, Eugene. "Religious Truth in a Relational and Processive World," *Cross Currents* 17 (1967): 283–315.

Gans, Herbert. *Popular Culture and High Culture: An Analysis and Evaluation of Taste* (New York: Basic Books, 1974).

Gelineau, Joseph. *The Liturgy Today and Tomorrow* (New York: Paulist Press, 1978).

Gelpi, Donald. *Charism and Sacraments: A Theology of Christian Conversion* (New York: Paulist Press, 1976).

————. *Experiencing God: A Theology of Human Experience* (New York: Paulist Press, 1978).

Gilkey, Langdon. *Catholicism Confronts Modernity: A Protestant View* (New York: The Seabury Press, 1975).

————. *Reaping the Whirlwind: A Christian Interpretation of History* (New York: The Seabury Press, 1976).

————. "Symbols, Meaning and the Divine Presence," *Theological Studies* 35 (June 1974): 149–67.

Greeley, Andrew. *The Mary Myth* (New York: Doubleday & Co., Inc., 1975).

————. *The New Agenda* (New York: Doubleday & Co., Inc., 1973).

————. *Unsecular Man: The Persistence of Religion* (New York: Schocken Books, 1973).

————. *The Crisis in the Church* (Chicago: Thomas More Press, 1979).

Greenleaf, Robert. *Servant Leadership: A Journey into the Nature of Legitimate Power and Greatness* (New York: Paulist Press, 1977).

Gustafson, James M. *Protestant and Roman Catholic Ethics: Prospects for Rapprochement* (Chicago: University of Chicago Press, 1978).

Gutierrez, Gustavo. *A Theology of Liberation* (Maryknoll, N.Y.: Orbis Books, 1973).

Hardon, John. *The Catholic Catechism* (New York: Doubleday & Co., Inc., 1976).

Häring, Bernard. *Prayer: The Integration of Faith and Life* (Notre Dame, Ind.: Fides Publishers, Inc., 1975).

Hart, Ray L. *Unfinished Man & the Imagination: Toward an Ontology and A Rhetoric of Revelation* (New York: Herder and Herder, 1968).

Hellwig, Monika. *What Are the Theologians Saying?* (Dayton: Pflaum Press, 1970).

Hillnan, James. *In Search: Psychology and Religion* (New York: Charles Scribner's Sons, 1967).

Hiltner, Seward. *Pastoral Counseling* (Nashville: Abingdon Press, 1949).

Hitchcock, James. *The Decline and Fall of Radical Catholicism* (New York: Herder and Herder, 1971).

Hulsbosch, A. *God in Creation and Evolution* (New York: Sheed & Ward, 1965).

James, Muriel. *Born to Love: Transactional Analysis in the Church* (Reading, Mass.: Addison-Wesley, 1973).

James, Muriel, and Savary, Louis M. *The Power at the Bottom of the Well: Transactional Analysis and Religious Experience* (New York: Harper and Row, 1974).

Jastrow, John. *God and the Astronomers* (New York: W. W. Norton & Co., 1978).

Johnston, William. *The Still Point: Reflections on Zen and Christian Mysticism* (New York: Harper and Row, 1970).

Jossua, Jean-Pierre, and Metz, Johannes B. (Editors). *Concilium: The Crisis of Religious Language*, Vol. 85 (New York: Herder and Herder, 1973).

Jung, Carl. *Man and His Symbols*, conceived and edited by Carl Jung. (Garden City, N.Y.: Doubleday & Co., Inc., 1964).

King, Robert, *The Meaning of God* (Philadelphia: Fortress Press, 1973).

Knox, Ronald. *Enthusiasm: A Chapter in the History of Religion* (Oxford: The Clarendon Press, 1973).

Larkin, Ernest E., and Broccolo, Gerard T. (Editors). *Spiritual Renewal of the American Priesthood* (Washington, D.C.: USCC, 1973).

Lane, Dermot. *The Reality of Jesus: An Essay in Christology* (New York: Paulist Press, 1975).

Lash, Nicholas. *Change in Focus: A Study of Doctrinal Change and Continuity* (London: Sheed and Ward, 1973).

Lawler, Ronald, Lawler, Thomas, and Wuerl, Donald (Editors). *The Catholic Catechism* (Huntington, Ind.: Our Sunday Visitor Press, 1976).

Lewis, H. D. *Our Experience of God* (London: Collins, 1974).

Lonergan, Bernard. *Philosophy of God and Theology: The Relationship between Philosophy of God and the Functional Speciality Systematics* (London: Darton, Longmans & Todd, Ltd., 1973).

Lynch, William. *Christ and Apollo* (New York: Mentor-Omega Books, 1963).

Macquarrie, John. *God-Talk: An Examination of the Language and Logic of Theology* (New York: Harper and Row, 1967).

———. *The Scope of Demythologizing: Bultmann and His Critics* (London: SCM Press, Ltd., 1960).

Malinowski, Bronislaw. *Magic Science & Religion* (Garden City, N.Y.: Doubleday & Co., Inc., 1954).

Marty, Martin, and Peerman, Dean (Editors). *New Theology No. 7: The Recovery of Transcendence* (New York: The Macmillan Co., 1970).

Mascall, E. L. *The Openness of Being: Natural Theology Today* (London: Darton, Longmans & Todd, Ltd., 1971).

Maston, Floyd W. *The Broken Image: Man and Science in Society* (Garden City, N.Y.: Doubleday & Co., Inc., 1966).

May, William. *Christ in Contemporary Thought* (Dayton: Pflaum Press, 1970).

McClendon, James. *Biography as Theology: How Life Stories Can Remake Today's Theology* (New York: Abingdon Press, 1974).

McFadden, Thomas (Editor). *American Theological Perspective* (New York: The Seabury Press, 1976).

McGuire, Michael. *The New Baltimore Catechism* (New York: Benzinger Brothers, 1953).

McKenzie, John. *The Roman Catholic Church* (New York: Holt, Rhinehart & Winston, 1969).

Merton, Thomas. *Contemplation in a World of Action* (Garden City, N.Y.: Doubleday & Co., Inc. 1971).

————. *Faith and Violence: Christian Teaching and Christian Practice* (Notre Dame, Ind.: University of Notre Dame Press, 1968).

————. *New Seeds of Contemplation* (Norfolk, Conn.: New Directions, 1962).

————. *Seasons of Celebration* (New York: Farrar, Straus and Giroux, 1969).

————. *The Seven Story Mountain* (New York: Harcourt, Brace, 1948).

Micklem, Caryl (Editor). *More Contemporary Prayers* (London: SCM Press, Ltd., 1970).

Moltmann, Jürgen. *The Crucified God: The Cross of Christ as the Foundation and Criticism of Christian Theology* (London: SCM Press, Ltd., 1974).

————. *The Theology of Hope* (London: SCM Press, Ltd., 1974).

Monod, Jacques. *Change and Necessity* (New York: Vintage Books, 1972).

Moreau, Jean. *The Meaning of Man* (Garden City, N.Y.: Image Books, 1961).

Murray, John. *The Problem of God* (New Haven, Conn.: Yale University Press, 1964).

Naranzo, Claudio. *The One Quest* (New York: Ballantine Books, 1972).

Needleman, Jacob, Bierman, A. K., and Gould, James A. *Religion for a New Generation* (New York: The Macmillan Co., 1973).

A New Catechism: Catholic Faith for Adults (The Dutch Catechism) (New York: Herder and Herder, 1970).

Newman, John H. *The Grammar of Assent* (New York: Image Books, 1955).

Niebuhr, H. R. *The Responsible Self: An Essay in Christian Moral Philosophy* (New York: Harper and Row, 1963).

Nouwen, Henri. *Creative Ministry* (Garden City, N.Y.: Doubleday & Co., Inc., 1971).

————. *Reaching Out: The Three Movements of the Spiritual Life* (Garden City, N.Y.: Doubleday & Co., Inc., 1975).

Novak, Michael. *Belief and Unbelief* (New York: Harper and Row, 1968).

O'Collins, Gerald. *What Are They Saying about Jesus?* (New York: Paulist Press, 1977).

O'Day, Thomas. *The Sociology of Religion* (Englewood Cliffs, N.J.: Prentice-Hall, Inc., 1976).

O'Grady, John. *Jesus, Lord and Christ* (New York: Paulist Press, 1972).

Panikkar, Raimundo. *Worship and Secular Man* (Maryknoll, N.Y.: Orbis Books, 1973).

Pelikan, Jaroslav (Editor). *Twentieth-Century Theology in the Making*, Vol. 2: *The Theological Dialogue: Issues & Resources*, translated by R. A. Wilson (London: Fontana Books, 1970).

Peterson, Severin. *A Catalogue of the Ways People Grow* (New York: Ballantine Books, 1971).

Polanyi, Michael. *Personal Knowledge: Toward a Post Critical Philosophy* (London: Routledge and Kegan Paul, 1958).

Powell, John. *Unconditional Love* (Niles, Ill.: Argus Books, 1978).

Rahner, Karl. *Bishops: Their Status & Function* (Baltimore: Helicon Press, 1963).

————. *The Dynamic Element in the Church: Quaestiones Disputatae 12* (Montreal: Palm Publishers, 1964).

———. "The Experience of God Today," *Theological Investigations*, Vol. 11 (London: Darton, Longmans & Todd, 1974): 149–65.

———. *Foundations of Christian Faith: An Introduction to the Idea of Christianity* (New York: The Seabury Press, 1978).

———. "The Future of Theology," *Theological Investigations*, Vol. 11 (London: Darton, Longmans & Todd, 1974): 137–48.

———. *Hearers of the Word*, revised by Johannes Metz (London: Sheed and Ward, 1969).

———. "The New Claims Which Pastoral Theology Make upon Theology as a Whole," *Theological Investigations*, Vol. 11 (London: Darton, Longmans & Todd, 1974): 115–36.

———. *The Priesthood* (New York: Herder and Herder, 1973).

———. "Reflections on Methodology in Theology," *Theological Investigations*, Vol. 11 (London: Darton, Longmans & Todd, 1974): 68–114.

Ratzinger, Joseph Cardinal. *Introduction to Christianity*, translated by J. R. Foster (New York: The Seabury Press, 1969).

Reich, Charles A. *The Greening of America* (New York: Bantam Books, 1971).

Richards, M. C. *Centering in Pottery, Poetry and the Person* (Middletown, Conn.: Wesleyan University Press, 1964).

Robinson, John. *The Human Face of God* (London: SCM Press, Ltd., 1972).

Roszak, Theodore. *Where the Wasteland Ends* (Garden City, N.Y.: Doubleday & Co., Inc., 1972).

Sabbas, Killian J. *Theological Models for the Parish* (New York: Alba House, 1977).

Savary, Louis, and O'Connor, Thomas (Editors). *The Heart Has Its Seasons: Reflections on the Human Condition* (New York: Regina Press, 1971).

Scheler, Max. *The Eternal in Man* (New York: Harper Brothers, 1960).

Schillebeeckx, Edward. *Jesus: An Experiment in Christology* (New York: The Seabury Press, 1979).

Schleiermacher, Friedrich. *Brief Outline on the Study of Theology*, translated by Terrence N. Tice (Richmond, Va.: John Knox Press, 1970).

Scott, Nathan A., Jr. "The Sacramental Vision," *The Wild Prayer of Longing: Poetry and the Sacred* (New Haven, Conn.: Yale University Press, 1971), pp. 43–76.

Segundo, Juan Louis. *The Liberation of Theology* (Maryknoll, N.Y.: Orbis Books, 1976).

Shepherd, William. *Man's Condition: God and World Process* (New York: Herder and Herder, 1969).

Simon, Arthur. *Bread for the World* (New York: Paulist Press, 1975).

Smith, John. *Experience and God* (New York: Oxford University Press, 1968).

Snell, Bruno. *The Discovery of Mind* (New York: Harper Torchbooks, 1960).

Sobrino, Jon. *Christology at the Crossroads: A Latin American Approach* (Maryknoll, N.Y.: Orbis Books, 1978).

Stuhlmueller, Carroll. *Women and Priesthood: Future Directions* (Collegeville, Minn.: The Liturgical Press, 1978).

Suenens, Leon Cardinal. *Coresponsibility in the Church* (New York: Herder and Herder, 1968).

Swidler, Leonard, and Swidler, Arlene (Editors). *Women Priests: A Catholic Commentary on the Vatican Declaration* (New York: Paulist Press, 1977).

Tillich, Paul. *The Dynamics of Faith* (New York: Harper Torchbooks, 1957).

Toffler, Alvin. *Future Shock* (New York: Bantam Books, 1971).

Torrance, Thomas F. *Theological Science* (New York: Oxford University Press, 1969).

Tracy, David. "Method as the Foundation for Theology: Bernard Lonergan's Option," *Journal of Religion*, 50 (1970): 292–318.

———. (Editor). *Toward Vatican III: The Work to be Done* (New York: The Seabury Press, 1978). Papers from an international meeting of theologians and sociologists representing Concilium and the Catholic Theological Society of America.

Troisfontaine, Roger. *I Do Not Die* (New York: Desclée, 1963).

Tyrrell, Bernard J. *Christotherapy: Healing through Enlightenment* (New York: The Seabury Press, 1975).

Vasoli, Robert. "Catholicism on the Catholic Campus," *Thought*, 47 (1972), 331–350.

Walgrave, Jan H. *Unfolding Revelation: The Nature of Doctrinal Development* (London: Hutchinson, 1972).

Watts, Alan. *Beyond Theology: The Art of Godmanship* (New York: Meridian Books, The World Publishing Co., 1964).

Whitehead, Evelyn Eaton (Editor). *The Parish in Community and Ministry* (New York: Paulist Press, 1978).

Whitson, R. E. *The Coming Convergence in World Religions* (New York: Newman Press, 1971).

Wojtyla, Karol Cardinal (Pope John Paul II). *Signs of Contradiction* (New York: The Seabury Press, 1979).

———. *The Acting Person* (Hingham, Mass.: Kluwer Boston, Inc., 1979).